ACTIVITIES: 1906–1914

The Collected Writings of John Maynard Keynes

J. M. Keynes about 1908
From a drawing by Duncan Grant in the possession of Dr Milo Keynes

THE COLLECTED WRITINGS OF
JOHN MAYNARD KEYNES

VOLUME XV

ACTIVITIES 1906-1914

INDIA AND CAMBRIDGE

EDITED BY
ELIZABETH JOHNSON

MACMILLAN
ST MARTIN'S PRESS

FOR THE
ROYAL ECONOMIC SOCIETY

© The Royal Economic Society 1971

Published by
MACMILLAN AND CO LTD
London and Basingstoke
Associated companies in New York Toronto
Dublin Melbourne Johannesburg and Madras

SBN 333 10740 3 (hard cover)

Library of Congress catalog card no. 76-133449

Printed in Great Britain
at the University Printing House, Cambridge
(Brooke Crutchley, University Printer)

3-19-84

CONTENTS

GENERAL INTRODUCTION

This new standard edition of *The Collected Writings of John Maynard Keynes* forms the memorial to him of the Royal Economic Society. He devoted a very large share of his busy life to the Society. In 1911, at the age of twenty-eight, he became editor of the *Economic Journal* in succession to Edgeworth; two years later he was made secretary as well. He held these offices without intermittence until almost the end of his life. Edgeworth, it is true, returned to help him with the editorship from 1919 to 1925; Macgregor took Edgeworth's place until 1934, when Austin Robinson succeeded him and continued to assist Keynes down to 1945. But through all these years Keynes himself carried the major responsibility and made the principal decisions about the articles that were to appear in the *Economic Journal*, without any break save for one or two issues when he was seriously ill in 1937. It was only a few months before his death at Easter 1946 that he was elected president and handed over his editorship to Roy Harrod and the secretaryship to Austin Robinson.

In his dual capacity of editor and secretary Keynes played a major part in framing the policies of the Royal Economic Society. It was very largely due to him that some of the major publishing activities of the Society—Sraffa's edition of Ricardo, Stark's edition of the economic writings of Bentham, and Guillebaud's edition of Marshall, as well as a number of earlier publications in the 1930s—were initiated.

When Keynes died in 1946 it was natural that the Royal Economic Society should wish to commemorate him. It was perhaps equally natural that the Society chose to commemorate him by producing an edition of his collected works. Keynes himself had always taken a joy in fine printing, and the Society, with the help of Messrs Macmillan as publishers and the Cambridge University Press as printers, has been anxious to give Keynes's writings a permanent form that is wholly worthy of him.

The present edition will publish as much as is possible of his work in the field of economics. It will not include any private and personal correspondence or publish letters in the possession of his family. The edition is concerned, that is to say, with Keynes as an economist.

Keynes's writings fall into five broad categories. First there are the books which he wrote and published as books. Second there are collections of articles and pamphlets which he himself made during his lifetime (*Essays in Persuasion* and *Essays in Biography*). Third, there is a very considerable volume of published but uncollected writings—articles written for newspapers, letters to newspapers, articles in journals that have not been included in his two volumes of collections, and various pamphlets. Fourth, there are a few hitherto unpublished writings. Fifth, there is correspondence with economists and concerned with economics or public affairs.

This series will attempt to publish a complete record of Keynes's serious writing as an economist. It is the intention to publish almost completely the whole of the first four categories listed above. The only exceptions are a few syndicated articles where Keynes wrote almost the same material for publication in different newspapers or in different countries, with minor and unimportant variations. In these cases, this series will publish one only of the variations, choosing the most interesting.

The publication of Keynes's economic correspondence must inevitably be selective. In the day of the typewriter and the filing cabinet and particularly in the case of so active and busy a man, to publish every scrap of paper that he may have dictated about some unimportant or ephemeral matter is impossible. We are aiming to collect and publish as much as possible, however, of the correspondence in which Keynes developed his own ideas in argument with his fellow economists, as well as the more significant correspondence at times when Keynes was in the middle of public affairs.

Apart from his published books, the main sources available to those preparing this series have been two. First, Keynes in his will made Richard Kahn his executor and responsible for his economic papers. They have been placed in the Marshall Library of the University of Cambridge and have been available for this edition. Until 1914 Keynes did not have a secretary and his earliest papers are in the main limited to drafts of important letters that he made in his own handwriting and retained. At that stage most of the correspondence that we possess is represented by what he received rather than by what he wrote. During the war years of 1914–18 Keynes was serving in the Treasury. With the opening of the 1914–18 records, many of the papers that he wrote have become available. From 1919 onwards, throughout the rest of his life, Keynes had the help of a secretary—for many years Mrs Stevens. Thus for the last twenty-five years of his working life we have in most cases the carbon copies of his own letters as well as the originals of the letters that he received.

There were, of course, occasions during this period on which Keynes wrote himself in his own handwriting. In some of these cases, with the help of his correspondents, we have been able to collect the whole of both sides of some important interchange and we have been anxious, in justice to both correspondents, to see that both sides of the correspondence are published in full.

The second main source of information has been a group of scrapbooks kept over a very long period of years by Keynes's mother, Florence Keynes, wife of Neville Keynes. From 1919 onwards these scrapbooks contain almost the whole of Maynard Keynes's more ephemeral writing, his letters to newspapers and a great deal of material which enables one to see not only what he wrote, but the reaction of others to his writing. Without these very carefully kept scrapbooks the task of any editor or biographer of Keynes would have been immensely more difficult.

The plan of the edition, as at present intended, is this. It will total twenty-four volumes. Of these, the first eight will be Keynes's published books from *Indian Currency and Finance*, in

1913, to the *General Theory* in 1936, with the addition of his *Treatise on Probability*. There will next follow, as vols. IX and X, *Essays in Persuasion* and *Essays in Biography*, representing Keynes's own collections of articles. *Essays in Persuasion* will differ from the original printing in two respects; it will contain the full texts of the articles or pamphlets included in it and not (as in the original printing) abbreviated versions of these articles, and it will have added one or two later articles which are of exactly the same character as those included by Keynes in his original collection. In the case of *Essays in Biography*, we shall add various other biographical studies that Keynes wrote throughout his work.

There will follow three volumes, XI to XIII, of economic articles and correspondence, and one volume, XIV, of social, political and literary writings. We shall include in these volumes such part of Keynes's economic correspondence as is closely associated with the articles that are printed in them.

The further nine volumes, as we estimate at present, will deal with Keynes's *Activities* during the years from the beginning of his public life in 1905 until his death. In each of the periods into which we propose to divide this material, the volume concerned will publish his more ephemeral writings, all of it hitherto un-collected, his correspondence relating to these activities, and such other material and correspondence as is necessary to the understanding of Keynes's activities. The first four of these volumes are being edited by Elizabeth Johnson; the later volumes will be the responsibility of Donald Moggridge. It is their task to trace and interpret Keynes's activities sufficiently to make the material fully intelligible to a later generation. Until this work has progressed further, it is not possible to say with exactitude whether this material will be distributed, as we now think, over nine volumes, or whether it will need to be spread over a further volume or volumes. There will be a final volume of bibliography and index.

Those responsible for this edition have been: Lord Kahn, both as Lord Keynes's executor and as a long and intimate friend of

Lord Keynes, able to help in the interpreting of much that would otherwise be misunderstood; Sir Roy Harrod as the author of his biography; Austin Robinson as Keynes's co-editor on the *Economic Journal* and successor as secretary of the Royal Economic Society. The main editorial tasks in the first four of these volumes have been carried by Elizabeth Johnson. She has been assisted at different times by Jane Thistlethwaite, Mrs McDonald, who was originally responsible for the systematic ordering of the files of the Keynes papers, Judith Masterman and Susan Wilsher, who in turn have worked with Mrs Johnson on the papers.

EDITORIAL FOREWORD

This volume, together with volume XVI, forms the first of a group of nine or more which will make available Keynes's more ephemeral writings, his letters and contributions to the newspapers, his memoranda while employed in the India Office and in the Treasury in two wars, and such correspondence as is directly related to the events about which he is writing or is necessary to the understanding of the documents that are published.

For his published contributions to the press, the main source is the series of scrapbooks which, as explained in the General Introduction, his mother indefatigably maintained throughout his working life. (Keynes, knowing that she was doing this, helped by sending her copies of all he published.) For the periods in Whitehall, first in the India Office and subsequently in the Treasury, dependence has been primarily on the files that are now available in the Public Record Office. In some cases, however, Keynes had himself retained an earlier draft of a memorandum that he had written. Almost all of the correspondence that is here published is among his surviving papers. At points the diaries of John Neville Keynes—Maynard Keynes's father—serve to illuminate Keynes's thoughts or state of mind at important moments.

This volume, like that which immediately follows it, has aimed to publish as much as possible of Keynes's writing of the period covered. In this early period there was none of the duplication in his contributions to the press, syndicated in different parts of the world, that sometimes is to be found in his later years. For the two Civil Service periods it has been necessary to be somewhat more selective and to confine publication to what is both clearly Keynes's work and of more than routine interest. During the later war years, for example, he wrote at intervals appreciations of the position regarding inter-allied finance, rehearsing much the same arguments about much the same problems in the light of progressively changing figures. We have selected for publication those examples of such memoranda which best illustrate a particular problem or best show his analytical handling of them.

It has been necessary, in order to make this material intelligible to a generation which did not live through the events and to whom the participants are unknown names, to provide a minimum of factual background. It has been sought to make this background information sufficient for clarity, but neither obtrusive nor argumentative. The purpose has been to provide the reader with the material from which to make his own judgment of Keynes rather than to attempt to impose the judgments of the editors.

No reader, we think, can fail to be impressed by the immensely detailed mastery which Keynes had achieved as a very young man of all the many ramifications of Indian finance. This capacity for mastery of detail remained with him through life. He was never content with a merely superficial understanding of the broad essentials of a problem. We suspect that a reader will find it equally fascinating to contrast Keynes's analysis of the economic problems of war as set out in volume XVI in some of his Treasury memoranda or other discussions of war finance of 1914–18 with the analysis that he developed twenty-five years later in *How to Pay for the War*. Finally, one sees there vividly through his own eyes and in his own words his agonies of despair as a rational handling of the problems of reparations became irretrievably frustrated by political ineptitude.

NOTE TO THE READER

In this and subsequent volumes, in general all of Keynes's own writings are printed in larger type. All introductory matter and all writings by others than Keynes are printed in smaller type. The only exception to this general rule is that occasional short quotations from a letter from Keynes to his parents or to a friend, used in introductory passages to clarify a situation, are treated as introductory matter and are printed in the smaller type. In those passages in this volume in which are printed extracts from the Minutes of Evidence of the Royal Commission on Indian Finance and Currency, Keynes's questions to witnesses are printed in roman type, their answers in italics. In the final chapter, where Keynes appears as a witness before the Babington Smith Committee, the questions to him are printed in italics, Keynes's answers are printed in roman type.

Most of Keynes's letters included in this and other volumes are reprinted from the carbon copies that remain among his papers. In most cases he has added his initials to the carbon in the familiar form in which he signed to all his friends. We have no means of knowing whether the top copy, sent to the recipient of the letter, carried a more formal signature.

Chapter 1

FROM THE INDIA OFFICE TO
CAMBRIDGE 1906-1913

The public life of John Maynard Keynes began with his appointment to the India Office as a junior clerk at the age of twenty-three. He stayed at the India Office only two years before embarking on his career in economics at Cambridge and during this time was much preoccupied with the writing of a dissertation on probability. The phase was crucial, however, in that it led to his acquaintance with the intricacies of the Indian financial system and eventually, through a combination of natural interest, the trust and encouragement of India Office colleagues, and a crisis that put the Indian currency situation in the foreground of public discussion, resulted in the writing of his first book, *Indian Currency and Finance*, and his creative role with the Royal Commission on Indian Finance and Currency. This is the main theme of the chapter that follows—although it was only one of the multifarious activities, academic and otherwise, crowding Keynes's early years at Cambridge.

The papers left from this period of Keynes's life are comparatively few and sketchy. What there are consist of a few memoranda written for the India Office, some lecture notes, some newspaper clippings, a small amount of correspondence. The correspondence, before the advent of the typewriter, is one-sided, unless Keynes considered a letter of his own to be of sufficient moment to make and keep a first draft in his own hand or to have a copy made—as he fortunately quite often did. Yet from these fragments, from the fact of what was kept, from the tone adopted by one correspondent or a Keynesian phrase echoed in the letter of another, there emerges a strong sense of personality, of attitudes taken, along with the concrete evidence of ideas pursued and work done.

Keynes had taken the Mathematical Tripos at Cambridge; he was twelfth Wrangler in 1905. He then stayed on a fourth year to prepare himself for the Civil Service examination and during this time attended Alfred Marshall's lectures and did some reading in economics with both Marshall and A. C. Pigou. Marshall (who had written on one of Keynes's essays: 'This is a very powerful answer. I trust your future career may be one in which you will not cease to be an economist. I should be glad if it could be that of an economist.') was eager for him to take Part II of the Economics Tripos, which was being held for the first time in Cambridge in 1906. The first letter in Keynes's collection from Marshall—it is dated 2 May 1906, from Balliol Croft, Madingley Road, Cambridge—reads:

My dear Keynes,

I was very sorry to get your letter this morning. But I must not urge you further. I think that if you went in for the Tripos, merely re-reading Economics in the ten days before it, you would *probably* get a first class: and that if you did not, you would not injure your position, since it would be known that you had had very little time free for economics. But I must say no more.

The list of Cobden Prize subjects is reprinted ('eighty' being substituted for 'thirty' in the second subject) in the current *Reporter*.

After you have taken your well earned holiday in August and September, I hope you may see your way to working at one of these, for your own good, for the glory of Cambridge and to the great satisfaction of

Yours very sincerely

ALFRED MARSHALL

It was not the first time that Marshall had coaxed, but Keynes had competing interests and seems to have been more excited, for example, by the philosophy of G. E. Moore. He persisted in his decision to concentrate on the Civil Service examination. While he was waiting for the results, he spent the well-earned holiday in Scotland with Lytton Strachey, James Strachey and Harry Norton, taking long walks and working at the subject of probability, on which he planned to write a dissertation for a King's College fellowship. 'I...am rather hopeful,' he wrote to his parents about it. 'My method is quite new, and I think amongst other things that I have got a formal proof of the problem of Inverse Probability.'

'We are admirably boarded and lodged for 3/6 a day each,' he added—a fact evidently noteworthy, since John Neville Keynes included it when he copied his son's letter into his diary 15 September 1906.

Keynes stood second of 104 Civil Service candidates. 'My marks have arrived and left me enraged', he wrote to Lytton Strachey, 4 October 1906. 'Really knowledge seems an absolute bar to success. I have done worst in the only two subjects of which I possessed a solid knowledge—mathematics and economics. I scored more marks for English history than for mathematics—is it credible? For economics I got a relatively low percentage and was the eighth or ninth in order of merit—whereas I knew the whole of both papers in a really elaborate way. On the other hand, in political science, to which

2

I devoted less than a fortnight in all, I was easily first of everybody. I was also first in logic and psychology and in essay.'

An advance proof of the *Oxford Magazine Supplement*, 7 November 1906, listing all the marks of all the candidates, which Keynes kept, shows that he ranked seventh in political economy and economic history (his marks were 356 out of a possible 600), eighteenth in mathematics and seventh in advanced mathematics, first in logic and psychology, second in moral and metaphysical philosophy, first in political science, second in English composition, twentieth in English history to 1485 and twelfth in English history 1485–1848. He obtained 3,498 out of a possible 6,000 marks, 419 marks less than the man who stood first, Otto Niemeyer, who was appointed to the Treasury.

Keynes was appointed to the Military Department of the India Office. On the authority of his father's diary, he started work 16 October 1906, so that a 'Draft Para. of Military Despatch to the Government of India', dated 18 October, arranging the shipment of ten young Ayrshire bulls to Bombay— kept in his files—was very likely to have been his first official responsibility. He also wrote a memorandum on the dating of lieutenants' commissions. Dr Keynes remarked in his diary that his son, with not enough to fill his time, was getting into the habit of doing his own work, i.e. the dissertation on probability, in office hours. He was soon offered a resident clerkship but declined, his father recorded (8 February 1907), because the evening work would interfere with the writing of his dissertation. At the beginning of March Keynes was transferred to the Revenue, Statistics and Commerce Department, and Dr Keynes said (7 March) that 'he is liking his work much better, has much reading, as he sees all papers that come into the Department'. Nevertheless, when a resident clerkship was again offered to him some months later, he wrote to the Permanent Secretary, Sir Arthur Godley, without enthusiasm.

To SIR ARTHUR GODLEY, *3 October 1907*

Dear Sir Arthur Godley,

I am still most unwilling to take up the resident clerkship. My fellowship work does not finish until December. But—apart from this special and temporary reason—now that I have settled down in London, I find the idea of sacrificing any of my out of office freedom repellent. I am, for instance, almost always away from London for weekends; and I should not like to have to give

3

this up. For these personal reasons, therefore, I shall be very grateful if you find it possible to make another arrangement.

Very truly yours,

J. M. KEYNES

On both occasions Sir Arthur Godley generously accepted this plea. Holding the fellowship, if Keynes were successful, would not necessarily have required him to give up the India Office for residence in Cambridge.

Keynes kept the drafts of some of the memoranda that he wrote: on a proposed grant of a monopoly of bonded warehouses in Cyprus, on the prevention of smuggling of liquor from Portuguese into British India, on a fixed licence fee to combat illicit distillation in the Punjab, and—at length—on the incorrect censure of a man in charge of the stamp office at Rangoon, an injustice about which Keynes felt strongly, to judge not only from the sentiments expressed but from the unusual amount of revision and crossing-out. In a mood of disgust with his department, he mentioned this case with some vehemence in a letter to Lytton Strachey, 13 September 1907. '...I have demonstrated quite clearly that he is wholly innocent of X, but that if he had been charged with a quite different offence Y, and if he had been allowed to reply and the thing had been investigated, he would probably have deserved censure for Y. But it seems to me that, whatever else is done, censure for doing X should be cancelled. They say—No, he deserves censure, and therefore censure must be maintained.'

In an earlier letter to Strachey, 13 July 1907, he said that he had been complimented on another minute—not kept with his papers—by the Secretary of State for India, John Morley. Keynes added, however: 'He did not say whether or not he had reversed the damned committee and agreed with me.'

The impression of reforming zeal coupled with impatience with bureaucratic procedure conveyed by these papers is present in the following draft, dated 19 March 1907, on the position of the jute trade. It is accompanied by a note to Keynes's superior, Thomas Holderness (later Sir Thomas Holderness).

Mr Holderness

The rough draft below is very long. If you at all agree that the Lieutenant Governor should be urged to follow up his suggestion of legislation for the *export* trade, I could throw it into a minute. I feel inclined to agree with the unanimous opinion of the trade that legislation might do something.

J.M.K.

19.3.07

To which Holderness replied:

We ought not to do anything until we receive the views of the G[overnment] of I[ndia] on the whole question. They have still to reply to our Desp[atch] of 15 Dec. 1905. I would put the present pages forward for information.

When we hear from the G. of I., you might reconsider what you have written and after revising it you might let me see it. We will then decide whether it should be put forward as a Departmental minute, or as a separate minute by you to which I call attention without agreeing with the final recommendation. I am disposed at present to agree with you that action might be taken as regards exported jute. But one has still to hear what the G. of I. say, and they may consult the trade as to confining action to exports before committing themselves.

T.W.H.

19.3.07

THE POSITION OF THE JUTE TRADE

The position of the jute trade is altogether peculiar, and the special circumstances governing it render dangerous all arguments from analogy. The Indian producer has in the past possessed a practical monopoly, but he has not been able or willing to increase the area under cultivation at a sufficient rate to keep pace with the increasing demand. As the bulk of the jute is manufactured into sacks this demand is likely to increase with the increasing carrying trade of the world, and in particular with the opening up of the wheat growing districts of America. The I[ndian] G[overnment] is fully alive to this fact and the Eastern Bengal jute specialist, Mr Finlow, has recently issued a report on the possibility of extending the area of cultivation in Bengal and of introducing jute into other parts of India. He reports on the whole favourably, but it is evident that the general conservatism of the ryot and the element of risk in all such experimental cultivation will render future extensions somewhat slow, although steadily progressive. In the meantime there is a period of transition, of abnormal profits, and of temporary circumstances giving exceptional opportunity to the cupidity of dishonest merchants.

The essence of the problem lies in the risk that these special conditions will lead to the discovery of some efficient substitute for jute or to its successful cultivation in foreign countries, before India is prepared to supply the normal demand at a normal price.

The monopoly in the past has been due to two causes: qualitative excellence at a relatively low price has enabled jute to defeat its possible substitutes (e.g. flax) and the initial physical advantages of India have kept it on the market at a price that has not stimulated the necessarily speculative attempt to grow it elsewhere. Both these influences are endangered by a period of high price combined (as is admitted) with deterioration of quality.

While this is the general problem, it is presented to Government in a special and narrowed form. The I.G. is already doing what can be done to stimulate production; it remains to consider whether the alleged deterioration can be usefully dealt with by legislation. This is the particular point immediately under discussion; but the general problem behind it must not be lost sight of.

The discussion falls into two parts, both of which can only be settled by an appeal to facts:

(i) Is the danger of a breakdown of India's monopoly (either by substitution or by rival production) real and considerable?

(ii) Is any part of this danger due to deterioration of quality which legislation can do anything to check?

There is some reason for thinking that the answer to the first is in the affirmative. Projects for growing jute elsewhere are very much in the air. Mr Malcolm, the President of the London Jute Association, on the occasion of the deputation to Sir A. Fraser, seemed to think it not at all unlikely that some country will soon step in as a competitor and instanced parallel cases. The German and Austrian representatives as well as others dwelt on the deterioration of quality due to adulteration and the tendency which this would have to drive trade from Bengal. Experimental cultivation is already on foot in several parts of the world. The Colonial Office has recently asked for seed for W. Africa, and the Brit. S. Africa Co. for Rhodesia.

But a more serious symptom is to be found in the actual trade statistics, which go to show that substitutes are already being used in several large markets.

The relative price of exported gunny bags in recent years is represented by the following figures: 1901–2, 137; 1902–3, 137; 1903–4, 147; 1904–5, 157; 1905–6, 173; and the price of the raw jute exported by the following: 53, 57, 57, 61, 80.

While the rise has been steady, the enormous increase in price was in 1905–6 although the total output in that year considerably surpassed that in previous years.

In the same period the exports to [the] U.S.A. and Germany have notably decreased:

	1901–2	1902–3	1903–4	1904–5	1905–6
			(thousands)		
Raw jute to U.S.A. (cwt.)	2,470	1,768	1,975	1,929	2,012
Gunny bags to U.S.A.	25,323	13,580	7,816	11,339	10,882
Raw jute to Germany (cwt.)	2,697	2,508	2,626	2,703	2,628
Gunny bags to Germany	9,806	10,316	4,245	3,601	3,609

There is also a slight diminution in the export to [the] U.K., while the diminution is made up by increases to various other countries (e.g. Chile).

The point of these figures is that the total use of jute in [the] U.S.A. and Germany has seriously diminished, and that as India has a monopoly and the demand for sacks is likely to have increased rather than decreased, something other than jute must already be used as a substitute in considerable quantities.

The foregoing argument is not very strong or conclusive, but it goes to show that India's monopoly should not be regarded as secure and altogether unassailable even so far as the immediate future is concerned.

The particular point of the desirability of checking deterioration by legislation now remains.

It is admitted that adulteration takes place on a large and increasing scale; it is also admitted that, apart from the question of commercial dishonesty, this adulteration spoils the quality of the jute and renders it unfit for use, or at any rate inferior, even after it has been cleaned and dried.

The causes of this adulteration are firstly the enormous profits to be made at the present prices and secondly (this is of course allied to the first) the keen competition amongst the dealers which prevents their picking and choosing too carefully from fear lest they should be boycotted by the whole trade.

> Mr Nimmo (quoted by Sir A. Fraser): 'If a buyer were to prosecute a seller for selling bad stuff, or to show him up, he would probably be boycotted by the whole trade.'
> 'It was not possible for want of space and in the hurry of the buying season to open out and dry every wet parcel.'
> The Director of Land Records: 'Competition is so keen that a voluntary combination of the merchants to boycott wet jute is almost an impossibility.'

The tendency of such adulteration is naturally to become universal; the general level of the excellence which is expected steadily sinks until dishonesty is so well known that it has become honesty again. Thus it is true that the trouble, like most commercial troubles, will, if left to itself, work itself out in time. The danger is that in the meantime irreparable damage will have been done to India's natural monopoly.

The whole trade is evidently alive to this danger, but they are not strong enough by themselves to meet it. While adulteration is plainly opposed to the interests of the trade as a whole, it is nevertheless to the interest of every individual to practise it. There is not sufficient sense of commercial solidarity for them to succeed in keeping a voluntary compact which it is to each separate firm's advantage to break. Under these circumstances

8

all branches of the trade, both in India and abroad, come with singular unanimity to the Government and ask for legislation and inspection, the cost of which is to be defrayed by a levy on jute itself. Not a single interest in the trade raises a voice of protest. The Lt. Governor replies in a carefully reasoned letter. He begins by admitting the greatness and reality of the danger to its full extent; but he goes on to say:

(i) A great departure from the hitherto accepted canons of legislation would be involved.

(ii) Legislation would be powerless so long as jute is at its present high price.

(iii) Legislation by the disturbance to trade and the rise in nominal price which it would occasion might cause ungrounded alarms amongst the cultivators leading to a diminution of production.

(iv) The experience of similar cotton legislation in Bombay is adverse.

(v) If legislation fixes a limit of saturation, *all* jute will be saturated up to this limit.

(vi) It would be difficult to obtain inspectors of the necessary integrity or to bring about any effective control over so large an area.

(vii) No one can protect the buyer as well as he can protect himself; if the methods of doing business which have grown up in the jute trade create special difficulties then those methods should be reformed by the trade itself.

(i) may be admitted; (ii) stands or falls with (vi); (iii) is highly doubtful: cultivators are not usually easily alarmed when their product is rising in price. As for (iv), the peculiar conditions of the jute trade prevent the cotton legislation from being altogether analogous; the present monopoly in Indian jute prevents the trade from coming to its senses as soon as would otherwise be the case, and the danger of losing the monopoly renders temporary aberrations more dangerous.

(iv) is however a serious argument.

(v) does not amount to much; jute is just as likely under present cond[itio]ns to become universally adulterated; it cuts both ways.

(vi) is most serious.

(vii) comprises an economic maxim of general truth; but reasons have already been given for supposing its application to the present cond[itio]ns of the jute trade doubtful. At any rate the buyers think so; and they are the people who, according to the maxim, know best.

The Lt. Governor is, however, prepared to admit that legislation for the export trade stands on a separate footing, and suggests that an order might be issued under section 19 of the Sea Customs Act prohibiting the taking by sea of adulterated jute. While bowing before his local knowledge, so far as internal legislation is concerned, especially on ground (vi), it is submitted that he should be strongly urged to follow up this suggestion.

There are several good reasons for dealing with the export trade separately. It is the bad quality of the exported raw jute which is most likely to encourage its cultivation elsewhere. The local manufacturers, it is admitted, are better able to protect themselves; and also they suffer less severely. The extent to which excessive moisture ruins the jute is largely a question of the time elapsing before its manufacture, and foreign manufacturers are therefore much more hardly hit by the adulteration.

Further, the local interference which, it was thought, might alarm the cultivator, would be unnecessary. Also reasons (ii) and (vi) lose much of their weight, since the control of the export trade, passing as it does almost entirely through Calcutta, would be infinitely simpler and consequently more effective. As the Lt. Governor points out, 'the number of exporters though large would be comparatively few, and it might be possible to arrange for the necessary inspection without any great dislocation of the trade'.

If the legislation proves a failure, it can easily be repealed. The request of the great jute buyers that there should be a penal clause against themselves is, as the Lt. Governor notes, remarkable proof of the desire for legislation in the trade.

It is greatly to be hoped that the question will not be allowed to drop.

J.M.K.

19.3.07

In January 1908 Keynes was entrusted with the editing of the 'Statement Exhibiting the Moral and Material Progress and Condition of India', the official annual report of the India Office to Parliament. This lengthy document—197 pages for 1906–7, the year that Keynes edited it—was made up from the annual reports of all the provinces of India, these in turn having been compiled from the reports of the local district and political officers. Keynes's report shows little evidence of his own hand, but something of his critical attitude towards the task may be conveyed in a comment by Sir Thomas Holderness, on seeing the proofs (28 April 1908):

> the only part about which I am exercised is that which deals with plague (pages 4 and 5). The facts are stated quite correctly, but the impression they produce is that the country has been terribly ravaged by plague, and that the Government has done nothing beyond issuing a circular and carrying on a coldblooded scientific inquiry. As we know that the only persons who read the M. and M.P. Report are persons who want to find fault with the Government, and who try to find in the report materials for faultfinding, some economy in statement is reasonable on our part.

Sir Thomas Holderness seems to have been most approachable, but there is no indication of how the following suggestion was received—if indeed it was sent. It is a memorandum in Keynes's handwriting, in what appears to be a careful copy.

Sir T. Holderness

In the despatch on the question of the appointment of a Director of Statistics, are not the Govt. of India underrating the extent to which the modern science of statistics has become complicated and specialised, in suggesting that the necessary attainments will be found in a Chartered Accountant?

Until quite recently there was of course no body of experience or of scientific theory upon which the statistician could draw, and each investigator in his own particular field had to apply general intelligence and start for himself. But this state of affairs has now quite passed away, and it is absurd to suppose that it is still possible to prepare and present statistics in the most compact, most informing and least misleading manner without special knowledge—and the more mathematics and economics this special knowledge includes the better (though of course it is still possible to be a fairly good practical statistician with no more than an elementary knowledge of mathematics). Such special knowledge the present D. G. of C. I. [Director General of Commercial Intelligence] has not got (as his otherwise admirable Review of Indian Trade immediately shows—e.g. his account of the balance of trade or the extremely unscientific character of the official index number which he publishes); and surely this is an admirable opportunity for supplementing his ignorance by the appointment of a real trained statistician. Such a class now exists—though hardly I should think amongst chartered accountants; and as it is a precarious and ill-paid trade in this country it ought to be possible to secure a good man at the salary proposed—not, I suppose, one of the leading experts, but at least one of their best pupils.

It would be easy to find out by enquiries from the Director of the London School of Economics, or Mr C. P. Sanger, or Prof. Karl Pearson, or by an editorial note saying that the creation of such a post is in contemplation in the Journal of the Royal Statistical Society, or from the Bd. of Trade who are constantly employing outsiders for their statistical work.

Of the above I should trust the *judgment* of Mr C. P. Sanger by far the most. He has a very wide knowledge of theoretical statistics and has also directed practical statistical operations on a large scale. This and the fact that he has long lectured at University College has made him well acquainted with the younger statisticians, and I think he is an exceptionally good judge of *ability*—but of course he is not of the standing of the others.

J.M.K.

9.2.[08]

Keynes had two weeks' leave in the autumn. 'Maynard has now gone into rooms at King's,' his father wrote in his diary, 19 October 1907. 'He wants to have another taste of college life.' He finished the dissertation on probability in December, but was unsuccessful with it in the fellowship election of March 1908. Shortly after this disappointment he received a rather cryptic letter from Alfred Marshall dated 3 April 1908.

My dear Keynes,

Quite recently, since your father left E[ng]land, I have heard in a round-about way, that it is just possible you might be willing to return to Cambridge, if you had work to do here. I have also heard that your chance of election to a fellowship at King's next year is good.

Under these circumstances, and taking account of the fact that [D. H.] Macgregor is going to Leeds, my course would have been clear if I had not been about to vacate the professorship. I should then have asked you to allow me to propose you to the Economics Board as a lecturer on general economics probably for the first year, but possibly for the second; and I should have said I would gladly pay you the £100 which I have paid in similar cases.

But I shall cease to be a member of the Economics Board on April 21st: and at its last meeting I said that I should do nothing to hamper the freedom of the reconstituted Board which will meet (probably on June 3rd) to make up its lecture list.

It has however been suggested to me by the same person, to whom the notion of your coming to Cambridge to teach economics is due, that there may be an advantage in calling your attention to the situation. I am in a position to state two things. First (subject to some reserve in the case of one possible election to the Professorship in May) if you approve, a suggestion will be made by a member of the Board on (probably) June 3, that you be asked to lecture. Secondly, if the Board concur—and I have no doubt that (subject to the above mentioned reserve) they will concur gladly—the sum of £100 will be forthcoming for you, just to make you feel that you really are a lecturer. I do not think that the £100 will be paid by me: but I can guarantee that it will be paid either from some other source or by me.

There is a certain air of mystery in this letter, and I dislike mystery. But later on you will understand that it was inevitable.

Answer at your convenience. There is no hurry.

Yours very sincerely

ALFRED MARSHALL

The person who suggested to Marshall that Keynes might come to Cambridge was Pigou. Marshall's reservation referred to the possibility of H. S.

Foxwell being elected to the professorship instead of Pigou. The letter was written while Keynes's parents were holidaying in the south of France. Keynes consulted his father who replied on his return to Cambridge, 23 April:

My dear Maynard,

I am glad that we shall see you Saturday. We shall then be able to talk over Marshall's proposal. I may as well, however, at once mention two points that occur to me.

(1) If you have to prepare a course of lectures on Economics it does not seem to me that you will have more time, or even as much, for your dissertation than if you remain at the India Office.

(2) Any stipend that Macgregor has received is a matter of purely private arrangement. Becoming his successor would not I think give you any University status beyond what you would have as a recognised lecturer and this position you could no doubt get at any time.

Is not Marshall's letter in some respects very vague? I am glad you have not in any way committed yourself at present.

Ever your loving father

J. N. KEYNES

This paternal caution was a reminder that at this time (and until 1926) only professors had any University status at Cambridge; while college lecturers might be approved for the official lecture list, they received no payment from the University but collected a fee of so much per head from the colleges of the students who attended their lectures. The £100 that had been provided by Marshall was entirely unofficial.

As it turned out, Pigou succeeded Marshall and Keynes was offered and accepted the opportunity to lecture, with the £100 being furnished by Pigou. In the letter of 10 June that follows Marshall disclaimed responsibility, but explained the mystery. The reference to J. N. Keynes being an elector is to his membership of the body of electors to the Chair of Political Economy. He became chairman of the Special Board for Economics and Politics at the same meeting as his son was appointed. (Maynard Keynes later served as secretary to the Board from 1910 until he left Cambridge for the Treasury in 1915.)

Dear Keynes,

I am delighted indeed that you are to join our economic staff. I think it is a brilliant, compact group of earnest men, full of the highest promise for the future. But you are wrong in supposing that I had anything to do with your coming back, any more than the postman had. It did not enter my head that you might do so till Pigou spoke to me of it. As your father is an 'elector', he could not approach you: so I put his message on paper and the postman delivered it: the postman and I are factors of the second order of smalls and may be neglected.

Yours very gladly

ALFRED MARSHALL

The 'brilliant, compact group of earnest men' that Keynes was to join in lecturing for the newly established Tripos consisted of Pigou, Walter Layton (later Lord Layton) appointed at the same time as Keynes, W. E. Johnson, Lowes Dickinson, J. H. Clapham, C. R. Fay, H. O. Meredith and L. Alston.

The Special Board met on 3 June; Keynes resigned from the India Office on 5 June, on his twenty-fifth birthday. His official resignation was addressed to Sir Arthur Godley but he also wrote from Cambridge to Sir Thomas Holderness explaining his decision.

To SIR THOMAS HOLDERNESS, *5 June 1908*

Dear Sir Thomas,

The new Professor of P.E. here has offered me a lectureship, and I have decided to accept. I have written to Sir Arthur Godley, therefore, resigning from the India Office, and asking to be released from work as soon as may be convenient, as I shall have a good deal of preparatory work to do here and should like to come into residence at Cambridge for the Long Vacation.

For many reasons I am very sorry to do this, and I have only made up my mind after a great deal of doubt and hesitation. But the desire for scientific and theoretical work and for life here is so great that I think I am probably right in giving way to it.

Please do not think that I have disliked my work in the Revenue Dept. or have been discontented. I have liked it very much and have learnt a great deal from it and from you. But the choice has been between two quite opposed ways of life, and on the whole I think, now at any rate, that the way here is better.

I hate doing this—I hope you won't misunderstand. I shall be back in the office on Tuesday morning.

Sincerely yours,

[Draft letter unsigned]

The drafts of these letters show that Keynes was concerned lest he seem ungrateful, in particular to Sir Thomas Holderness ('to whom I owe a great

15

deal. I specially regret leaving him,' he wrote to Sir Arthur Godley), and that he got his mother's help with some of the wording—there are pencilled suggestions in her handwriting, some adopted, some not.

Sir Arthur Godley replied the next day: 'I have received your letter with great regret. If you had stayed in this office you would, I firmly believe, have been very soon in one of its highest places: but, as you say, the choice is between the two careers, and I personally am one of the last to quarrel with your decision...'

Sir Thomas Holderness wrote the same day as Godley (6 June 1908), even more personally and sympathetically.

> Your letter is a blow to me. I had hoped to have your cooperation for some time to come, until Godley should annex you for Private Secretary work. At the same time I think I can enter sufficiently into your views to understand the motive which urges you to strike for intellectual freedom and leisure for research, and I am not sure that I would not do the same if I were in your place. I have never been quite able to satisfy myself that a government office in this country is the best thing for a young man of energy and right ambitions. It is a comfortable means of life and leads by fairly sure, if slow, stages to moderate competence and old age provision. But it is rarely exciting or strenuous and does not make sufficient call on the combative and self-assertive elements of human nature.

> I suppose I ought to counsel reflection before you plunge, and paint the possible successes of official life in attractive colours—and I undoubtedly think you have the ball at your feet in this office, such as the ball is. But I won't do this, because I take for granted that you have fully weighed the cost...

Keynes left the India Office in July and after a holiday in the Orkneys with Duncan Grant, during which he worked on a new version of the dissertation on probability, he settled in Cambridge for the Michaelmas term. His first lectures were not to be given until the following January, and in the meantime he finished the dissertation (which in this version was to bring him the fellowship) and wrote his first major article, 'Recent Economic Events in India', published in the *Economic Journal*, March 1909 (*JMK*, vol. XI).

In this article Keynes examined the recent rise of prices in India; he attributed it to a flow of foreign capital into India rather than the drain of capital that was commonly supposed to be taking place. The article's reception was encouraging. In India, four newspapers thought it important enough to print long reviews, and the Director General of Commercial Intelligence (whose knowledge of statistics Keynes had disparaged) wrote: 'Even after a preliminary glance I can see that it suggests many reflections to the officer in charge of this Department.'

'I sincerely hope', Sir Arthur Godley said in a letter dated 30 March 1909, 'that you will continue to keep an eye on Indian affairs, and to write about them as opportunities occur.' Keynes's departure from the Indian Office did not break his connection with it; indeed, from this time onward the association seems to have expanded. He had submitted the proofs of his article to the criticism of Lionel Abrahams, Financial Secretary and later Under-Secretary of State for India. His former colleagues were generous in their interest and repeatedly furnished him with information, figures and discussion.

The *Economic Journal* article was not Keynes's first publication; a small green-covered notebook, in which for a few years he recorded his early writings and their earnings, starts with the year 1908 and shows on the first page:

		1908	£	s	d
1.	March	Stat. Journal. 'West Ham' Review	1	6	3
2.	March	Statement exhibiting the Moral and Material Progress and Condition of India 1906–07	50	0	0
3.	Septr	Econ. Journal. 'Rents, Prices and Wages'		7	6
4.	Decr	Econ. Journal. Further Note on the same subject.			
5.	Decr	'The Principles of Probability'. Fellowship Dissertation.			

Keynes's first publication then, by this authority, was a review signed 'J.M.K.' in the *Journal of the Royal Statistical Society* of a statistical analysis of the social and industrial problems of the West Ham area of London (*JMK*, vol. XI). The two notes in the *Economic Journal* that followed were a criticism of the method of using index numbers employed by a Board of Trade investigation (*JMK*, vol. XI).

Keynes's first known letter to a newspaper, signed with the initials J.M.K., was addressed to *The Economist*. Although it appeared as a letter to the editor, an acknowledgement and the green notebook show that *The Economist* paid £1 10s for it as an editorial contribution, probably because it elaborated on an editorial theme. The main political issue of the day was the movement of the Tariff Reform League for a 'scientific tariff', a cause which the free-trading *Economist* vigorously opposed. George Wyndham, a leading tariff reformer, had rather ineptly promised in a speech at Liverpool that the scientific tariff would operate to the detriment of profiteering bankers, brokers and shippers. *The Economist* delightedly seized on this occasion for an editorial ('Should London Become a Free Port?', 30 January 1909) envisaging the eclipse of the big northern commercial cities under tariff reform and ironically suggesting that London should become a free port to compensate for the consequent waning of her warehouse, banking, broking and shipping business. Keynes's letter was in somewhat the same vein.

To the Editor of The Economist, *6 February 1909*

Sir,

All tariff reformers will thank you, I feel sure, for your very suggestive article in the last number of *The Economist*, commending to their notice a proposal that, temporarily at least, London should remain a free port; for there are many who, in spite of their preferences for other occupations as a basis of national wealth, do not altogether agree with Mr Wyndham in despising the subsidiary trades and professions of shipping, banking, and broking. The example of Hamburg, too, is one which cannot but create a desire for imitation on the part of London. May I, therefore, submit a few reflections to which your article has given rise?

In the first place, it should not escape the notice of the Tariff Reform League, when they come to consider this matter, that the detriment to London's position as the leading emporium of the world's trade is not proportional to the height of the duties which may be imposed. Bonded warehouses and an elaborate system of rebates would be as necessary with a low as with a high tariff, and the interference with merchants in the free transactions of their business in shipping, warehousing, and re-exporting is not much less with an all-round duty as low as the league proposes in its most conciliatory moments, than it is with the tariff wall which free-traders predict when the prospects of the future seem to them gloomiest. Nor must we forget the close though sometimes hidden bond which connects with the freedom of trade the interests of the banking community. The centralisation in London of the world's banking has been due, of course, to more causes than one. But who can doubt that the immense volume of bills drawn by merchants of all countries, which circulate in the City, has been in the past a necessary condition, or that this volume could never have reached its present dimensions without the huge trade which London transacts as an importer both for home consumption and for eventual re-export?

In spite, however, of these special reasons for preserving, so far as London is concerned, the present system, there are certain difficulties in the way of the practical solution which you, sir, have proposed. If London is to be a free port, it will be necessary, I presume, to separate by a tariff wall the metropolitan districts from the rest of the country. It will be necessary to establish at the railway stations and at selected points on the leading thoroughfares a cordon of customs officers such as is necessitated in some continental towns by the system of *octroi* duties, who will hold up, for fear of contraband, the County Council trams on their journeys to Outer London. Apart from this, the port of ultimate re-export is not invariably the place of original import, and, if we are to leave the entrepôt trade unhindered, we must provide facilities for duty-free transport between London and the principal ports of departure. Even so, would Liverpool, Glasgow, and the rest permit themselves to be deprived of privileges which had been accorded to London? It might, one foresees, be most expedient in the long run to raise the tariff wall round Birmingham and declare as a free port the rest of the country.

In any case, the problem is one whose solution deserves close and immediate attention. You, sir, have proposed a method to which, in spite of its advantages, some practical objections can, I submit, be raised. It remains for those numerous tariff reformers, who recognise the importance of the interests endangered, to endorse your scheme or to put before the public some alternative means of mitigation.

Yours, etc.,

J.M.K.

2-2

Shortly afterwards Keynes began a lengthy correspondence in *The Economist* on a statistical problem he had encountered in his researches for 'Recent Economic Events in India'. One of the claims of the tariff reformers was that too much British capital was being invested abroad. In an article attempting to determine scientifically the total amount involved, *The Economist* ('Our Investments Abroad', 20 February 1909) made use of two estimates, one by 'a correspondent' and one by H. Beaumont, a member of the London Stock Exchange. Although Keynes had found in his article that there had been a rapid influx of capital into India, he questioned the figures given for India in both of these estimates as being too high.

To the Editor of The Economist, *27 February 1909*

Sir,

In your analysis of investments abroad in the last issue of *The Economist*, you attempted a very important enterprise. Some investigations, which I have recently undertaken for another purpose, lead me, however, to question your figures, so far as they relate to India. You quote a correspondent who estimates Indian indebtedness to Great Britain at £470 million, and you compare with this Mr Beaumont's estimate of £500 million. Accuracy in such a matter is, of course, impossible, but I should be interested to know on what kind of evidence these enormous totals are based. My own inquiries suggest a much smaller figure.

The definite evidence seems to be as follows. The rupee and sterling Government debt held in London in 1906 amounted, roughly, to £160 million. The ordinary and debenture capital of companies working in India, but registered in London, was, in 1905, about £96 million, the greater part being accounted for by railways, tea plantations, and mines. The capital of joint-stock companies registered in India amounted to about £28 million, to which must be added not more than £20 million on account of the debt of municipalities and port trusts, but it is probable that by far the greater part of this total sum of £48 million is held in India. For the remaining items our evidence is necessarily unprecise. We must add a large sum for the foreign banking capital employed in India, but £50 million is probably

an outside estimate under this head. There remain the unknown resources of the great foreign merchants and private
firms trading in India. Unless I have altogether omitted some
important item, it seems difficult to account for foreign investments in excess of some sum between £300 million and
£350 million.

I should trespass unduly on your space if I were to analyse
the Indian balance of trade. But this supplies, I think, an additional argument against any estimate which approaches £500
million. For, allowance being made for probable new investments and other known items on both sides of the account, the
sum left over is quite insufficient to pay the interest on so large
a sum.

I have no means of checking your estimates under other heads.
The compilation of more accurate figures than have been available hitherto regarding capital and interest transactions with
foreign countries is most essential if any safe deduction is to be
made from the figures of foreign trade regarding the financial
position of this country.

Faithfully yours,

J. M. KEYNES

Beaumont replied in a letter to *The Economist*, 6 March 1909, that Keynes
had underestimated the amount of capital involved by quoting figures from
1905 and 1906. The present market value of Indian railway securities listed
on the Stock Exchange was £137 million. If British investors held £160
million of Indian Government stocks in 1906 and account was taken of
subsequent borrowings, the total present British holdings of Indian *and
Ceylon* Government and railways securities must be 'fully £325 million'.
He accounted for the remaining £175 million in his own total of £500 million
by the considerable quantity of floating debentures issued by Indian railways
and held in London.

Beaumont added: 'I fail to see how any analysis of India's trade balance
could settle the point at issue, as it is difficult to ascertain how far payments
due for interest are cancelled by fresh borrowings at the time. India's yearly
debt to us is largely settled by her trade balance of £35 million due to her
from the United States and Europe.'

Keynes answered:

21

To the Editor of The Economist, *20 March 1909*

Sir,

Mr Beaumont's letter partially explains the discrepancy between his estimate of foreign investments in India and mine, but is not adequate, I think, to account for his total of £500 million. Perhaps I may be permitted to take up briefly one or two points. In the first place, I had not understood that he intended 'India' to include 'Ceylon', and I do not know how much difference that makes. In the second place, the discrepancy between my total for the capital of private railways and his is entirely due to his including the capitalised value of the annuities, and also certain Government railway debentures, by means of which the companies have been from time to time bought out. These annuities are paid by the Secretary of State, and are not naturally included amongst the liabilities of private companies. I had, however, omitted a part of these, and there has been an increase in the Government debt since the year 1906 to which my figures avowedly referred; on the other hand, a deduction must be made from the capital of private companies on account of the recent purchase of the Madras Railway. Making the necessary corrections and taking market values, as Mr Beaumont suggests, some net addition must be made to the items in question. I had allowed in my total estimate for a considerable error in defect in regard to these details, and I still doubt whether we can reasonably assess the unascertained banking and private trading capital employed in India at much more than £50 million. This about makes up the estimate of £350 million for India, excluding Ceylon.

With regard to the balance of trade, it is true, as Mr Beaumont suggests, that India pays a large part of her debt in a roundabout way, but the only figure relevant to the present argument is her *net* balance of exports over imports. Due allowance being made for Government transactions, we know for certain that practically the whole of this balance is required to meet the Secretary of State's various liabilities, the balance of private trade between

1903 and 1908 being almost equal on the average to the drawings of Council bills. We can certainly infer from this that the new capital annually loaned to India and remitted by private persons, together with any small miscellaneous amounts which may be due to her, must equal the payments due from her on account of interest, freight, insurance, banking charges, and other remittances. If, as Mr Beaumont holds, the foreign capital in India, exclusive of Government debt, is not far short of £300 million, the fresh capital annually loaned to India, exclusive, it must be carefully remembered, of Government borrowings, to enable her to pay the interest on this and the charges for freight, etc., must exceed £15 million. There is no visible trace of so large an amount of new private investment, and this is the argument, drawn from the balance of trade, to which I referred in my former letter.

Faithfully yours,

J. M. KEYNES

Beaumont replied (*Economist*, 27 March 1909) that if, as Keynes argued, practically the whole of the Indian balance of trade was needed to meet the Secretary of State's liabilities, it was difficult to see how the yearly interest on investment in India was to be met. Even if the £8 million of new capital that was subscribed in 1908 was the yearly average, the total interest bill would still not be covered. He criticised Keynes for taking an average of only five years of Council bills and transfers sold in London when the fluctuations from year to year were so great. 'Whatever the balance of trade figures seems to prove,' he asserted, 'I am convinced the larger total, viz., £500 million, is nearer the truth, and my view is, I find, confirmed by several in the City who should know.'

Beaumont gave his own calculation, emphasising that his figures were only a rough estimate. The items were £180 million, representing the part of the £245 million Government debt of India and Ceylon that was held in the United Kingdom; £160 million sterling railway debt (including £20 million of floating debentures), and £30 million invested in tea plantations—totalling £370 million. To this he added £100 million as an estimate of the investment in all other British enterprises in India.

At this point 'a correspondent', whose figures *The Economist* had originally quoted with Beaumont's, entered the discussion with an article on 'British Investments in India' (*Economist*, 10 April 1909), furnishing the data on which he based his own estimate of £470 million. His calculation took into account more items than either Beaumont's or Keynes's did, including not only Government stock and rupee paper, the market value of Indian railways with the capitalised value of their annuities, and Ceylon stocks, but also the total capital of a detailed list of commercial enterprises located in India (assuming this to be entirely British), the total capital of Anglo-Indian banking and merchant houses and of British shipping, telegraph and insurance companies, and finally a half of all the capital of Indian-registered joint-stock companies and Indian local authorities, which he took to represent the amount of British interest in these. Adding all the items together, he reached the sum of £470 million.

As to the balance of trade, 'a correspondent' argued both that the available figures were unreliable and that they were 'not inconsistent with' his estimate of a capital sum of £470 million. Using figures for the year ending 31 March 1908, he added the net balance of India's exports over its imports of £2,626,000 (including Government transactions) to the net amount subscribed in Britain for investment in India—£15,200,000—and arrived at the sum of £17,826,000. This, he concluded, capitalised at 25 years' purchase, represented a total sum of over £445 million.

Keynes replied to the article from Versailles, where he was spending the Easter vacation with Duncan Grant and writing an essay on index numbers (*JMK*, vol. XI) that won the Cambridge Adam Smith Prize.

To the Editor of The Economist, *8 May 1909*

Sir,

I feel unwilling to trouble you again on the above subject, but your correspondent's full discussion of my criticisms requires perhaps a reply. My criticisms were based on two distinct lines of argument—the direct argument from the available figures of capital investments, supplemented, where necessary, by doubtful estimates, and the indirect argument from India's balance sheet as a whole.

With regard to the first, I have nothing to add to my former letters. Your correspondent points to no factors of which I was not already aware, and the difference between our estimates arises from his allowing, in every case of doubt, what seems to me, but not of course to him, a total excessively generous to his own view. My estimates referred to 1908, since in most cases late

24

figures are not available. No tables of reference are at hand as I write, but even the comparatively definite figure of Indian Government stock held in this country he overestimates, I think, at £185 million. Further, if we take the *market* values of annuities and railway stock, we must be consistent, and deal with Government stock similarly, deducting an appreciable sum from the total nominal value.

With your correspondent's estimate of the capital of miscellaneous companies working in India and registered in London I concur. But if we assume that not a penny of this is held in India, can we also assume that no less than half of the capital of the companies and public bodies, *registered in India*, is held abroad? Is it reasonable, for instance, in the case of those Bombay cotton mills which work with rupee capital, and are, to all appearances, purely Indian concerns? And is it natural to suppose that a sum of £25 million, belonging to miscellaneous companies and trusts registered in India, is held abroad, no part, or no appreciable part, of which is quoted on any foreign stock exchange? In supposing, for the purposes of my estimate, that sterling companies are owned in England and rupee companies in India, I believed myself to be making two assumptions, the errors in which might be fairly taken in the present state of our knowledge to balance one another. Whatever may have been the case formerly, we can no longer act on the assumption that the invested savings of the inhabitants of India are of no account. Your correspondent's estimate can be based on no positive evidence, and is most improbable.

Finally, his estimate is brought up to the required amount by an allowance of £65 million for foreign banking and trade capital, and of £25 million for shipping, telegraph, and insurance companies. The first figure does seem to me, in spite of your correspondent, much too high. In my own estimate, I allowed £50 million, and thought this possibly beyond the mark; but the data are so scanty that it would be unreasonable to insist too much on any estimate. The inclusion of the second figure is, I expect, an afterthought of your correspondent's. It is inconvenient, and contrary to usage, to regard the capital of the P. and O. Steamship Company as partly situated in India. When we reckon the amount of British capital which has 'left the country' it is unusual, and rightly so, to include in this category the capital of our shipping companies. In any case, the principle of division would be obscure, and the actual figure named excessive.

The second part of my argument—from the balance of trade—still seems to me to be strong, and to be untouched by your correspondent's criticism. In the case of most countries no cogent argument could be derived from this source. But in the case of India there are two special circumstances to aid us. In the first place, we have precise information regarding a large part of the total volume of transactions—that part transacted through the Secretary of State. In the second place, we can safely assume that the miscellaneous payments due to India are small—much smaller at any rate than those due *from* her.

Since the element of doubt in our argument refers to private transactions, we can introduce the great simplification of first deducting all Government transactions. We find, by the process of comparing the volume of Council bills, and the balance of private trade during the last five years, that the source of remittances towards England arising out of the latter is almost wholly swallowed up by the sales of the former. The proceeds of Council bills, together with the Secretary of State's borrowings in London, go to meet interest on the public debt, and on most of the railways, the cost of Government stores, of silver, railway materials, etc., bought in England, the gold standard and currency reserves, and other miscellaneous charges. We know, therefore—and there is no room up to this point for arbitrary estimates—that during the last few years the fresh capital annually loaned to *private* companies in India must about equal the sum of the interest on capital previously loaned to them, *plus* the payments due from India on account of freight, insurance, banking charges, etc. Deduction being made for Government and railway debt, the interest on which is paid through the India Office, your correspondent estimates that investments in private companies are not less than £215 million. As this excludes all guaranteed debt, and includes much private trading capital, the rate of interest cannot be less than 5 per cent and is probably higher. New investments to India, *excluding all debt raised through the Secretary of State*, must amount, therefore, over a course of years to an average exceeding £10,500,000 annually, *plus* the amount due from India for freight, etc. Your correspondent quotes the figure of £15,200,000 for 1908. But this, which was a larger figure than usual, was mainly made up of *Government* borrowings, which we must altogether exclude from the present calculation. He has given no evidence whatever which meets the force of the indirect argument, and until he can do so we ought to refrain from accepting a direct estimate, inconsistent with it, which is based on much that is arbitrary and excessively uncertain.

I may add that, while the year 1908 was specially favourable to your correspondent's argument in respect of capital investment, it was, on the whole, *unfavourable* to him on account of the unprecedentedly small trade balance of that year. His selection of a year unfavourable to his argument is counterbalanced by his omission of the Secretary of State's home charges, beyond those for treasure, stores, and interest, of the growth of his reserves, and of the sums due from India for freight, etc. His example does not do his argument justice, but the argument is for these reasons bad.

Yours, etc.,

J. M. KEYNES

(The estimate of £215 million for British investments in private companies which Keynes attributed to *The Economist*'s correspondent was apparently arrived at by deducting from the total for British investment of £470 million the estimated £185 million of Government stocks and approximately half of the estimated railway debt of £138 million, the latter deduction representing the portion of the total on which interest was paid through the India Office.)

The somewhat questionable evidence of a statement by the Bombay Presidency Association in a loyal address to Queen Victoria in 1887, that 'nearly 500 millions' of British capital was invested in Indian 'agriculture, manufacture and trade', was offered by a member of the Indian Educational Service in the next issue of *The Economist* and the correspondence ended. It had, however, attracted the notice of the Under-Secretary of State who mentioned it in the House of Commons debate on the Indian Budget.

Sir Thomas Holderness, writing (23 March 1909) to congratulate Keynes on his election to the King's College Fellowship—he was elected 16 March, on the basis of the revised dissertation on probability—remarked concerning the first two letters:

> ...It seems to me that you have [the] facts on your side. In your economic studies don't forget the field for observation which India offers. We here have not the time (and possibly not the technical training) for a close examination of the economic phenomena of India. You will help us if you will do what we fail to do.

When, three years later, Sir Thomas Holderness answered a correspondent's request for an estimate of the amounts of Indian and non-Indian capital invested in India, he sent Keynes a copy of his reply (14 February 1912). He suggested a comparison of some official figures which gave 'such information as we have'—imperfect because they did not include some of the most important undertakings in India—with figures given by George Paish in some papers read to the Royal Statistical Society. 'But I am not sanguine, as the obstacles are many', he said.

> ...In most cases the bulk of the capital is European. But there is probably not a single company in which many native names do not figure in the list of shareholders; and it is impossible to say what proportion of the total capital their aggregate shareholding represents...Broadly speaking, I should say that in the Bombay Presidency possibly the Parsis and other non-Europeans own a half or more of the mills and other industrial concerns; but that elsewhere in India the non-European share is less than one-fourth and may not exceed one-sixth or even one-eighth.

Keynes retained a copy of his own letter to Holderness. The review that he mentions was of *The Economic Transition in India* by Sir Theodore Morison, which he had written for the *Economic Journal* (*JMK*, vol. XI).

To SIR THOMAS HOLDERNESS, *22 February 1912*

Dear Sir Thomas,

Wakely has forwarded to me a copy of your letter to Mr Percy Ashley relating to foreign investments of capital in India. I have thought about this question a good deal from time to time, but have never yet hit upon any method of making a really accurate estimate; and I think the general tenor of your reply is the only one possible.

Paish's estimate, which is quoted by [G. Findlay] Shirras in the *Indian Trade Journal*, did not when originally published distinguish between India and Ceylon. Shirras does not mention this, and the only correction he has made has been to reduce the figure for investments in railways by about 11 millions, leaving the other items unaltered. This is clearly not accurate, for a considerable part of the capital invested in tea and coffee (apart from other minor items) must be accounted for by Ceylon. But how inaccurate it is I do not know.

When Paish originally read his paper, I complained to him of his having combined India and Ceylon together, and he told me that there would be no special difficulty in separating them. But I have not heard that he has ever done this. I enclose a copy of his paper. The relevant table is on p. 7.

I enclose also a copy of a review, which I wrote last year, of Morison's new book. On pp. 429, 430 I made some calculations relevant to the present problem, attacking it from the point of view of the balance of trade. You will see that I arrived at the conclusion that during the last ten years new *private* investments approximately balanced interest on *private* capital already invested. But the value of each of these two items is of course very conjectural.

I am inclined to think that considerations derived from the balance of trade justify one in supposing that that part of the foreign capital invested in India, on which the interest is *not* paid through the Secretary of State, lies at the present time between 100 and 140 millions, the latter figure being an absolutely outside limit.

In some countries, where the bulk of foreign investment is put into public companies, one is in a very much better position for estimating its amount than in India—where so much of the foreign capital employed is in banks and private businesses. This latter circumstance makes the argument from the statistics of public companies peculiarly unreliable. I prefer, therefore, to pay attention to the light which the balance of trade can throw upon the problem. But calculations arrived at in this manner are necessarily vague.

[Copy unsigned]

Keynes gave his first lecture, according to his father's diary, on 19 January 1909. The course was entitled 'Money, Credit and Prices'; he lectured on this subject twice a week during his first four terms of work. In the Lent term of 1910 he branched out into eight extra lectures on 'The Stock Exchange and the Money Market'. 'Maynard's Stock Exchange class yesterday numbered 52, and there wasn't even standing room', Dr Keynes wrote in his diary, 20 January 1910.

During Keynes's first year as a don a covertly prejudiced and patronising article on 'The Indian Student at Cambridge' appeared in the *Cambridge Review*, 13 May 1909. The occasion for the article was a proposal for an information bureau and advisory committee to help both Indian students in England and the colleges to which they applied. Its tone may be gathered from the anonymous writer's account of the need for such bodies.

...The present stamp of Hindu undergraduate is not so good as his forebears: he is often morally, socially, and intellectually inferior...Selection is important, but mistakes may sometimes be made. Absolute restriction as to numbers is a further safeguard...On one point there can be no dispute, and that is if the Indian undergraduates are allowed to congregate at two or three colleges or hostels, the tendency is naturally for them to make their own exclusive society; they keep to themselves, the difficulty of their mixing with the British undergraduate is made more difficult, and the opportunity of their gaining in 'character' is lost. Not only so: there is political danger...If they have returned [to their country] embittered against the British Government in India, many of them with one sole object, to help in expelling the British administration, what is the outlook for India but what Lord Morley said, 'Anarchy and bloody carnage'? The University cannot calmly disregard an open intention to destroy a part of the British Empire, or to those who hold those views hospitably open her doors and grant degrees, and call herself their dear Mother!

The article continued: 'Indians *will* seek access to the colleges at Cambridge, and *concerted* action on the part of the colleges is necessary to make their residence here a benefit and not a bane to all concerned.' The author invoked 'the sacred duty of hospitality to lead the white man to make allowances'; with a unique flash of sympathy he recognised the torture for an Indian of dining in Hall—'those hunks of mutton and beef, beef and mutton!' But this was spoiled by a final paragraph enjoining Indians (among whom, one of their prominent well-wishers had admitted, were numerous 'bounders') to learn to tell the truth and pay their debts and 'show no mercy to those who advocate the dismemberment of the British Empire'.

Keynes never visited India but he had some appreciation of the feelings of his Indian contemporaries. His India Office reading made him familiar with Indian periodicals and pamphlets. It was a period of considerable political unrest. At one time, probably while in the India Office, he amused himself by copying out quotations from nationalistic editorials. The language and sentiments were high-flown, but the message was clear. His reaction to the *Cambridge Review*'s article appeared in the next issue.

To the Editor of the Cambridge Review, *20 May 1909*

Sir,

Many of your readers will have regretted that you found a place last week for an article so lacking in discernment and good feeling as that on 'The Indian Student at Cambridge'. When one reads such expressions of opinion, it is easy to understand *why* we have an 'Indian problem' in Cambridge, and why, in the past, we have sometimes sent young Indians back to India embittered against us. Your contributor was so evidently unaware of the real nature of his own sentiments, that he will probably regard this criticism as most unjust. Yet it is he and people like him who *create* the problem as it exists here.

It is not necessary that I should recall the various charges and complaints with which he led up to the conclusion that Indians are 'bounders', who may hope to gain, by mixing with us, a little 'character'. These were the commonplaces of prejudice, which should not have been brought forward anonymously and unsubstantiated.

The question of the future action of the colleges, however, and of their relation to the new advisory committee raises a

31

matter of much importance. The plan of distributing Indian students evenly amongst the colleges is the most valuable of all practical suggestions, and would probably go far towards curing some of the existing evils. If each college would agree to take two applicants a year, the matter would be settled. In providing information upon which the tutors can exercise their judgment, the advisory committee may give valuable assistance, and tutors, who have been wisely unwilling in the past to admit candidates about whom they knew nothing, may now agree to take their share in a scheme of distribution. The danger lies, of course, in the possibility that one or two tutors may not choose to exercise their discretion, and may thus collect together all those Indians who should have been discouraged from entering the University.

The absolute limitation of total number, which your contributor suggests, is an unwise proposal. For it might work indiscriminately. Furthermore in considering plans of limitation, we must not forget that to prevent a student from coming to Cambridge is not necessarily to dissuade him from coming to Europe, and that life here is probably much better for him in many ways than in London or Paris. Since we fill up the Indian Civil Service and the Indian Medical Service through examinations held in England on the lines of English education, since qualifications for the higher posts in the scientific departments can only be obtained at a European university, and while a call to the English bar is thought to be an advantage in India, it is our duty to give full opportunity to all Indians whose ambitions lie most properly in these directions. By putting obstacles in the way we should create a real and heavy grievance.

There remains the censorship of political discussion which appeals so strongly to your contributor's instincts. I can conceive nothing more contrary both to expediency and to the proper spirit of a university. I am not one of those who dispute the wisdom of restrictive measures in India, where an ignorant populace may be excited, not so much through the preaching of a political creed, as by mis-statements and distortions of fact. But to stifle free discussion, even of the British Empire, in an English university involves completely different considerations. Many Indians, I know, use their influence to discourage anti-British rhetoric, and to promote the reasonable discussion of India's future. But, in any case, suppression of debate or a refusal to grant degrees is not the right way to dissuade from his opinions a rash and enthusiastic undergraduate. British rule in India has little to fear from free criticism, but it is not necessary to regard such criticism as the certain symptom of a vicious and debased spirit.

The prospect for the future is better, I think, than it has been in recent times. The calmer temper which now prevails in India is reflected here. The feeling aroused a few years ago by some bitterly contested elections at the [Cambridge] Union has died away, and the Indian community are prepared on their side with friendlier feelings. We too have realised the unsatisfactory state of affairs which succeeded the interested curiosity with which the first comers were greeted. The colleges are awakening to their proper duty in the matter, and there is now an advisory committee to make the tutor's task easier. There will be difficulties and misunderstanding to overcome. But it should be possible, without restriction of entry or suppression of opinion, to bring about such a state of affairs, that embittered personal feeling will be, no longer, even a part cause of antagonism to the British Government, amongst those who return to India from this university.

I am, your obedient servant,

J. M. KEYNES

The editing of the report on the Moral and Material Progress of India had given Keynes some ideas for its improvement, and his successor in the task at the India Office, at the suggestion of both Sir Thomas Holderness and Lionel Abrahams, consulted him on its organisation. When the report was published Keynes wrote *The Economist* review of it: the review is unsigned but his notebook lists it as earning three guineas.

From The Economist, *3 July 1909*

INDIA DURING 1907–8

The new issue of the India Office's annual statement (price 1s 3d), exhibiting the Moral and Material Progress and Condition of India, is a mine of general information which ought to be better known. Several changes have been introduced this year, and they effect, so far as we can judge, great improvements. The volume is, however, still marked by a too rigid economy of statement upon many interesting and controversial subjects, which is somewhat characteristic of the India Office. Some reticence may be wise. A government is not bound to supply unfriendly critics with fuel. But if the officials prefer to maintain silence touching the difficulties they have to encounter and the imperfections which exist in spite of their efforts, they must not be surprised that the public sometimes derive their information from less trustworthy sources, or complain of British ignorance respecting the peculiar difficulties of Indian administration. The period covered by the report was one of the most trying in the recent history of the country. Plague, famine, and political unrest quickly followed one another. Prices rose to an unprecedented level, revenue fell off, and the currency system seemed at one moment to be in danger. We do not get from the pages of the statement an impression of the anxieties which have been successfully overcome, or realise the stability of a system which such shocks have been unable to disturb. Of political unrest there is, in effect, no mention; the account of plague dwells on the remedial measures of Government, and does not emphasise the extraordinary mortality in certain districts; in the chapter on finance we are left, for the most, to draw our own inferences from the figures. Of the famine, however, there is an admirable, if rather colourless, account. In the United Provinces alone, we are told, it is estimated that the loss of food grains amounted to 7,000,000 tons, valued at £28 million, equal to nine months' food supply, and the loss of other crops (cotton, oilseeds, etc.) to

£10 million. The extraordinary depletion of stocks resulting from this may be some explanation of the slow rate at which the Indian wheat crop of the present year is being moved forward for export.

Turning to the more permanent features of Indian administration, we find material for a just appreciation of the steady advance in nearly all departments. The currency system and the constitution of the gold standard reserve are explained for the first time. There is a separate chapter on Manufactures and Industrial Development; and the numerous scientific departments, which have been so greatly expanded since Lord Curzon initiated his new schemes, are now grouped together. One of the most interesting of the new movements in India is that towards the formation of co-operative credit societies amongst agriculturists. The movement, which began in 1904, has already made great progress, and seems to have received no serious setback on account of the recent famine. The societies steadily increased in number from 41 in 1905 to 1,358 in 1908, with a membership of nearly 150,000 and total resources amounting to about £300,000. There is an enormous field for further development, but a good beginning has been made in what may prove to be a powerful agency for the emancipation of the peasant from the village moneylender and for the much-needed direction of new capital into agriculture. Members are charged, as a rule, from 9 to 12 per cent on loans, and are allowed from 6 to 7 per cent on deposits, as compared with the 15 to 75 per cent charged by the local capitalists for agricultural loans on ordinarily good security. A good number of the loans are used at present for the repayment of old debts bearing exorbitant rates of interest, but an increasing number are for productive purposes, such as cultivation and the purchase of cattle.

A new chapter on the condition of the people is, perhaps, the most interesting in the volume. We are confronted here, however, with the extreme unreliability of many Indian statistics. It is a good general rule that where detailed figures are collected for a definite administrative purpose, they can be relied on; but where their sole purpose is to satisfy the simple but legitimate requirements of the merchant, or the troublesome and often trifling curiosity of the academic statistician, neither speed nor accuracy can be looked for. But it is unfortunate that the commercial departments laboriously collect estimates, and publish them after their practical value is lost. If you grow fruit you might as well pick it when it is ripe, even if it involves a little extra expenditure. We can hardly ask the Indian Government to spend large sums at the present time on the collection of such facts, but they do not, perhaps, quite realise to what an extent accurate and easily accessible information oils the wheels of commerce. We have already called attention in these columns to the inefficiency of the machinery for collecting and disseminating the crop forecasts. The great bulk of the statistics relating to agriculture, prices, and wages is open to similar criticisms. The apologist of our Indian administration still asks in vain for the simple statistical data which would upset the statistical fiction of an India declining under British rule.

Recent movements of prices and wages in India raise a number of interesting questions. Until 1903 prices were, on the whole, falling, but between that year and 1907 the official index number for articles consumed or exported rose from 103 to 148, and that for food grains from 126 to 180. Such a change is enormous, and must, if these figures represent the facts, have profoundly affected the condition of the people. Whether the rate of wages has fully responded to the increased cost of living, it is almost impossible to say. The tendency has certainly been upwards but, apart from the wage census taken in the United Provinces during 1906, all statistics relating to wages are most unprecise. The official view may be too optimistic, and there has been probably much local distress, where wages are not paid in kind. Where, on the other hand, the ravages of plague have been worst, wages have risen even more than prices. It is not fully realised in this country how devastating plague has been in particular localities, especi-

36

ally in the Punjab. The population of large tracts has been more than decimated, and in a few places nearly half the population have perished since the first outbreak of the disease. Under such conditions there have been districts in which the crops were left standing on the ground for lack of labourers to harvest them, and the favourable harvests of this year have naturally caused a demand for labour which exceeds the supply. The *Pioneer* has recently reported that labourers have been able in some parts of the Punjab to earn a rupee a day in the fields, with the result that on the North-Western Railway and the new canal works it has been difficult to keep gangs together. The permanent effect of these circumstances on the position of the labourer may be profound, and one recalls the parallel of the Black Death in England. The labourer finds himself master of the situation. Every year, we are told, he becomes more mobile, and moves of his own accord to places where remunerative employment exists. But the above is not true, of course, respecting India as a whole. In the United Provinces, for instance, the agricultural labourer earns from $1\frac{1}{2}d$ to $3d$ a day according to the locality, and in the centres of industry the wages of unskilled labour are from $3d$ to $4d$. It is not clear that real wages may not have diminished in some cases as the result of high prices. In some parts of Eastern Bengal, for example, the price of rice doubled in four or five years.

It is consoling to turn from these rather disturbing figures to the chapter on finance. Never before, probably, has taxation sat so lightly on the people of India. The reduction of the salt tax by successive stages from Rs $2\frac{1}{2}$ per maund of $82\frac{2}{7}$ lb in 1902 to Rs 1 in 1907 has benefited the consumer to its full extent, as the returns of retail salt prices throughout India clearly show, and has led to an increase in consumption of 20 per cent. Let us hope it may soon be abolished. The Government's commercial undertakings, the post office, railways, and irrigation, now yield from £2 to £3 million a year in excess of the interest charges, and the deadweight debt has been reduced to £38 million, with an annual interest charge of less than £1 million. About 40 per cent of the net revenue of the country is derived from land revenue, the most economical and least oppressive of all forms of taxation. By immemorial right the State is part landlord of the country, and can derive its revenue from this source of wealth without injustice to individuals or disturbance to industry. The evidence shows that the real share of the rent, measured in kind, taken by the State, has steadily decreased during the last 50 years. It may be added that the burden of land revenue per head of the population of British India was in 1907–8 1s 6d.

To form a judgment on the political condition of India at the present time we must go to non-official sources. But a more widespread knowledge of the facts and figures contained in this annual report would go some way towards removing misconceptions as to the economic effects of British rule in India. A useful bibliography of Indian official reports is given at the end of the volume.

Keynes's mentor was Lionel Abrahams, the moulder and manipulator of India's involved but efficient financial system. He submitted to Abrahams' criticism everything that he wrote concerning Indian finance and the discussion was carried on both by conversation and by letter. In Keynes's papers only Abrahams' side of the longhand correspondence remains, but the intellectual stimulation seems to have been mutual. '...I take the opportunity of thanking you for the assistance that I derived from the methods used in your paper in the *Economic Journal*', Abrahams wrote in a letter dated 31 October 1909. It presumably was Keynes who arranged a week earlier for Abrahams to bring some of his staff (Dr Keynes in his diary, 24 October, described it as 'an embassy from the India Office') to Cambridge to discuss Indian currency and prices with Alfred Marshall. Marshall had been interested in Indian economic problems since his early lecturing days in Oxford and in 1899 he had given some elaborate evidence to the Fowler Committee on Indian Currency—to which Abrahams had been the Assistant Secretary. Commenting in the same letter on their meeting, Abrahams said:

I found Marshall instructive as well as interesting. You know what my views were before our conference: and what I was specially concerned to know was whether a careful economist, considering the questions from a point of view different from my own, would tell me that I must temporarily or permanently abandon my views on account of considerations to which I had not attached due weight. I was relieved to find that he did not do this and that, in the more important respects, you agreed with him. My final conclusion is not that I may slumber in peace because we are dispensed from the necessity of changing the currency system—but rather that we could not make any change without doing more harm than good...

As a free-trading Liberal Keynes was engaged in battling with the tariff reformers in the two general elections that began and ended the year 1910. He was secretary of the Cambridge University Free Trade Association, a non-party organisation, and as a partisan he spoke from the platform for Liberal candidates. He addressed the Majlis, the Indian undergraduate debating society at Cambridge, on 'India and Protection'. He also defended the free trade position in the local press.

Both the Liberal and Conservative parties were split over tariff reform, and the Liberals were split over Home Rule for Ireland as well. The election issues were extremely tangled, involving not only free trade and Home Rule but Lloyd George's controversial People's Budget of 1909, the reform of the House of Lords which had rejected that Budget, and a growing preoccupation with national defence. A fellow of Trinity College, Basil Edward Hammond, wrote a letter to the *Cambridge Daily News*, 28 December 1909, on the 'Thoughts of a Unionist Free Trader on the Coming Election in Cambridge', demonstrating the dilemma of the voter attempting to arrive at a rational decision. He argued that bad as the protectionist policy might be, its social results would not be so disastrous as the 'sapping of the manhood of the working classes' by Lloyd George's plan for old-age pensions, and that tariff reform could be neither so prompt nor so irrevocable in its consequences. On other questions he looked to the tariff reformers to defend the Union against Asquith's desire for Home Rule; he feared that Asquith would eliminate the Lords in favour of a single chamber; he expected that the Unionists would do more for national defence than a party that had put old-age pensions ahead of the Navy. Under the circumstances he hoped 'that Mr Asquith should not have a large majority' and would vote for Almeric Paget, the Conservative candidate, rather than S. O. Buckmaster, the Liberal.

Keynes's answer appeared the very next day.

To the Editor of the Cambridge Daily News, *29 December 1909*

Sir,

Mr Hammond's letter in your issue of yesterday, in which, disliking much in the policy of both parties, he comes to the conclusion that he will do most wisely to vote for Mr Paget, probably represents a balance of opinion not uncommon, and worthy, therefore, of close attention. His argument depends, broadly, upon the belief that those Liberal measures which he dislikes can be rapidly and irrevocably put into effect, but that the positive results of a Conservative victory might be long postponed. He seeks to demonstrate, in fact, that the traditional reason for a moderate man's voting Conservative, namely, that the Conservative party in office will leave things substantially as they now are—exists at the present time.

The fact that I differ most profoundly from this conclusion is the main reason why I, personally, attach unusual importance to a Liberal victory in the forthcoming election. This must be my excuse for writing to you with the object of showing that permanent changes of the greatest possible moment, as objectionable to Mr Hammond, I expect, as they are to me, are really the probable result of a Conservative victory now or in the immediate future.

Let us consider from this point of view the plans of the tariff reformers. In the first place, it is surely plain that the Conservative party could not hang together for a session unless these plans were to take instant effect. The Tariff Reform party are in earnest, if ever a party was, and they are strong enough within the Conservative machine to prevent even Mr Balfour's snatching from them the legitimate fruits of victory. Nor are the practical difficulties in their way insurmountable. The negotiation of the necessary commercial treaties would, it has been argued from the experience of Germany, effect a delay. I do not believe that this is the case. We have no complicated treaties to supersede, such as those in the way of an already protectionist country which seeks to change from one tariff to another. I see nothing to prevent the imposition of a tariff system on food and manufacture within a year. In what respect would such a system be less irrevocable than the provisions of Mr Lloyd George's Budget? Does Mr Hammond's knowledge of history teach him that even those tariffs, which were assuredly temporary at the beginning, have been actually so in fact?

Mr Hammond's objections to the Budget, on the other hand, are directed rather against the possible exaggerations of it, which may follow, than against the Budget itself. I do not think that he need fear such exaggeration in the near future. If this Budget, which provides much more money for future years than for the present, is carried, I think we may expect that the Liberal party will rest awhile from budgeting. In the present Budget Mr Hammond knows the worst, I think, of the finance of this Liberal administration. But does he know the worst that the tariff reformers may inflict? If they really intend, and it is not absurd to believe them, to raise sufficient revenue by tariffs to support the Navy and old-age pensions, where may not the attempt to fulfil this intention lead us? I repeat that the Liberal Budget really does raise the money, and we know the worst. Of Tariff Reform finance we know scarcely the beginning.

Secondly, those in the House of Lords. Mr Hammond assumes that the Liberal party intend to establish what would be, substantially, a single chamber system. They have, I believe, neither the intention nor the power to do so. The Lord Chancellor is by no means the only 'two chamber' man in the Cabinet, and Mr Buckmaster is not the only member of the rank and file of the party who would oppose it. It is not necessary to probe the secret desires of extension to know that the thing is not possible. The immense preponderance of opinion against it in the country is fully reflected in the Liberal party. A Conservative victory, on the other hand, would, it is unnecessary to point out to Mr Hammond, involve a change in the constitutional custom of the country and in the powers of the House of Lords so tremendous that permanent toleration of it would be impossible. The progressive parties, as a necessary condition of their continued existence, must reverse it even at the expense of a generation of political unrest.

I must not take up your space much further. With regard to

Home Rule, it is true that the Liberal party is pledged to give to the Irish the control of their own affairs, and Mr Hammond must, in so far as he is opposed to this, place it on the other side of the account. But he need not fear separation or a breach of the fundamental principles of the Union. This, like the establishment of a single chamber system, is not, in the present temper of the Liberal party itself, politically possible. But if there is any risk of more concession to the Irish party than is wise, it would arise out of that narrow balance of power between the two great political parties which Mr Hammond seems to desire.

Lastly, I do not understand how if, as Mr Hammond believes, we are on the brink of an international crisis, national defence is to gain from an indecisive result to the present election, which would prolong, perhaps for years, agitation and inflamed feeling between classes and parties. The interests of the nation, I submit to Mr Hammond, demand that we should have now a decisive answer to the questions before it. And I urge all those of his opinion to remember that only a decisive defeat can make the Conservative party repent of tariff reform, that only a decisive victory can leave the Liberals free to deal with Ireland and with the problems of labour as reason rather than immediate expediency directs, and that only a decisive result, one way or the other, can give us a stable Government, strong to deal with troubles from abroad, if it be indeed true that these troubles are upon us. What do we gain from delay, in Mr Hammond's opinion? The country must make up its mind sooner or later which of the two policies now before us it really prefers.

I am, sir, yours, etc.

J. M. KEYNES

Two weeks later Keynes again addressed a letter to the *Cambridge Daily News* in reply to Archdeacon William Cunningham, the economic historian, who had chosen the statements of two professors as occasion to expatiate on the idiosyncrasies of professors in general and the advantages of protectionism in particular. The Archdeacon interpreted a recent book by J. S. Nicholson, Professor of Political Economy at the University of Edinburgh, as a gratifying abandonment of the writer's well-known free trade principles. He went on to refute a declaration by the Slade Professor of Fine Art at Cambridge, Charles Waldstein, that free trade was the system by which this country had prospered, by a summary of British trade policy from the protectionism of Elizabeth to its present low ebb following the adoption of free trade in 1850. Keynes's letter was written from Birmingham, where he was speaking in support of his friend Edward Hilton Young, who was campaigning against Austen Chamberlain, the chief protagonist of tariff reform, in Chamberlain's long-held seat of East Worcestershire.

To the Editor of the Cambridge Daily News, *13 January 1910*

Sir,

Archdeacon Cunningham's letter in your issue of yesterday is calculated to leave the impression in the reader's mind that the interesting and important book, which Professor Nicholson has recently published, involves a partial recantation of his former free trade opinions. I should like, therefore, to inform those of your readers who have not seen Professor Nicholson's *Project of Empire*, that a principal object of this book is to show that an admission of the preponderant importance of investing as much capital as possible in Great Britain, rather than abroad, is no help whatever to the protectionist argument, that protection has no tendency to retain capital at home, and that this aspect of the matter was fully dealt with by Adam Smith in some chapters of his famous work, which are not known so well as they should be. It is surprising to find Archdeacon Cunningham probing with approval an author whose text from beginning to end is 'Back to Adam Smith', and whose object is the development on free trade lines of Adam Smith's imperial ideals.

The Archdeacon's other conclusion, that it was protection which enabled us to defeat the Spanish Armada, was put forward, no doubt, for amusement's sake. It is never easy to know when to take the Archdeacon seriously.

Yours, etc.

J. M. KEYNES

The radical Budget of 1909—with its provisions for a rising income-tax, super-tax on incomes over £5,000, higher death duties, levies on unearned increments, and heavy taxes on the liquor trade—was attacked as a demonstration of how Liberal policies would drive British investment out of the country. Keynes refuted this claim by the tariff reformers—who pledged themselves to keep capital at home—in a full-length article which was published by Desmond MacCarthy in the *New Quarterly*.

The article was a forerunner of the kind of political-economic essay that Keynes was later to write for the *Nation*. He was apparently rather diffident about it, fearing that it was 'dull', but he was encouraged by MacCarthy who wrote to him 23 September 1909: 'I don't think you do justice to your own work; it is much more interesting than you think.'

From the New Quarterly, *February 1910*

GREAT BRITAIN'S FOREIGN INVESTMENTS

Nothing has been more noticeable in the campaign between free trade and tariff reform than the gradual growth of the importance attached by the latter party to the charge that the policy of their opponents is driving capital from the country to the detriment of British enterprise and labour. Only comparatively recently has the charge been heard at all; but for the last few months the reiterations of it have risen in a crescendo culminating in the House of Lords' debate, when no other single subject received greater prominence.

The charge is the outcome of an entirely new way of regarding this particular question, which is, however, not at all inconsistent with the manner in which international relations generally are now viewed by the party which advances it. The strength of England's international position, arising out of her pre-eminence as a creditor country, used formerly to be a matter of general admiration. The extraordinary advantages to which, partly by chance, she owed this commanding position, have naturally in some degree passed away. But by permitting a part of her foreign loans to accumulate at compound interest, she has maintained a position hardly less strong than formerly. We used to make no complaint, therefore, against the process by which part of the interest due to us is not paid for the present and is reinvested to swell the amount which will be due in the future. But another side to the question has now been discovered. To place our resources at the disposal of foreigners is to strengthen those who may ultimately overthrow us, and to send capital out of the country is to impoverish our own people. The object of this article is to discover whether such a view has in this particular case any real basis. For it is at least plausible to suppose that circumstances *might* exist in which foreign investment was a symptom of decaying enterprise at home and the agent of national weakness.

I begin, therefore, by admitting that a large and increasing export of capital *might* be the symptom of a decaying polity, and that the arguments of those who urge that this is actually the case deserve examination. The result of the examination must chiefly depend upon two questions of fact, of which the first is easily answered, but the second is partly a matter of opinion. We must inquire to whom the capital is sent, and in what manner it is employed. And, secondly, we must determine what considerations influence investors in placing their savings at home or abroad. We must also examine into the truth of the underlying hypothesis that the export of capital abroad has actually grown out of proportion to the increase in the national wealth.

Let us examine first the considerations which influence investors. It is evident that the volume of foreign investment entirely depends on the nature of the advantages which that kind of investment can offer. A change, therefore, in the relative volume of home and foreign investment can only be brought about by a change in the kind or the degree of the advantage which the average investor believes that he can obtain from each. The determining factors are principally the following:

1. The rate of interest;
2. The kind and degree of risk;
3. The ease with which the capital value can be recovered;

4. The desire to further some cause or enterprise for other reasons than those of economic profit.

Not much need be said about the rate of interest. The investor will naturally be determined by the *net* rate; and if the amount of taxation which he must pay varies in the case of different classes of investment, this must be taken into account. Moreover, he will be affected, as is obvious, not by the net income which he will actually receive from his investment in the long run, but by his expectations. These will often depend upon fashion, upon advertisement, or upon purely irrational waves of optimism or depression. Similarly by risk we must mean, not the real risk as measured by the actual average yield of the class of investment over the period of years to which the expectation refers, but the risk as it is estimated, wisely or foolishly, by the investor. His desire that the net rate of interest shall be as high as possible will be modified by the usually conflicting desire that the rate of risk shall be as low as possible. But no mathematical rule can be laid down respecting the exact compromise which will be struck between the fear of loss and the desire for a high rate of interest. The ordinary investor would prefer a certainty of four per cent to an even chance of eight per cent or nil. But how great an evil he considers it depends upon his individual circumstances and psychology. There is probably a difference, for instance, at the present time between English and French investors in this respect.

Since the risk of which we must take account is the subjective risk, the feeling, that is to say, in the mind of the investor, its magnitude very largely depends upon the amount of relevant information regarding the investment that is easily accessible to him. What would be a risky investment for the ignorant speculator may be exceptionally safe for the well-informed expert. The amount of the risk to any investor principally depends, in fact, upon the degree of his ignorance respecting the circumstances and prospects of the investment he is considering. It will, however, also depend upon what we may term the objective risk, so

46

far as that is known to him, arising, for instance, out of bad and unstable government or the uncertainty of the seasons.

The third factor—the ease with which the capital value can be recovered—is more important than is sometimes supposed. Consols provide an extreme instance, the ease with which they can be pawned or sold and the low rate of the charges involved in transfer compensating in the eyes of many investors for their exceptionally low yield; and the difference between the rates of interest on Consols and on a high-class mortgage is hardly due at all to the difference of risk. This factor naturally tells severely *against* foreign investment. Just as many local securities which are quoted on provincial stock exchanges are not quoted in London, so many foreign securities have no regular market at all. This need not be due to their being specially risky or in any other way undesirable, but solely to the relatively small extent to which they are bought and sold in this country. Even in India, for instance, where the predominance of English capital is most marked, there are companies having in the aggregate a capital of £50 million which are not quoted on any English exchange. The difficulty and delay which must ensue if an investor wishes to dispose of such shares in this country naturally deters him from purchasing them. There are numerous South American bonds, to take another example, in which the relatively high yield is counterbalanced, in the eyes of the investor, by the difficulty of reselling them.

The fourth factor is less important. There is no evidence that extra-economic motives are effective in more than isolated cases, or that their influence is steadily either for or against foreign investments. There are no doubt persons who are appreciably influenced in making their investments by a desire to develop the Empire or to support home industries, who put their money into tea plantations rather than into breweries, and prefer garden cities to Congo rubber. But there is no reason to suppose that, in the aggregate, their action either swells or diminishes appreciably the stream of foreign investment, foreign investment

47

always meaning, for the purposes of this article, investment out-side the United Kingdom.

Now it is clear that the yield of investments in new countries with great unexploited natural resources must tend to be greater than in old countries where the more profitable forms of business have been already developed. Nor can there be any doubt that there is more profit to be made on the average and in the long run from rubber or from Canadian land and railway development than from extensions or improvements in English railways. We only refrain from the former class of investment, first, on account of the disadvantageous position in which most of us find our-selves for determining which of the various companies, from which we must choose, are honest enterprises likely to be success-ful; and, secondly, in some cases, on account of the difficulty of selling out again when once we have embarked upon them. If investors in England possessed the same knowledge regarding the prospects of successful enterprise all over the world as they possess regarding the prospects of business in England, the amount of foreign investment would be immensely greater than it is.

It is, in fact, ridiculous to suppose that any possible policy could make a small country, in which many thousand million pounds have been already invested, a better field, in all respects, for further investment than a new and undeveloped continent. And it is natural to expect, as we progress in wealth and as our annual savings increase, that we should tend in the course of time to invest a larger absolute amount abroad. But there are also other explanations of an increasing tendency in this direction in the decreasing influence of the two great checks to foreign investment, which have been already referred to. Every year the volume of foreign securities which can be bought and sold in England with ease and certainty increases, and at the same time the difference of risk between foreign and home investment has been growing steadily less—not because the risk in England is greater than it was formerly, but because the risk abroad is diminishing.

The risk of foreign investment is growing less both for objective and for subjective reasons. On the one hand, foreign systems have been acquiring everywhere greater stability. Consider, for instance, the uniformity and integrity of the currency systems of the world compared with their state not many years ago. On the other hand, the subjective risk in the mind of the investor has been yielding before the steady dissemination of easily accessible knowledge about all kinds of enterprise.

If we were to come seriously to the conclusion that these tendencies are damaging and ought to be resisted, there are obvious measures which the Government might take to that end. The increasing number of foreign securities which are quoted on the stock exchanges and are freely bought and sold in England might be quickly checked by a special duty levied on their transfer or as a condition of their being quoted on the London Exchange. There is no practical difficulty in this, and a somewhat similar plan has been actually adopted in France. City men are perhaps sufficiently in earnest about their desire to cause more employment for the British working man by diminishing the flow of foreign investment, to accept some check of this kind upon their daily transactions. Furthermore it would not be difficult for the Government to hinder that part of the increased investment which is due to the spread of information and to the ability of Englishmen to find openings abroad. They could, for instance, immediately abolish the consular service; they could direct our ambassadors to obstruct rather than assist British enterprise in such countries as China or Turkey; and they could take such minor steps as to raise, so far as possible, the rates of postage between England and Canada or the Argentine. Is it not a stupid inconsistency on the part of politicians to weep loudly over the aggregate amount of foreign investment and to complain bitterly if in every individual case the Government do not do their utmost to foster it?

There exist influences, therefore, apart from the policy of any particular government, inducing investors to send their savings abroad increasingly. Let us now turn to the specific charges, under this head, which are levelled against the Liberal administration. They are three in number. First, that by the neglect of tariff reform the field for enterprise at home is restricted. Second, that high income tax and high death duties discourage the employment of capital in England. Third, that recent legislation has influenced investors by inducing in their minds a fear of Socialism.

The answer to the question, whether tariff reform would stimulate home industries taken as a whole or whether it would only stimulate some at the expense of others, is bound up with the answer to the general problem, which it would not be in place to discuss here. But it is worth pointing out that the claim of tariff reformers, that their policy would check the flow of foreign investment, is utterly inconsistent with their other claim that the diminution of imports which they seek to bring about will not be accompanied by a corresponding diminution of exports. For the policy of diminishing the present excess of imports over exports is simply another name for the policy of investing more capital abroad than is invested at present. The statement that imports are paid for by exports is not correct if it is taken to imply that present imports are paid for by present exports. Present imports may be paid for by past exports—they may represent, that is to say, interest on or repayment of former foreign investment. And present exports may be in anticipation of future imports—they may represent, that is to say, new foreign investments. Tariff reformers, therefore, must remember that there are only two ways of immediately reducing foreign investment—by increasing our imports or decreasing our exports; and that a policy which aims at decreasing our imports without decreasing our exports, must incontrovertibly have the effect, in so far as it is successful, of stimulating still further the flow of foreign investment.

The argument, that high income tax and high death duties discriminate against home investments, rests upon the assumption that these taxes will induce those who pay them either to leave the country or to make false declarations. With regard to the first alternative there is no evidence that rich men, who are investing abroad, do this as a measure preliminary to emigration or, taking into account existing taxation in other countries, that they would be wise from their own point of view if they had such an intention. With regard to the second alternative there is reason to believe that the ease with which taxation on foreign investments can be evaded is immensely exaggerated. No doubt evasion of income tax is very common, though decreasingly so, and that some part of this evasion is on the interest from investments in companies not registered in this country paid by means of coupons through foreign bankers. But successful evasion on a large scale is far commoner with the profits of private businesses in this country. It is the business man who develops a new enterprise here whose profits can be easily concealed, without its being necessary for him to take any special measures, from the officers of Inland Revenue. Furthermore a very large number of the companies worked abroad with English capital have registered offices in London. In the case of these companies, which are, as a rule, those in which English investors can most easily put their money, income tax is deducted at the source, and evasion is just as difficult as in the case of a home security. Also, apart from these, the income, disclosed in 1906–7 to the Commissioners of Inland Revenue by *agents* for the payment of interest on foreign and colonial government securities, companies and corporations, and by bankers and coupon dealers, amounted to no less than £60 million. Thus a would-be evader must first choose very carefully a *special class* of foreign investment, must then take precautions for remittance to this country through other than the usual channels, and must finally fill up a false declaration. Indeed evasion is, in general, easily practicable only for merchants and manufacturers who, in any case, bank in some foreign country as well as here and have placed capital abroad privately. These investments, moreover, are precisely those which do not appear in the lists of foreign securities which have been publicly subscribed in this country, and which are the ground of the complaint that more capital is going abroad now than formerly. Account being taken of all these considerations, it is more than doubtful whether an extra $2d$ on the income tax, which would reduce the yield of a security previously yielding 5 per cent to $4\frac{23}{24}$ per cent, would make it worth the while of the private investor to evade, at considerable expense of trouble, money, and legality, a charge costing him in the aggregate about $\frac{1}{4}$ per cent, if it was not worth his while before. It is within human nature that a strong party man would be willing at first to go to the necessary trouble and expense and to the risks attendant on perjury, in order to justify the prophecies of his political leaders; but it is questionable whether he would long continue so un-businesslike and emotional a practice.

There remains the alleged fear of Socialism. It is not clear, however, in what way socialistic legislation would discriminate in favour of the investor in foreign securities, unless it were to take an unlikely form. If the confiscation of property was expected, this might reasonably diminish saving. But confiscatory death duties or income tax on savings would fall equally on investors in every kind of security. Heavy duties on land would diminish its selling value but, as someone would still own it, no additional capital would be released for investment abroad. Only if it were thought that the Government proposed to seize private factories, while leaving the owners of securities unmolested, or if the investor were preparing eventually to leave the country and become naturalised elsewhere, would it be reasonable for him to invest his wealth abroad from a fear of Socialism at home. The prospect of legislation detrimental to private property might, in fact, work in the opposite direction by deterring foreigners from investing in English securities, and so by leaving a larger power of absorption of capital at home, diminish the investments of Englishmen abroad. If England were a borrowing instead of a lending country, heavy taxes on property, or the fear of them, would have a much greater effect in diverting the flow of capital than is actually the case.

We must remember, however, at this point, that the relative amount of foreign investment is determined, not by what is actually reasonable, but by what the average investor believes to be reasonable. Politicians, therefore, who persuade their hearers that the probable course of future legislation makes it reasonable to invest abroad, may have some influence, whether what they say is or is not true, in sending away capital.

If Mr Balfour's speeches induce investors to place their money abroad, and if his speeches are due to a fear of Socialism, then, in a sense, no doubt, the fear of Socialism is ultimately responsible. This part of the argument was extremely well put in a recent issue of the financial supplement of *The Times* in a passage which is worth quoting:

The unpopularity of home investments is a stubborn fact, abundantly testified in private by scores of stockbrokers, and placed beyond all doubt by Lord Revelstoke's public testimony in the House of Lords. But how far is it due to the facts of the case and how far to the picturesque utterances of the politicians? When Mr Chamberlain determined to alter the fiscal system of these islands, he thereby found it necessary to maintain that British industries were dying; that if our present system is maintained, disaster and destruction must be the ultimate fate of the Empire. The tune that he performed so ably has been repeated with variations by the whole host of his lieutenants and followers, and a chorus of Cassandras has sung our approaching doom in crashing and crushing harmony. The investing class, being largely in sympathy with the party which has adopted tariff reform, takes all that it hears about the inevitable doom of the country as literally correct, naturally begins to prefer to put some of its money abroad, and so one of the causes of the comparative unpopularity of home investments arises from the necessity with which one of the great parties is faced, of proving that we are on the road to irretrievable ruin.

It may be added that, in spite of the first sentence of this quotation, the best index to the position of home securities—their market price—shows that their unpopularity cannot have grown to a very alarming extent. Although the Duke of Marlborough lately asserted in the House of Lords that the high rate of interest upon Consols shows beyond doubt that the emigration of capital cannot be due to the difficulty of finding suitable investment here owing to its abundance, nevertheless Consols still yield far less than any corresponding foreign stock. And, to take one out of a large number of analogous examples, Messrs Guinness and Co., representatives of the trade which is said to have most to fear from discriminatory taxation, can still borrow as cheaply for the manufacture of stout as the German Empire can for the development of a navy.

Passing from the motives which influence investors to the manner in which their capital is invested, we enter upon questions regarding which some fairly definite information is available. The figures which I shall quote are derived from a paper read recently before the Royal Statistical Society by Mr George Paish. His estimates do not pretend to be accurate in detail, but may be assumed to show reliably the dimensions of the sums in question. He reckons the total income derived by Englishmen at the present time from foreign investments at £140 million annually. In existing circumstances not the whole of this amount is actually paid to us, but a large part is reloaned to the debtor nations and thus allowed to accumulate at compound interest. Our annual income from previous foreign investments exceeds, as a rule, the amount of new investments which are sent each year abroad, and we may, therefore, regard the whole of the fresh capital, which is usually said to 'leave' the country, as old interest due to us which remains by agreement in our debtors' hands to accumulate at compound interest. If we were to reduce the volume of our foreign investment, this would mean that we were insisting on our debtors paying back to us a larger proportion of the interest due than formerly.

What would be the effects of our insisting on such payment from the countries whose resources we have been developing? Unless some other great country took our place, many of them would be faced with partial bankruptcy, and works which had been begun would never be brought to completion. India, Argentina, and Canada, for instance, would meet with financial disaster if they were prevented from liquidating the interest they owe us by new loans. The development of these countries is in a stage when we must put more money into them, and not, for the present, take much out, if we are to gain the full fruit of our enterprise. In the second place, a considerable part of our export trade would be faced with extinction. We sell a large amount of goods to those countries to whom we lend. Our export trade is carried on, that is to say, on a basis of credit. If we were to withdraw this credit the trade could not continue. Lastly, it would involve the slow decline of London as the financial centre of the world, as the volume of our foreign trade and of our foreign loans declined, and the work of opening up new countries fell gradually into other hands.

We will now examine in more detail the enterprise in which British capital has been chiefly employed. This is an important part of our investigation. For a want of enterprise at home is likely to be reflected in a want of enterprise abroad, and circumstances may arise in which excessive foreign investment is an unfavourable symptom. It is questionable, for instance, how far French investment abroad in recent years may not have been at the expense of French industry, and whether it has not been sometimes due to a want of enterprise on the part of investors and an excessive unwillingness to undertake reasonable risk in industrial development. It may well be the case that part at least of the £500 million which France is said to have lent Russia in recent years, and which yields a relatively low rate of interest, would have been better employed in France itself. French investors seem to be too fond, on the one hand, of unenterprising investment in the bonds of other continental countries (not only

Russia), and of speculation in mines or other excessively risky undertakings, on the other. Whether or not this is actually the case in France, foreign investment may be a sign of lethargy at home, and of failure to take advantage of opportunities for internal development. We can decide a particular case only by an examination of the facts. No concrete evidence has been advanced, I believe, to show that there is, at present, an undue want of enterprise in England. Expansion abroad seems to have been accompanied by, and not to have been at the expense of, expansion at home. The character of the investments shows that they have been due, not to a spirit of excessive caution, but to a desire for new enterprise in countries where great profits can be expected. So far from lending great sums to support the extravagance of foreign governments, England has loaned to Europe an almost negligible amount, and has spent her savings on railways, finance and land, in such countries as India, Canada and Argentina, from whence she obtains her food and the raw material of manufacture, and in assisting colonial governments. South America, India and the colonies have absorbed in recent years the greater part of our new capital.

A few figures may be usefully quoted in support of this. Mr Paish estimated the aggregate amount of foreign investments up to 1907–8 at about £2,700 million, or, with allowance for further investment since that time, at nearly £3,000 million. This total agrees substantially with other independent estimates which have been recorded, although it differs from them in detail very greatly. Of this £2,700 million nearly £1,700 million has been expended upon railway construction; nearly £200 million by development companies, under the heading 'Financial, land, and investment'; £54 million in banks, these yielding *on the average* a rate of 13·6 per cent interest; £243 million in mines; £52 million on nitrate, oil, rubber, tea and coffee; over £100 million in canals, docks, electricity, gas, telegraphs and telephones, tramways and water-works; and £95 million in various commercial and industrial undertakings, of which breweries and distilleries account for £17 million. With regard to the destination of this capital, £1,312 million has been supplied to India and the colonies, and £1,381 million to foreign States, mainly to the United States, Central and South America, Japan and China. If we consider quite recent times only, of the £170 million nominally invested between July 1908 and June 1909, £70 million was destined for India and the colonies, and £56 million for South America and Mexico.

Assertions, therefore, that the exported capital goes mainly, or to any important extent, either to the industries abroad which compete with ours, or to the countries which are our international rivals, are untrue. Our investments have been directed towards developing the purchasing power of our principal customers, or to opening up and supplying with credit and the means of transport our main sources of food and raw material. To quote one final figure: of £170 million invested in 1908–9, £47,000 went to Germany and £335,000 to France. It is probable that France and Germany invest at the present time more largely in English securities than we do in theirs.

The recent controversy has arisen, of course, out of the very large scale on which foreign loans were taken up during the year 1908–9. Although the volume of foreign investment during this year and the years immediately preceding it greatly exceeded their volume in the period 1898 to 1904, when war expenditure had much diminished the national savings, it is doubtful whether it bore a higher proportion to the total volume of investment than during the late eighties. The large total of foreign loans offered for subscription during 1908–9 was due, however, to a variety of causes. In the first place, it must be remarked that the figures usually quoted are in excess, by an amount which it is difficult to estimate, of the sums actually subscribed by English investors. The increasingly international character of the London market leads to a great deal of stock being placed there in the first instance, which is ultimately absorbed by foreign investors; and it is known, for example, that purchases on French account in London have been recently on a large scale. A security, which is not of sufficient importance to be divided for subscription between several markets, will often be offered as a whole in London; but this does not mean that some part will not ultimately find its way abroad. In the second place, the amount offered for subscription within a given year does not accurately represent the capital actually sent abroad within that period. Even if the whole amount is paid up, a large part may be left for a time with London bankers, and gradually withdrawn as it is expended. Thirdly, the condition of the money market and the smallness, on account of the industrial depression, of the amount of money required to finance production, made the greater part of the year 1909 a specially suitable period for financiers to float loans which had been some time in prospect, or to dispose to the public of liabilities which they had already contracted.

A correct comparison of these figures with the amount of new investment at home is not possible. The comparisons which some politicians have attempted to make are entirely vitiated by the fact that the vastly greater part of foreign investment takes the form of loans to governments or joint-stock companies, while the greater part of home investment takes other forms which escape tabular valuation. The vast annual expenditure in this country on fixed capital in the form of dwelling-houses, shops and factories, for instance, does not appear in the comparisons. Nor does more than a very small part of the enormous amount of capital sunk in their businesses and factories during recent times by the manufacturers of Lancashire and Yorkshire figure in these accounts. Finally, the estimates given do not, I believe, even include capital publicly subscribed, unless the subscription was opened in London. While foreign capital is all, or almost all, subscribed in London, capital for local investment, unless it is on a very large scale, is, it is well known, largely obtained from local sources. In fact, if we take the test of the amount offered for subscription in London, home investment will only *appear* to be on a large scale when manufacturers think it a favourable moment to convert their businesses into joint-stock companies.

It would be possible to enumerate a number of other advantages, which have not yet been referred to, which England derives as a nation from her foreign investments. It must be sufficient to mention two. In the first place, the great variety of sources from which she draws her income greatly increases its stability. In the second place, these investments provide a source from which a great mass of wealth can be taken at need without disturbance to domestic enterprise. In the years during and immediately succeeding the Boer War, for instance, the diminution of foreign investment, the additional amount of wealth drawn in, that is to say, from abroad, was almost sufficient in itself to defray the whole cost of the war, and prevented home producers from being pinched by the want of their usual supplies of capital. It is scarcely possible to exaggerate the importance in time of war of being able to draw very largely upon foreign supplies *without incurring debt*, and merely in virtue of not lending so freely as before.

Our argument, therefore, taken as a whole, leads us to the conclusion that, in existing circumstances, complaints respecting the volume of England's foreign investments are baseless. It is not unplausible to suppose that their existence is mainly the result of chance. The course of the campaign in favour of tariff reform has shown that the advocates of this change base complaints in any given year on whatever statistical figure chances at the time to be somewhat unusual, quite independently of the underlying causes. It is easy to imagine the complaints of tariff reformers if the amount of capital invested abroad was diminishing instead of increasing. Suppose, in place of the actual facts, Germany or America were assuming the premier place as the creditor country of the world, and these countries, instead of ourselves, were financing the development of India, Canada and South America, would a free trade government have escaped blame, or the protectionist party have refrained from proclaiming that the Empire was virtually passing out of our hands into those of foreigners?

Keynes's papers show that during 1910 and 1911 he was making a study of British gold reserves. In February 1910 he also wrote the memorandum that follows: it comments specifically on a report of a United States government commission in 1903 favouring the introduction of the gold exchange standard to China and other silver currency countries; the British Foreign Office took the opposite view. While the green notebook lists the memorandum as a letter, it is not possible to tell for what or whom it was intended; it is given here as it appears in manuscript.

MEMORANDUM ON A CURRENCY SYSTEM FOR CHINA

Two problems: (1) to provide a currency system for internal use; (2) to devise some method of moderating the disturbance to foreign trade arising out of fluctuations of exchange.

1. Any uniform system of currency not easily liable to alteration would solve this problem. The customs of the people and the value of the units of currency most needed for circulation point with certainty to *silver* as the proper medium.

For actual purposes of circulation, *gold* is probably out of the question for three reasons:

(*a*) China would have great difficulty in obtaining a sufficient quantity of the metal.

(*b*) Gold never has been, so far as I know, an important medium of exchange in China.

(*c*) A gold coin of the smallest convenient size would have too large a value for most of the exchanges for which currency is required.

The only third alternative is *paper money*. I am very strongly of opinion that, at the present stage of development, China should have as little as possible to do with paper. It is true, of course, that the use of paper money is in accordance with the genius of the people. But in a long experience, extending over some centuries, the use of it in China has been invariably accompanied, I believe, by instability and ultimate disaster. Any large admixture of paper in the currency will involve the whole of any scheme, however carefully constructed, in danger, until a much firmer control of such things than is at present possible can be established.

There is also this further argument against the use of paper:

In the interior of China, I understand, as in many parts of India, even at the present time barter exists to a very considerable extent. It must be a principal object of any currency scheme to hasten, so far as possible, what is known as the process of adæration, or transition from barter to money. While paper will, no doubt, circulate with ease in the mercantile centres, any difficulty, even a slight one, in the way of obtaining metallic coin will greatly hinder the use of the new currency in country districts and in the more remote provinces of the Empire.

Furthermore, for reasons which will be given later, the introduction of a silver currency will yield great profits, and there need be no temptation, therefore, at present after the even greater but much more dangerous profits arising out of the use of paper.

The use of paper money, I feel, is the most dangerous factor in the situation—the rock on which currency reform is most likely to split.

2. A currency system which will stimulate foreign trade by reducing the fluctuations in exchange must, it is clear, bear some fixed relation to the standard of nearly all other countries, namely gold.

Our argument points, therefore, to a system of currency whose medium of circulation shall be silver, and whose standard shall be gold.

To a system of this kind, which is called a gold exchange standard, the monetary history of recent times has been steadily tending, especially in Oriental countries.

When the proposals for international bimetallism finally broke down, few countries were in a position to introduce pure gold monometallism. In the Latin Monetary Union, therefore, and elsewhere, what is known as the 'Limping Standard' was adopted. In this system the silver coins are legal tender to an inhibited amount and form, in fact, a great part of the currency in active circulation. But their value is maintained at a fixed ratio in relation to gold by means of a gold reserve which is available for their redemption at this fixed ratio, when a drain of gold from the country for the purpose of making international payments would otherwise lead to the depreciation of the silver token coins.

More recently, a more scientific and economical system than this has come into use. If the gold is only required for foreign payments and not for internal circulation, it is cheaper to maintain a credit at one of the great financial centres of the world, which can be converted with great readiness into gold when it is required, and which earns a small rate of interest when it is not required.

A system, somewhat of this kind, has long been adopted in Holland. It was the transitional system of Russia, when they were passing from inconvertible paper to gold under Count de Witte. And it is, substantially, the system of Austria-Hungary.

Passing from Europe to Asia, we find that it has been adopted, in most cases within very recent years, in India (where it has been very severely and successfully tested during the last two years), Straits Settlements (British possessions), Philippines (U.S.), Indo-China (France) and Java (Dutch). In America it has been adopted for Mexico (a great silver-producing and -using country which has furnished China in the past with a large part of the currency in use in her mercantile centres near the coast) and Panama.

This system, the *Gold-Exchange Standard*, in which the medium is silver and the standard gold, is in my opinion the only feasible system for introduction into China.

I am, therefore, in very general agreement with the proposals of the Commission appointed by the U.S. Government in 1903 to report on the introduction of the gold exchange standard into China and other silver-using countries. The precise nature of a gold exchange standard is fully explained in that report, and the details of such a system, suitable to Chinese conditions, is discussed. I have nothing to add to the matter collected in the body and appendices of the report (see especially pp. 14–24 and pp. 103–17).

Attention may be called, however, to the following points:

1. Will the Chinese trader easily learn to accept a coin at more than its bullion value? In spite of his long traditional practice to the contrary, experience elsewhere shows, I think, that he will. In the Philippines he has accepted such a system after some preliminary objections. In India it was found that the distinction between the value of the rupee as bullion and as money was very quickly learnt. If a new currency system is a good and useful one it will soon be accepted, and the difficulty of change on account of popular feeling is, I suspect, much exaggerated. The details of the gold exchange standard are difficult and complicated, but there is not the least need for anyone who uses the coin to understand the system on which it is based. In India very few traders ever understand it. Only those who actually control the system need appreciate the details.

2. In the interior of China the new silver coin would, of course, be absolutely inconvertible, so far as the Government is concerned, in terms of gold. Only in a very few of the principal trading centres near or on the coast would drafts be sold at a fixed rate in terms of the local currency commanding gold in London.

3. The building up of a reserve in London or elsewhere which could be utilised for cashing these drafts, if at any time it were to become necessary to sell them, is of course a very vital point. I do not think that this would be difficult. The Indian Government's great problem, of raising a pre-existing currency to a higher level, does not exist in China. The profits on the new coinage would from the beginning be sufficiently large, if the scheme were at all successful, to form an adequate reserve. Foreign traders would obtain the new coins, in order to exchange

them for Chinese products, by buying bills from the Chinese agent in London. Part of the proceeds of the sale of these bills would be required for the purchase of silver bullion for the Chinese mints; the rest would be invested in London in easily saleable securities as a reserve. If the scheme were to be successful, the profits would be so enormous that some part might be diverted from the reserve eventually and devoted by the Chinese Government to capital expenditure in China—e.g., railways.

4. I see no reason why the scheme should not be adopted initially by one province only. In this case it might be desirable to utilise the services, as an agent, of some powerful and independent bank such as the Hong Kong and Shanghai Bank. Bills, that is to say, might be sold through them as agents. But this is entirely a matter for local knowledge.

5. It must be remembered that if exchange is falling and bills have to be sold in China to support the new currency, it is vitally necessary to withdraw the coins, in exchange for which the bills are sold, from circulation, until it is proved by a rise in the exchange that there is again a demand for them.

6. While it is true that Japan has not, in a sense, adopted a full *gold-exchange* standard, her system is in practice not unlike the latter. Gold scarcely circulates at all in the country, and is held in the bank for the purpose of international payments only. Furthermore the Government of Japan holds a considerable amount of its reserve in the form of English Treasury bills in London—precisely in the form in which it is proposed that China should hold her currency reserve. The Japanese example is not, therefore, truly opposed to these proposals.

During the summer vacation of 1910 Keynes worked more on probability and reported to his father that he was making good progress. He also became involved in a controversy with the statistician Karl Pearson, as the result of a review that he wrote for the *Journal of the Royal Statistical Society* attacking the methods of a study of the effects of parental alcoholism on offspring. The dispute gathered adherents on both sides and raged for half a year, spilling over into the *British Medical Journal* and *The Times*, where contributions on Keynes's behalf appeared from Marshall and Pigou (*J.M.K.* vol. XIII).

Meantime, after an Easter term free of lectures, Keynes embarked on five new courses in turn. Through the Michaelmas term of 1910 he lectured on the Theory of Money and on Company Finance and the Stock Exchange. During 1911 he lectured on Currency and Banking in the Lent term, the Money Market and the Foreign Exchanges in the Easter term, and Principles in the Michaelmas term. With a single exception he kept up these five courses until the end of 1914, lecturing on the first two in the Lent term, the second two in the Easter term, and Principles through all three terms.

He was appointed Girdlers' Lecturer in Economics to succeed H. O. Meredith in January 1911. A congratulatory message from Alfred Marshall on the back of a picture postcard of Brixham fish market (postmarked 14 December 1910) reads thus:

> I am very glad you, who have girded up your loins so well, are now well-girdled.
> This is the shed in which I have seen prime soles sold to the wholesale dealer at 2/6 a pound.
>
> A.M.

In May 1910 Keynes was asked to give a series of six lectures on Indian finance at the London School of Economics, to be delivered in the following year. His subsequent correspondence shows that he was gathering material for them. 'I am very glad that your eye is on our currency operations', Lionel Abrahams wrote, 29 August 1910, in a letter commenting on the proofs of Keynes's review for the *Economic Journal* of *The Rupee Problem* by M. de P. Webb (*JMK*, vol. XI). 'The paucity of well-equipped observers and honest critics is sometimes disheartening', he added. Sir Thomas Holderness, thanking Keynes for pointing out the inaccuracy of some figures on the sea-borne trade of India in an official publication, said in a letter dated 19 October: 'I am very glad to have your criticisms. They serve to keep the Department more up to the mark than it is at present.'

Keynes gave the lectures on 'Currency, Finance and the Level of Prices in India' at the London School of Economics—and at Cambridge, in place of his Company Finance and Stock Exchange lectures—early in 1911. There is a lively, up-to-date quality to his notes: newspaper clippings pinned to the pages provide the latest figures; part of a letter in the handwriting of Lionel Abrahams, cut out and pasted in, explains a point. Keynes quoted from *The Times* City column to illustrate the 'confusion which exists in regard to the Indian system even in well-informed circles'. He also tossed off this sort of typically Keynesian *obiter dictum* (cf. *Indian Currency and Finance, JMK*, vol. 1, pp. 24–5):

> Leading financiers, being unable to follow an argument, will never admit the feasibility of anything until it has been demonstrated to them by practical experience. It follows, therefore, that they will never give their support to anything new.

These lectures provided the material for a paper on Indian currency which Keynes read to the Royal Economic Society at its quarterly meeting on 9 May 1911; the paper, in turn, he developed into *Indian Currency and Finance*. Lionel Abrahams wrote in anticipation (29 April 1911):

> I am sure that we have much to learn from you. Our official discussions are sometimes narrow; and outside criticism is often dogmatic and impractical, like that in a German pamphlet that I was looking at the other day, which said that we had on the whole done the right thing, but with no proper knowledge of the metaphysical and world-historical significance of our action. Your knowledge of both the practical official's and the economist's standpoint will enable you to say much more helpful things.

In a later letter Abrahams enquired especially into the arguments Keynes would use against the establishment of a gold mint in India, a question coming much to the fore. When the paper arrived, he thought it (writing 28 May) 'most useful and interesting. As you know, I agree with you on many points but not on all.'

Abrahams had a copy of Keynes's draft made for the use of the India Office and the Government of India. Those who received it were told that it had been prepared solely for the purpose of Keynes's address and was an abstract of ampler material which he hoped to expand for later publication. The version which follows was printed at Simla by the Government of India for internal use.

The appendix appears to have been added, after Keynes gave the paper to a meeting of the Royal Economic Society, as the result of a correspondence with Sir James Wilson, a former finance commissioner of the Punjab, who wished to strengthen the rupee by having more gold and fewer rupees in circulation and wanted the gold standard reserve to be held entirely in gold and entirely in India. Keynes made a copy of an extract from a letter that he wrote to Wilson on 21 June 1911 (he sent a copy to Lionel Abrahams as well) —which is substantially the same as the appendix and an argument he developed in *Indian Currency and Finance*. (Sir Guy Fleetwood Wilson, whose sponsorship of gold currency Keynes mentions in the appendix, was the Finance Minister of the Viceroy's Council in India and not to be confused with Sir James Wilson.)

RECENT DEVELOPMENTS OF
THE INDIAN CURRENCY QUESTION

The evolution of the Indian currency system since 1899 has been silent but rapid. There have been few public pronouncements of policy on the part of Government, and the legislative changes have been insignificant. Yet a system has been developed, which was contemplated neither by those who effected nor by those who opposed the closing of the mints in 1892 and which was not favoured either by the Government or by the Committee of 1898, although something resembling it was brought before them. I do not know that it is possible to point to any special date at which the currency policy now in force was first deliberately adopted by the Government of India. The fact that the Government has drifted into a system and has never plainly set it forth, is responsible for a great deal of the misapprehension regarding its true nature which exists in the minds not only of the public, but also of some Government officials.

Few are now found who dispute on broad general grounds the wisdom of the change in 1892. In fact recent complaints against currency policy have all been occasioned by the tendency of prices to rise; whereas it is plain that the great change of 1892 tended to make them fall and that they would, in all probability, be higher than they are now if the change had not been carried through. Time has dealt satisfactorily with what were originally the two principal grounds of criticism: first, that the new system was unstable; and second, that a depreciating currency is advantageous to a country's trade. Time also has muffled the outcries of the silver interests. And against some depreciation in the value of the ryot's hoards on account of the fall in the value of silver, there is to be set the fact, which was pointed out by Mr Gokhale in the Budget debate of 1910, that the remission of six crores of taxation during the period from 1898 to 1908 was rendered possible by the saving on the Government's home remittances, due to the rise in the value of the rupee, which almost exactly balanced it. The criticisms, therefore, of 1893 are no longer heard, and the currency problems with which we are now confronted are new.

In this paper I wish to discuss briefly one or two of the chief questions of current controversy and also to give some account of the stage of development which has now been reached.

In 1893 four possible systems of currency seemed to hold the field: debased and depreciating currencies usually of paper, silver, bimetallism, and gold. It was not to be supposed that the Government of India was adopting the first, the second it was deliberately upsetting, and the third it had negotiated for and failed to obtain. It seemed to follow that its ultimate objective must be the last—namely, a gold standard. The Commission of 1892 did not commit themselves in advance, but the system which they established was supposed to be transitional and to lead ultimately to gold. The Committee of 1898 declared themselves to be in favour of the ultimate establishment of a full gold standard. Since that time this intention has never been repudiated, so far as I am aware, by Government, and speeches have been made by its officers implying that it is still maintained. In 1900–1, Sir Clinton Dawkins announced that it had been decided to constitute a branch of the Mint at Bombay for the coinage of gold. More recently, in the Budget debate of 1910, Mr Meston, Financial Secretary to the Government, spoke as follows:

The broad lines of our action and our objects are clear and unmistakable and there has been no great or fundamental sacrifice of consistency in progress towards our ideal. Since the Fowler Commission that progress has been real and unbroken. There is still one great step forward before the ideal can be reached. We have linked India with the gold countries of the world, we have reached a gold-exchange standard, which we are steadily developing and improving. The next and final step is a true gold currency. That, I have every hope, will come in time, but we cannot force it. The backwardness of our banking arrangements, the habits and suspicions of the people, the infancy of co-operation—all stand in the way. But the final step will come when the country is ripe for it. I trust that will not long be delayed; for when it comes, it will obliterate all the mistakes, all the inconveniences, all the artificialities of our present position.

68

Further in the Imperial Legislative Council this March Sir Fleetwood Wilson replied, in answer to Sir Vithaldas Thackersey, who had argued that a 10-rupee gold coin ought to be minted and put into active circulation in India, that 'much has happened since 1902 which justified the re-opening of the question', and that he 'will have pleasure in examining the subject again at an early date'. The actual policy of the Government of India as regards currency since 1900 has been, in my opinion, exceedingly well judged. But the above passages show that some of its officers are still doubtful as to the advantages of the existing system.

I will endeavour to give reasons for thinking that this existing system, to which the name of gold-exchange standard has been given, is something much more civilised, much more economical, and much more satisfactory than a gold currency. I should like to see it openly established in India on a permanent basis and all talk of an eventual gold currency definitely abandoned.

The Government of India has been the first to adopt the gold-exchange standard on a large scale. But every year there are fresh converts; nor will it be long before it becomes, in effect, the standard of half the world. And out of it, in my belief, will be evolved the ideal currency of the future.

I will endeavour to give some account of the gold-exchange standard as it now exists in India, and will then give reasons against the granting of further facilities for the use of gold in India and in favour of curtailing, perhaps, those facilities which already exist.

In 1870, England was the only country in the world of any importance which possessed a true gold standard. All the rest of the world had silver, bimetallism, or depreciated paper. For the next ten years a gold standard was the ideal which currency reformers had before them, and a number of the principal countries in Europe succeeded in making the change in greater or less degree. During the eighties the doubtful outcome of the bimetallic controversy, by making the future uncertain, retarded changes. During the nineties, after the final defeat of bimetallism, numerous other countries succeeded in establishing a gold standard, but this was accompanied by the establishment of a gold currency to a much less extent than had been the case after the changes effected in the seventies. Since 1900 almost all the rest of the world, with the exception of China and one or two South American states, have been able to regulate their currencies on a gold standard. But none have established a gold currency and most have introduced some form or other of the gold-exchange standard upon the Indian model.

The countries which now possess, in effect, a gold-exchange standard are the following: Holland, Austro-Hungary, Mexico, Panama, the Philippines, Indo-China, Java and the Dutch Colonies, Straits Settlements, Siam, and India. It is, therefore, at the present time the prevailing form of currency in Asia. And in Russia and Japan, while there is nominally a full gold standard, the system works in practice in a manner more like the gold-exchange standard.

Finally those countries which made the change in the seventies, some of whom, Germany for example, endeavoured formerly to force as much gold as possible into circulation, now endeavour to keep as much of it as possible in their central reserves and as little of it as possible in circulation.

It may fairly be said that, while a gold *standard* has become almost universal, a gold *currency* is becoming rapidly obsolete.

The gold-exchange standard, which resembles the currency proposed at the time of the bullionist controversy by Ricardo, who pointed out that a currency is in its most perfect state, when it consists of cheap material, but of an equal value with the gold it professes to represent, arises out of the discovery that, so long as gold is available for payments of *international* indebtedness at an approximately constant rate in terms of the national currency, it is a matter of comparative indifference whether it actually *forms* the *national* currency; and that there is in fact an enormous saving of expense in using some cheaper material for the actual medium of exchange, India for example, having saved 20 millions in this way during the last ten years.

The gold-exchange standard may be said to exist when gold does not circulate in a country to an appreciable extent, when the local currency is not necessarily redeemable in gold, but when the government or central bank makes arrangements for the provision of foreign remittances in gold at a fixed maximum rate in terms of the local currency.

The gold-exchange standard in the form in which it has been adopted in India is justly known as the Lindsay scheme. It was proposed and advocated from as early as 1876 down to the Committee of 1898 by Mr A. M. Lindsay, deputy secretary of the Bank of Bengal, who always maintained that 'They *must* adopt my scheme despite themselves'.

The provisions of the Indian system as now established are as follows:

1. The sovereign is legal tender in India at 15 rupees to £1.

2. The Government is bound to give rupees for sovereigns at this rate.

3. It is, as a rule, willing to give sovereigns for rupees at this rate, but is under no legal obligation to do so, and will not, in fact, exchange *large* quantities at all times. This third provision I will deal with later when I come to the general question of the use of gold in India.

We come next to the essential of the gold-exchange standard and of Lindsay's scheme:

4. The Secretary of State will usually sell bills in London on India in unlimited amounts at a maximum rate of 1s 4⅛d, and will always sell bills in India on London at 1s 3⅞d.

It is not necessary in the present connection to take account of telegraphic transfers.

The upper limit is determined by the gold import point, by the expense, that is to say, of sending sovereigns from London to Calcutta. For, if the Secretary of State were to refuse to sell at this rate, it would become more profitable to send sovereigns and exchange them for rupees than to buy bills. The upper limit to the fluctuations of exchange is, therefore, automatic and independent of the momentary policy of the Secretary of State. His power to carry out his legal obligations to provide rupee currency in exchange for gold, tendered either in India or England, depends upon his having at all times an adequate reserve of coined rupees.

A year or two ago it was found (though I believe the practice has been since rendered impossible) that gold could be sent more cheaply than before by remitting sovereigns to Paris and sending them on from there by parcel post. If the Alexandria exchange is suitable, it is not at all unusual, particularly during the winter months, to send sovereigns from Egypt. Sovereigns which have been minted in Australia from Australian gold may also prove at times the cheapest form of remittance. Thus the cost of sending gold to India is not constant, and at times the gold import point exceeds $1s\ 4d$ by less than $\frac{1}{8}d$. A further cause for fluctuation arises out of the rate of discount; for the loss of interest arising out of the time of transmission of gold varies with this. But the cost will seldom exceed $\frac{1}{8}d$ by an appreciable amount and, if the Secretary of State refuses to sell freely at $1s\ 4\frac{1}{8}d$, gold will flow.

But since the Secretary of State is not bound to give sovereigns for rupees and in fact will not do so in large quantities, the lower limit is not automatic and there is no legal provision which prevents exchange from falling below $1s\ 3\frac{7}{8}d$. Before 1898 exchange was habitually below this rate, and even after the closing of the mints fell as low as $1s\ 1d$.

Lindsay perceived that the closing of the mints and the Secretary of State's management of his remittances *to* England, and the corresponding remittances of the public *from* England would not necessarily be adequate to maintain the solidity of exchange, unless he also provided a mechanism ready to work at all times in the opposite direction. By his readiness to sell drafts in Calcutta on London at $1s\ 3\frac{7}{8}d$, although under no legal obligation to do so, such a mechanism is provided.

I think that the time has now come when the Secretary of State might safely place himself under an obligation to sell drafts in Calcutta on London at $1s\ 3\frac{7}{8}d$ at all times. At any rate, whether he does or not, the currency system will have broken down completely if he ever takes advantage of his legal right to refuse drafts at this rate.

The stability of the Indian system depends, therefore, upon the Secretary of State's keeping sufficient reserves of coined rupees to enable him at all times to exchange international currency for local currency, and sufficient liquid resources in sterling to enable him to change back the local currency into international currency, when he is required to do so.

The actual arrangements he makes to this end are somewhat complicated, but the principle underlying them is simple. He must have a certain amount of coined rupees, a certain amount of coined gold, a certain amount of very liquid resources in the form of money at call, and a certain amount of fairly liquid resources in the form of investments. These various forms of resources he keeps distributed according to rules, the origin of which is largely historical, between what are called the currency reserve and the gold standard reserve. The amount of the currency reserve depends upon the volume of notes in circulation (i.e., the resources released through the use of *paper* token currency) and the amount of the gold standard reserve depends upon the profits which arise when additional rupees are coined (i.e., the resources released through the use of *silver* token currency). Thus the currency system pays for itself and in addition a certain amount of the profit, amounting to about a quarter of a million annually, is transferred to the exchequer.

The distribution of the various forms of resources between the two reserves is as follows:

1. The reserve of coined rupees is held partly in the currency reserve, and partly in the gold standard reserve.

2. The reserve of gold is held wholly in the currency reserve.

3. The reserve in the form of loans at call or short notice is held wholly in the gold standard reserve.

4. The reserve in the form of sterling securities is held partly in the currency reserve and partly in the gold standard reserve.

73

The policy of holding part of the reserve of coined rupees in the gold standard reserve has been subjected to much criticism. But the only point of importance is that the aggregate reserve of coined rupees should not be larger than is necessary, and its location is mainly a matter of book-keeping.

The present theory of the matter seems to be that the reserve of rupees which may be required to meet a reduction in the volume of notes is kept in the currency reserve, while the reserve of rupees which may be required to meet unexpectedly heavy sales of Council bills in London is kept in the gold standard reserve.

The adequacy of these reserves to meet all probable calls upon them is frequently disputed. I am myself inclined to think that the Government of India tends to be over-optimistic in this matter, but that the position is not really serious and that the reserves will soon reach an adequate amount if their natural growth be encouraged in all reasonable ways; if, that is to say, an increased use of notes is stimulated and encouraged, and if none of the profits on coinage or of the interest accruing to the gold standard reserve be diverted to other purposes.

With regard to the first—the encouragement of the use of notes—the Government have embarked upon a new and wise policy of far-reaching importance.

The system of note issue in India, which was established in 1862, divided the country up into eight circles, which roughly corresponded to the principal provinces, and speaking broadly, notes were obligatory currency in their own circle of issue only. Certain extra-legal facilities were in fact allowed by which notes could often be cashed in other circles, but virtually for the purposes of paper currency, India was divided up into eight different countries. The reasons for these restrictions are obvious. India is a very large country, and there is a considerable flow of rupees from one part of the country to another at different seasons of the year. The Government shrank, therefore, from issuing notes under conditions which would lay upon them the responsibility of providing rupees in different parts of the country in accordance with the needs of trade.

But, although the growth of the note issue for many years past has been very steady, these restrictions have naturally retarded it. Since 1900 the importance of supporting a gold-exchange standard system by means of the reserves of a popular and well-devised system of paper currency has been plain, and the question of abolishing these restrictions has been prominent. After some tentative changes in 1903 and 1909 which affected 5-rupee notes only, steps have been taken in February 1910 and this year which virtually have the effect of abolishing the old system of circles and of making India into a single country for the purposes of the paper currency. The notes of the denominations Rs. 10, Rs. 50 and Rs. 100 are now to have universal currency throughout India. The change has already caused a very great increase in the volume of notes in circulation and, consequently, in the amount of reserve which can be held in the form of gold sterling securities.

With regard to the growth of the gold standard reserve through the profits of coinage, the Government have announced that they will divert half of the future profits to capital expenditure on railways. But it is to be hoped that this decision will be reconsidered before the time comes.

At present the reserve of coined rupees is admittedly excessive and is being reduced. When this process is complete the sterling reserves ought not to fall far short of £35 million or 50 crores of rupees, let us say. I estimate the total number of rupees in India at between 200 and 225 crores. The Government is able, therefore, to withdraw nearly one-quarter of the total circulation if exchange shows any tendency towards the depreciation of the rupee. This takes no account of the Secretary of State's credit on the London money market, and his capacity to borrow in the event of the resources in his reserves proving insufficient; nor does it take account of his cash balances in London which are, at the present time, very great. The position is not critical but

Amount of Various Reserves

	Rupees	£ million
Reserve of coined rupees in:		
currency reserve	2,35,000,000	
gold standard reserve	30,000,000	
	2,65,000,000 =	17½
Reserve of gold in:		
India	97,500,000 =	6½
London	75,000,000 =	5
	1,72,500,000 =	11½
Reserve of securities in:		
currency reserve	40,000,000 =	2½
gold standard reserve	=	15¼
		18
Reserve of cash at short notice in gold standard reserve	=	1½
i.e.		
Sterling securities		18
Cash at short notice		1½
Gold		11½
		31
Rupees		17½

the experience of 1907–8 shows, I think, that the reserves have not yet reached a figure which is at all excessive and that the time has not yet come for relinquishing any of the existing methods for strengthening them. In 1907 the Secretary of State had to face the results of only one bad harvest and the situation was not complicated by any serious political trouble in India or in Europe. Yet he found it necessary to withdraw from circulation not far short of 30 crores of rupees.

This must conclude a very compressed account of the existing system in which, while omitting many important points of detail, I have endeavoured to emphasise what seem to me to be its salient and characteristic features. One further point, I think, requires explicit recognition. From the point of view of English merchants or bankers, of Indian manufacturers or agriculturists or ryots, the system works undistinguishably from a full gold system. They would run no risk and would have no reason to change the price of any article, if they were to believe that it was a full gold system. The differences, therefore, between the existing system and a full gold system have nothing whatever to do with the recent upward movement of prices. Prices are, of course, at a different level from that at which they would be if the mints were still open to the free coinage of silver or if the rupee had been fixed at 1s or 1s 6d; but they are not, except to a small degree due to indirect causes, at a different level from that at which they would be if the mints were open to the free coinage of gold and rupees were freely exchangeable in India in terms of it.

I wish to devote the rest of my paper to considering in more detail the present position of gold in India. We have seen that the Government is under a legal obligation always to give rupees for sovereigns at the rate of 15, and that they are willing, when their gold reserves permit it, to give sovereigns for rupees at this rate. These arrangements are survivals of the time when the ultimate establishment of a full gold standard was the declared policy of Government. It is now proposed on some hands that these facilities for the use of gold in India should be extended. So far from this I am myself of opinion that the existing facilities ought to be abolished, although I dare say that public opinion has not yet reached the point when this is practically possible. Closely bound up with this is the vexed question as to whether the gold portion of the currency reserve should be held mainly in England or in India.

Up to 1870, the English currency system was the envy of the rest of the world and it was supposed that the excellences of the practical working of this system were due to the fact that the actual circulating medium of the country was gold. This, it was thought, must be the only really safe way of maintaining absolute stability. Germany, accordingly, when she instituted her gold standard, prohibited the issue of notes of a less denomination than 100 marks, in order that gold might actually circulate from hand to hand to a maximum possible amount. For similar reasons the business community showed themselves immovably hostile to Lord Goschen's proposals for the issue of one-pound notes in England. While other countries, who have with few exceptions found the expense of a gold medium of exchange prohibitively heavy, have nevertheless envied those who could afford it, and have adapted their laws, even when they could not afford to adapt their practice, to a currency of gold.

But since 1900 the evolution of currency has embarked upon a new stage of development and all this is changed. In England the use of a cheque currency has become so universal, that the composition of the metallic coin has become a matter of secondary importance. In Germany the policy of 1876 has been deliberately reversed by a recent revision of the Bank Act, and 20-mark notes are now issued with the deliberate object of keeping as much gold in the bank and wasting as little as possible in circulation. And in other countries, where actual currency is the principal medium of exchange, the attempt to introduce gold as the medium passing from hand to hand has been for the most part abandoned. By far the greater part of the new gold during the last ten years has flowed into the reserves of the state banks, and only a very small amount can have found its way into circulation. The reasons for this change are easily seen. It has been found that the expense of a gold circulation is insupportable and that large economies can be safely effected by the use of some cheaper substitute; and it has been found further that gold in the pockets of the people is not in the least available at a time of crisis or to meet a foreign drain, and that for these purposes the gold resources of a country must be centralised. This view has long been maintained by economists. Mill, for example, argued that 'gold wanted for exportation is almost invariably drawn from the reserves of banks, and is never likely to be taken from the outside circulation while the banks remain solvent'. While Goschen spoke as follows in 1891 before the London Chamber of Commerce: 'We only have as an effective circulation that which is required for the daily wants of the people. You cannot tap that to any extent so as to increase your central stock of gold. You may raise your rate of

78

interest to 6 per cent or 8 per cent., but the bulk of the people will not carry less gold in their pockets than they did before, and I doubt whether, from other quarters, you would be able to get much addition to your central store.'

At last governments have been converted to this view and it is now as much their anxiety to keep gold out of circulation and in their reserves as was formerly the opposite. A preference for a tangible gold currency is no longer more than a relic of a time when governments were less trustworthy in these matters than they are now, and when it was the fashion to imitate uncritically the system which had been established in England and had seemed to work so well during the second quarter of the nineteenth century.

Let us now apply these general considerations to the case of India. In 1900 an attempt was actually made to get sovereigns into actual circulation in India in accordance with the recommendations of the Committee of 1898. It was decided to pay out gold to the public as soon as the stock should exceed five millions sterling, and such payments commenced on 12 January 1900 at the currency offices in Calcutta, Madras and Bombay. The instructions issued were to tender gold to all presenters of notes, but to give rupees if they were preferred. Later on the Comptroller-General was authorised to send sovereigns to the larger District Treasuries. And in March the post offices in the Presidency towns began to give gold in payment of money orders, and the Presidency Banks were requested to issue sovereigns in making payment on Government account. These arrangements continued in force throughout the financial year 1900–1, and by 31 March 1901 the amount put into the hands of the public reached the considerable total of £6,750,000. But of this amount part was exported, not far short of half was returned to Government, and it was supposed that the greater part of the remainder went into the hands of bullion-dealers. Further attempts to force gold into circulation were therefore abandoned, and a large part of the gold which had accumulated in the currency reserve in India was shipped to England in order to be held 'ear-marked' at the Bank of England.

79

The defeat of this experiment was due to a variety of causes, but mainly, I should suppose, on account of the long habituation of the Indian public to the use of silver, and on account of the unsuitability of the sovereign, by reason of its high value, for so poor a country as India.

But it is not by any means so certain that an attempt at the present time to put a 10-rupee gold coin into circulation would not meet with more success. Its value would be somewhat less. But, more important than this, the taste of India for gold, as against silver, has been very considerably developed during the last ten years.

During the past year bullion-dealers and other observers seem to have been reaching a very clear conviction that gold, in the form of sovereigns and not of bars only, is entering very much more than formerly into the hoards of the people and is actually displacing rupees. In 1909–10 the net absorption of gold reached £16½ million, and I believe that for this year it has been about £18 million, figures greatly exceeding those for any years previous to 1906–7. In 1909–10 gold to the value of no less than £9¼ million was imported in the form of sovereigns. Apart from this it seems probable that the number of sovereigns actually in circulation has been slowly increasing. Although no attempt has been made since 1911 to force sovereigns into circulation, they are legal tender in India and can usually be obtained in exchange for rupees, in small quantities at any rate, from the Government treasuries. Accordingly a not inappreciable number have found their way into circulation in the Presidency towns and other large centres, although accounts agree that not many are to be met with up-country. There are no data for any accurate estimate of this number. In 1909 the Paper Currency Department thought that the amount, circulating previous to the crisis of 1907–8, cannot have been less than two millions, but that a considerable proportion of this was exported during 1908. It is probable that the amount in circulation at the present time again exceeds two millions. A proposal to introduce a gold currency into India is, therefore, exceedingly dangerous; because it is not at all impossible that its introduction, if it were systematically attempted, might meet with some considerable measure of success.

I have attempted in the first part of this paper to show that no advantage over the present scheme would accrue through the success of such a policy. It only remains to point out how heavy a loss and expense it might involve. During the last ten years alone the Government has been able to accumulate a sum of no less than twenty millions sterling from the profits of rupee coinage; and the interest on the invested portion of the paper currency reserve now exceeds £300,000 annually. Both these sources of profit would be jeopardised if the introduction of an Indian gold coin were to meet with any considerable measure of success. It would also be specially unfortunate if a competitor to the paper currency were to be introduced, before the virtual abolition of the system of circles has had time to have its full effect in the direction of popularising the use of notes.

India, as we all know, already wastes far too high a proportion of her resources in the needless accumulation of the precious metals. The Government ought not to encourage in the slightest degree this ingrained fondness for handling hard gold. By import taxes on *both* precious metals and by their elimination, to the utmost extent that public opinion will permit, from amongst the circulating media of the country, they ought to counteract an uncivilised and wasteful habit.

I wish in conclusion briefly to give my reasons for thinking that even the existing facilities for the use of gold should be abolished. It would be a good thing, I think, if sovereigns were to cease to be legal tender, if no gold reserve whatever were to be held in India, and if no facilities were granted for the exchange *locally* either of sovereigns for rupees or rupees for sovereigns. I do not regard this as of first-rate importance, for these facilities amount, as it is, to so little, and I dare say that public opinion has not yet reached the point when it would readily acquiesce in such a policy; but there is at present, as I will show in a moment, a not inappreciable pecuniary loss, and a good deal would be gained if it were possible to put an end to the rumours and the uncertainty arising out of the apparent flirtation with a gold currency on the part of the Government of India, for which the existing arrangements afford colourable ground.

The rule by which rupees are given in exchange for sovereigns only comes into operation, speaking generally, when the Secretary of State refuses to sell bills below what is at the moment gold point. He may do this for three reasons:

1. Deliberately, to replenish his Indian reserves.

2. To relieve the London money market, when the gold which India will get will flow from Australia or Egypt.

3. Accidentally, when he has miscalculated the gold point.

The first circumstance can only arise out of the practice of giving gold for rupees, which I will deal with in a moment. The second could be met, as it often is at present, by buying the gold from Australia or Egypt for Council bills at suitable rates for delivery in London. The third would be altogether avoided, if the existing rule were abrogated.

There is no need, therefore, that gold should ever flow to India. When it does flow to India, loss is involved for the following reasons:

If it leaves the Indian reserve, it goes either into circulation or into the hands of the bullion-dealers for hoarding or for ornaments. If the sovereigns go into circulation, they must displace rupees or notes, and thus reduce the profits on coinage. But there is reason for supposing that relatively few find their way into circulation and that the majority go to the bullion-dealers. The Currency Department publishes figures which show the number of sovereigns withdrawn from the treasury each month. It appears from these that very few are withdrawn in the winter months during the busy season, when the demand for currency is at its height, but that in the summer, when it is most improbable that an extra supply of currency is required, there is always a steady and, in the aggregate, a heavy drain. A brief arithmetical calculation provides what must, I think, be the explanation of this. Since the price of bullion in London is (normally) £3 17s 9d per oz., while the price of sovereigns is £3 17s 10½d, the bullion import point of Indian exchanges will be a little below the sovereign import point. Thus when exchange is fairly high, an Indian purchaser of gold finds it more profitable to buy drafts on London, purchase gold in the bullion market and ship it to India, than to purchase sovereigns from the treasury at 1s 4d; but when exchange is low, the reverse is the case and it is cheaper to get as much gold as the treasury will let you have at 1s 4d. I do not know exactly where the dividing line comes; but when telegraphic transfers are at 1s 4⅛d, it is certainly more profitable to get gold in London, and when they are at 1s 4$\frac{1}{32}$d it pays to get it in India.

These considerations are modified in practice by the fact that many Indian purchasers of bullion have a preference for small gold bars which are manufactured in England. Thus these bars are worth more than an equivalent weight of sovereigns, and consequently importation of bullion in this form takes place throughout the year. But for many non-currency purposes sovereigns are as good or nearly as good as other forms of bullion, and for these purposes the Indian treasury is the bullion-dealer's cheapest source of supply when exchange is low. Thus in the summer months the bullion-dealers will always draw their supplies from the treasury, so long as the treasury is willing to supply them. Whenever, therefore, gold in India is available to the public throughout the year, the Government will lose during the summer months whatever amount the bullion-dealers require. On every sovereign thus drawn out, the Government loses about 1½d. For the gold could have been kept in England by selling bills at a rate more advantageous than the par of exchange by about this amount. The annual amount which is drawn out by bullion-dealers when gold is available all the year round, is almost certainly underestimated at £2,000,000. Thus the main effect of the present practice is to allow bullion-dealers to get

6-2

their gold in the summer months cheaper than they otherwise could.

If, on the other hand, the gold remains in the reserve, it can only be wanted when the balance of trade is unfavourable and it is necessary to ship it to London. In this case there is double loss involved in having allowed it ever to reach India, the cost of getting it there and the cost of getting it back. Sterling reserves held against a drain it is plainly much more economical to keep in London where, eventually, they will be wanted.

These losses are not large in relation to the questions at stake, and it may be worth while to incur them as an inexpensive sop to a public opinion which likes to see the gold in India. I do not argue, therefore, that this public opinion ought to be over-ridden. I argue only that it is not well founded and ought to be discouraged in every possible way by the Government and others.

May 1911   J. M. KEYNES

APPENDIX

There is one point in connection with the proposals of Sir Guy Wilson, Sir V. D. Thackersey and others, for the introduction of a larger quantity of gold into the Indian circulation, with regard to which I should like to add something to the preceding remarks.

It is suggested that the currency should be composed of rupees, gold and paper, rupees still predominating, but gold forming a larger proportion than at present, this greater infusion of gold being necessarily at the expense either of the currency reserve or of the gold standard reserve.

It is tacitly assumed that the greater part of what has to be withdrawn from the circulation at a time of crisis, would come from the gold portion of the circulation.

This assumption seems to me to be unwarranted and contrary to general experience. At a time of crisis it is the fiduciary coins with which the public are most eager to part. It would be rupees (in great part) and not gold that would be paid into the Government treasuries. Bankers and others would keep as much of their surplus currency as they possibly could in the form of gold, and it would be *rupees* that the Government would have to withdraw.

The infusion of more gold into the circulation would necessarily weaken the existing reserves and would not, in my opinion, correspondingly reduce the amount of such reserves which Government ought in prudence to keep. When it became necessary to contract the volume of currency, Government would be in a *worse* position than at present, unless the greater part of what was withdrawn came from the gold portion of the circulation and not from the rupee or paper portion. This is not an expectation upon which it would be prudent to act.

There are, in fact, two ways of maintaining stability in a country whose demand for currency varies widely from year to year—either it must consist almost *wholly* of gold or a sufficient reserve must be *concentrated* in the hands of Government. If only one-quarter or one-fifth of the circulation consists of gold, I do not think that a government can rely on getting more than a *fraction* of this, when it becomes necessary to contract the circulation by one-sixth or one-seventh; whereas if the gold is in the government's reserves, the *whole* of it is available.

For obvious reasons of convenience and of economy the greater part of the Indian circulation must continue in any case to consist of rupees. It is vain to suppose that the advantages of a true gold currency can be obtained by the compromise of somewhat increasing the gold element. If the Government dissipates some part of its sterling resources over the country—and any proposal for a greater infusion of gold into the currency amounts to this—it must plainly stand in a weaker position to meet a crisis than if they are concentrated in its own chests.

Keynes was appointed editor of the *Economic Journal* in October 1911; he also had a heavy lecturing load and began to be involved in college and faculty administration. While the book on Indian currency lay temporarily in abeyance, he received the mistaken impression that the Government of India in Calcutta might have published the draft of his paper which they had printed and distributed privately. He wrote to Sir James Meston, the Secretary of the Finance Department, inquiring about this and received a reassuring explanation in reply (7 February 1912). 'You cannot realise how much we appreciate the independent opinion of a trained mind who studies these matters from outside', the letter added, and went on to say that Meston would like to talk over with Keynes 'the present disposition of the Government of India...to ask for permission to open a gold mint tentatively, for the use of any who desire to convert their bars into sovereigns'.

Keynes had a copy made of his answer to this letter and added in his own hand the part that follows it. It is not clear whether he sent the postscript to Meston or, as seems more likely, simply kept it as notes for his book.

To SIR JAMES MESTON, *24 February 1912*

Dear Sir James Meston,

Many thanks for your letter. I did not really suppose that the Government of India would publish my paper without express permission. But I wished to avoid all risks.

I shall be very glad indeed if we have an opportunity of meeting when you are in England in the early part of the summer. If you can come and stay here with me for a night I shall be very glad. But if you cannot spare the time for this I am frequently in London and we can probably arrange to meet.

I am sorry to hear that the Government of India is disposed to open a gold mint—rather because it suggests preference for what seems to me a doubtful line of policy than because it is of any great importance in itself. Provided that only sovereigns are coined (and nothing of a lower denomination) I should not expect it to have much influence in further popularising the use of gold in India; and indeed I should be surprised if many gold bars were to be brought to it (I am assuming that sovereigns would not be given for bars on demand, but that, as is the case in England, an interval for mintage would elapse before the applicant could get his coins). In this case the cost of the mint would be so much money thrown away. But no further harm would be done.

If there is a strong public opinion in India in favour of a gold mint, it may very well be worth while to placate it at this comparatively small expense.

Yours truly,

J. M. KEYNES

Since writing the above, I have been trying to figure out in what circumstances gold bars are likely to be brought to an Indian mint. Provided no specific Indian coin is minted and that you do not mint on easier terms than is the case in England (two conditions to the observance of which I should attach importance), would bars be brought in any quantity unless

(*a*) the habits of the people were changing, the importation of new bars from England had ceased, and the people were wanting, therefore, to get rid of their bars; or

(*b*) in time of famine or depression when the people were wishing to turn their hoards into money?

In both cases it seems to me likely that the minting of the bars would be preliminary to changing the sovereigns for rupees or to exporting them.

Might it not, therefore, be advisable to publish terms on which bars could be exchanged for rupees *direct*? (I don't clearly remember whether such an exchange is already provided for, but fancy not.) It might be a real convenience if Government notified its readiness to purchase bars tendered in India at 58 rupees 5 annas per ounce (payable in silver or notes). Sovereigns might be obtainable at the same rate (i.e., £3 17s 9d per ounce) *when convenient to Government*. Such a notification would, I feel, be much more in the true spirit of the Indian currency system than the establishment of a gold mint would be; and it would serve the convenience of the public just as efficiently, at less expense to Government. What it would *not* accomplish would be the encouragement and placation of a certain type of public opinion. But then, of course, I regard this type of opinion as ill-informed, and any encouragement of it as an encouragement of a standing danger to the whole system.

87

During the summer vacation of 1912 Keynes continued his work on probability; his father's diary reported twenty-seven out of thirty chapters ready for a book at the end of the summer. But a situation was developing that soon concentrated his energies on Indian finance. Elements of it appear in his correspondence; R. W. Gillan, Finance Secretary to the Government of India, writing (10 August 1912) from Simla after a tour of the Presidency towns, remarked:

> Ideas which in the light of experience we have been able to leave behind us are still current and accepted among those of the public who concern themselves with currency matters. There was for instance a debate in Council last cold weather, on the subject of a gold currency in India, and it was almost ludicrous to note the way in which one speaker after another quoted from the Fowler Commission, and called on the Government without further delay to carry out its recommendations *literatim et verbatim*.

The recommendations of the Fowler Committee of 1898–9—that the Indian gold standard reserve should be held in gold, that gold should be coined in India and a gold currency established—were repeated in England by Sir Edward Holden, chairman of the London City and Midland Bank, who addressed the Manchester Statistical Society on the subject of British gold reserves at a meeting reported in *The Times*, 24 October 1912. His main thesis was that Britain must increase her own gold reserves, and he spoke of the absorption of gold by India, where the bulk of it appeared to have been hoarded, as a potential menace to the British supply. In particular he criticised the holding of the Indian gold standard reserve in securities and rupees. In conclusion, he called for a commission to investigate.

Keynes rose to the defence of Abraham's system.

To the Editor of The Times, *26 October 1912*

Sir,

Sir Edward Holden, in his address to the Manchester Statistical Society, reported in *The Times* of yesterday, does not, I think, do full justice to the policy of the India Council in the matter of the reserves they hold.

The stability of the Indian system depends upon the India Council's keeping sufficient reserves of coined rupees to enable them at all times to exchange international currency for local currency, and sufficient liquid resources in sterling to enable them to change back the local currency into international currency when they are required to do so.

The actual arrangements they make to this end are somewhat complicated, but the principle underlying them is simple. They must have a certain amount of coined rupees, a certain amount of coined gold, a certain amount of very liquid resources in the form of money at call, and a certain amount of fairly liquid resources in the form of investments. These various forms of resources they keep distributed according to rules, the origin of which is largely historical, between the currency reserve, the gold standard reserve, and the cash balances.

It happens that all the coined gold, held in reserve, is credited to the currency reserve, where it is just as available for meeting an adverse balance of trade as if it were in the gold standard reserve. Some part of this gold could be immediately transferred to the gold standard reserve, were this desired, by a mere book-keeping transaction.

Sir Edward Holden, in criticising the India Council for holding insufficient reserves in coined gold, makes no allusion to their enormous holding of gold—now about £26,000,000—in the currency reserve, and seems to suggest that they ought to hold an additional £18,000,000 in gold. Such a policy, whatever its utility to the London money market, would be a wanton extravagance from the point of view of India. If he had suggested that a larger proportion of this £26,000,000 should be held in London (approximately £3,660,000 is now held here and the rest in India), this would have been a practicable policy, and in the interests both of India (for in times of emergency there would be some delay and expense in sending the gold here) and of the London market.

It may be added that the most probable danger, against which the India Council have to provide, is that a large sum, due to a sudden failure of the exports, should be due for immediate payment from India to this country. This contingency is quite as adequately guarded against by holding large sums at call in this country as by holding gold; and there is no reason why the use of these sums in such an emergency should lead to exports of gold from this country or should inconvenience the London money market.

In the last part of his address Sir Edward Holden complained of the possible inconvenience to London of the heavy drain of gold, now habitually required by India, and seemed to suggest that the establishment of a gold currency in India would be some remedy for this. Probably the report of his address has been compressed at this point. The establishment of an effective gold currency in India would plainly increase rather than diminish the drain of gold thither. The present policy of the India Council economises the use of gold in India more than would any of the alternative policies now in the field.

Your obedient servant,

J. M. KEYNES

It was just at this time that the rumour of scandal precipitated a public discussion of the whole Indian currency question. Earlier in the year the Council of India had arranged for the secret purchase of large amounts of silver through the bullion-brokers Messrs. Samuel Montagu and Company. The sole reason for secrecy was to avoid speculation and the transaction was conducted according to the customary procedures of the India Office; nevertheless, Parliamentary critics made much of the coincidental circumstances that a member of the House of Commons was a partner in the firm and that the senior partner was the brother of the Under-Secretary of State for India.

At this point *The Times* published a series of five long articles by an anonymous correspondent, revealing 'a state not only of affairs but of opinion which calls for thorough and immediate consideration' (1, 2, 4, 6 and 7 November 1912). The writer's criticisms were based on the recommendations of the Fowler Committee. A rash of questions erupted in the House of Commons concerning the cash balances of India, the selling prices of the securities held in the Indian gold standard reserve, the market price for silver, the approved list of borrowers from the India Office balances, etc. Keynes was curious as to the identity of the writer of the articles and asked Lionel Abrahams, who replied (8 November):

I fancy that someone on the staff of the *Times of India*, inspired by M. de P. Webb [chairman of the Karachi Chamber of Commerce and one of the most vociferous of the currency critics], writes the articles, but I don't know for certain. The work of replying to Parliamentary questions through ignorant mouths is very wearing.

I am delighted to hear about your book. I am sure that it will do much good. But can't you send a letter to *The Times* as well in a day or two? There is so little said on our side. I should be most grateful.

Keynes immediately obliged with a letter, dated 9 November, which he must have written the same day as he received Abraham's note—there was a short delay in its publication. This was reproduced by the *Times of India*, 13 December 1912.

To the Editor of The Times, *14 November 1912*

Sir,

The series of articles which you have lately published from 'An Indian Correspondent' has clearly shown that the true character of the Indian currency system is easily misrepresented. For this, as you justly point out in the very judicious leading article in *The Times* of today, the Government of India must be held partly responsible. For ten years they have kept silence even from good words. But the question whether the Indian authorities have adequately explained themselves is quite different from the question whether their currency system is actually a good one. It is in regard to this latter question that I wish to make a few comments.

One of the chief objects of a good currency is to combine cheapness with stability. Against the attempts of the Government of India to achieve this your correspondent has advanced two main criticisms—first, that they have established a gold standard without encouraging the circulation of gold; and second, that they have kept a part of their reserves in London earning interest.

With regard to the first, he supports the doctrine that every increase in the proportion of gold actually circulating increases *pro tanto* the stability of the system. The late Lord Goschen was one of the first to point out the fallacy in this. Gold reserves to be effective must be centralised and not scattered through the pockets of the people. So long as a large part of the currency is token, it will be this part that the government will be called on in times of trouble to redeem for purposes of export. The more troublous the times, the more obstinately will the gold in the pockets of the people remain there. The trend of currency policy, therefore, in recent times has been to encourage the use of some relatively cheap material, cheques or notes or token silver, as the actual medium of exchange; and to ensure stability by centralising the reserve of gold to the utmost degree, so that the local currency can be immediately changed for gold, when gold is needed to meet foreign obligations. It is now the anxiety of governments and central banks to prevent the dissipation of their gold out of the reserves into the circulation.

Take, for example, France, Russia, Austria-Hungary, Holland, or Japan. They all have in varying degrees a gold standard. In some of them a small amount of gold circulates from hand to hand. In others the gold circulating outside the reserves bears a negligible proportion to the total volume of media of exchange. In all of them the authorities keep as much of the gold as they can in their own hands; and in none of them do they encourage the circulation of gold coin from hand to hand. If the Government of India were to follow your correspondent's advice and give additional facilities for the circulation of gold, they would be acting counter to what is now one of the most widely accepted of currency maxims. This, then—the centralisation of the gold reserves—is one of the guiding principles of the Government of India's policy, in opposition, as your correspondent truly points out, to the policy recommended by the Fowler Commission.

There remains the question of the amount, the form, and the location of these central reserves. To deal with this matter adequately is obviously beyond the scope of a letter. The Government of India enter their reserves under three heads—the gold standard reserve, the currency reserve, the cash balances. All three have a sterling branch and a rupee branch. When it is necessary to change rupees into sterling, the holdings of the rupee branches are swollen, and sterling resources are released.

In discussing the adequacy of the reserves and the suitability of the forms in which they are held, the only sensible course is to regard them as a whole. Your correspondent puts himself out of court as a serious student of this question by treating them as if they were in watertight compartments. He first of all criticises the gold standard reserve on the ground that it is not liquid enough, and then criticises the cash balances on the ground that they contain excessive liquid resources in sterling. This question of the proper size and form of the reserves is one of great complexity, well worth discussing, but his is not a useful point of view from which to approach it.

When the reserves have been centralised and raised to an adequate amount, the next question is whether they need lie wholly idle. These reserves are accumulated, it must be remembered, to meet foreign demands in case of need. For such a purpose liquid balances in some foreign country where there is a stable money market are just as useful, if the amount of them is kept within proper limits, as gold—in fact more useful, since the remission of gold from a distant country involves expense and delay; and in addition these balances can be made to earn a small but not negligible sum by way of interest. It is a principal ground of your correspondent's complaints that some part of the Indian reserves are thus held in this country earning interest.

In this policy India is not, as he seems to suggest, alone. Austria-Hungary, Russia, Sweden, and Japan, for example, habitually keep a considerable part of their reserves in foreign balances or foreign bills, while numerous other countries practise the same policy on a smaller scale. In October of this year the Russian balances abroad were about £26,000,000; and the Swedish were nearly £5,000,000 (or almost half of their total liquid resources). The bills held by the Austro-Hungarian Bank bear a smaller proportion to their total reserves, but are nevertheless important. I know of no regular statement of the Japanese balances abroad; but Mr Yamamoto, the Japanese Minister of Finance, stated in the spring of this year that they were then a

93

little over £37,000,000 (in Europe and the United States). Regard being had to the relative liabilities of India and Japan, compared with the Indian balances these figures are large. Yet no one accuses the Japanese Government of acting thus through partiality for the London money market, or of taking up Treasury bills at a low rate of discount (in spite of the notoriously high rate of interest in Japan) out of a corrupt affection for the Chancellor of the Exchequer.

The Government of India's policy only differs from policies lately adopted in all parts of the world in being more complete, more systematic, and, compared with some of them, more public. Within the last few years, moreover, they have established their currency in a position of almost unassailable stability; and have managed at the same time to save considerable sums for the taxpayer. This policy of theirs has been evolved gradually. Hence follows, no doubt, some part of the misapprehensions that exist regarding it. But it has been taken as the model for several small countries which have lately, without much public notice being taken, put their currencies in order; a commission of the House of Representatives of the United States has pressed it on China; and it has received the approbation of numerous students in Germany and America. One notes with regret, though with acquiescence and without surprise, that in this country financial ability in departments of State must be accompanied by public eloquence if it is to rest free from ungenerous and ill-founded charges.   Your obedient servant,

J. M. KEYNES

'The best statement on our side that has yet appeared, and my only regret was that *The Times* did not print it in letters of gold and silver and issue it as a special supplement!' commented William Robinson of the India Office (31 December 1912), sending Keynes copies of the latest Paper Currency Reports for his book.

Many other letters and articles were published by *The Times*, which later had to acknowledge that 'the views of our Anglo-Indian correspondent have altogether failed to secure widespread support' (20 January 1913). This, however, did not disturb *The Times*' editorial campaign, ultimately successful, for the appointment of a Royal Commission to inquire into the whole financial management of the India Office.

While the Parliamentary questions continued Keynes was making progress with his book on Indian currency. In March 1910 he had arranged to publish his work on probability with the Cambridge University Press and in November signed a half-profits agreement with them. However, during the autumn of 1912, according to his father's diary, he became annoyed with some action —unspecified—that the Press had taken. The records of the Press show that because the manuscript was now about 100 pages longer than the 320 stipulated in the agreement, Keynes was being asked to contribute £30 to the cost—which he refused to do. On 1 December 1912, Dr Keynes wrote, he brought the publisher Maurice Macmillan to tea at his parents' house, and on 15 December he had signed agreements for both the book on probability and the book on Indian currency to be published by Macmillan and Company. Keynes had already reported on manuscripts on logic and Indian economics for Macmillan's; Daniel Macmillan, son of Maurice Macmillan, had been a friend of his at Eton.

By February 1913 Keynes was sending out proofs of *Indian Currency and Finance* to those whose criticism he sought. Among them were Hartley Withers, a financial journalist with *The Times* who had also written on the subject, his father, and Lionel Abrahams.

Abrahams greeted the proofs 'with admiration and general but not unvarying agreement' (24 February 1913) and took much care in reading and discussing them. Many times he supplied or corrected matters of information. The discussion was carried on both by letter—sometimes two letters despatched the same day—and in person. Abrahams wanted Keynes to disassociate his argument for making loans in India out of the paper currency reserve from his treatment—with which Abrahams disagreed—of all the English balances as part of the same reserve. 'The one fundamental error of our angry critics that you have not quite succeeded in avoiding is the error of regarding the Secretary of State's balances as primarily a loan fund or a reserve fund, whereas their primary purpose is to serve as a working balance from which the India Office can pay its way' (24 March 1913). He had difficulties about a point concerning sovereigns in transit to Australia, which Keynes revised to meet his objections (29 April 1913). In another letter the same day he took issue with the psychological implications of Keynes's plan for providing for Indian railroads. A postcard pleaded for a less severe treatment of the Government's broker in order not to '...hurt a worthy, harmless man'—whose income, rivalled only by the Viceroy's, Keynes felt was too high for the amount of work he did. Later Abrahams relented because, as he wrote (12 May 1913), 'fortunately his [the broker's] tastes do not run to literature (or economic science)'.

Keynes went to Egypt for the Easter vacation. On 28 March Dr Keynes wrote in his diary:

> Maynard is offered the secretaryship of the approaching Royal Commission on Indian Currency. He would evidently like to accept but there are difficulties in the way, and his absence in Egypt makes negotiation difficult.

He returned from Egypt, not secretary to the Commission, but a member. All but one of the chapters of the book were in type, and he hurriedly finished it 'without the addition of certain other chapters which had been projected', as he noted in the preface. 'I am going to try to index Maynard's book for him', Dr Keynes wrote, 4 May. 'He seems to have been somewhat overworked.' The Commission held its first meeting 5 May. On 18 May Dr Keynes reported that 'Maynard has now finished his book' (the preface was dated 12 May 1913) and that he himself had finished the index. *Indian Currency and Finance* was published 9 June 1913.

Chapter 2

THE ROYAL COMMISSION ON INDIAN FINANCE AND CURRENCY 1913-1914

Keynes was in Alexandria during the Easter vacation when he received a letter from Sir Thomas Holderness at the India Office dated 11 March 1913 and marked 'Private and Confidential'.

Dear Keynes,

You know that a Royal Commission is to be appointed to inquire into certain aspects of the Indian currency system and the part played therein by the India Office.

Would you be willing to be Secretary to it on suitable terms as to remuneration? I imagine that if you should take the appointment, it would mean more or less continuous work from, say, the beginning of April until the end of July. By that time I should hope that the taking of evidence would be finished, and that the Commission would adjourn until the autumn, when a draft report would be put before them.

I think I can say that if you will take the appointment, it would be offered to you.

Perhaps you would like [to] see me about it before deciding.

Yours sincerely

T. W. HOLDERNESS

Keynes cabled his reply (he kept the draft worked out on a scrap of hotel writing paper):

Holderness India Office London
Back April 14 sooner if essential Cambridge requires two days weekly until May 22 thereafter free book Indian Currency printing attach importance freedom respecting this proofs with Abrahams writing

Keynes Governorate Alexandria

A sequence of cables from Holderness tells the story.

[22 March 1913]
Mr Keynes Savoy Hotel Luxor
From London your telegram received glad no serious difficulty April 14th probably early enough for return but will let you know if earlier date desirable
Holderness

[22 March 1913]
Mr Keynes Savoy Hotel Luxor
From London have now seen your proofs will let you know within few days if proposed book should present difficulty
Holderness

[29 March 1913]
Keynes care Furness Governorate Alexandria
I don't think your book will stand in the way will wire again next week no need to hurry back
Holderness

[3 April 1913]
Keynes care Furness Governorate Alex[andria]
Am instructed to offer you seat on commission this is considered in view of book more suitable than secretaryship and will give greater scope hope you will accept
Holderness

These telegrams explain the 'difficulties' mentioned by Keynes's father in the way of his appointment to the Royal Commission on Indian Finance and Currency and how they were resolved. Marshall wrote in congratulation (12 April):

My dear Keynes,
I am delighted to know the youngest member of the youngest Commission; and I think almost the youngest of any. You are the right man for the place. But you will need to husband your strength

Yours happily

ALFRED MARSHALL

Keynes wanted to make certain that his freedom in publishing *Indian Currency and Finance* would not be compromised by his membership on the Commission. He sent the proofs to the chairman, Austen Chamberlain— leader of the tariff reformers and financial authority of the Conservative opposition. Chamberlain had been Financial Secretary to the Treasury 1900–2; his official position at this time was Member of Parliament for East Worcestershire, where three years earlier Keynes had taken part in the unsuccessful free trade campaign against him. He wrote to Keynes 21 April 1913:

Dear Sir,

I reply even before receiving your proofs because I do not think that whatever is in them it ought to affect my answer. The selection of the Commission was entirely a matter for Lord Crewe [the Secretary of State for India]. He knew, before he proposed your name to the King, that you were publishing this book and told me that he had seen the proof-sheets, and thought that the character of the work and its subject were a qualification and your method of treating the subject no bar to your appointment.

In these circumstances you are obviously at liberty to publish it forthwith, and whilst I appreciate your kindness in laying the facts before me, I certainly should not wish to interfere in any way with your judgement. It is just possible that you might wish to modify a phrase here or there or to hold in suspense a conclusion in view of your subsequent appointment to the Commission but of this you should be the sole judge. The point would be that you should not seem to *prejudge* questions which you are now to *judge*.

Your proofs have come by a later post even while I am writing this letter. I shall be very interested to read them.

Yours very truly

AUSTEN CHAMBERLAIN

Most reviewers, bar one or two dissenting voices, shared Chamberlain's attitude when the book appeared in June and greeted with approval both the decision to publish and the appointment of one so obviously well qualified. The Commission held its first meeting 5 May 1913 and heard evidence until 6 August. It was not until it adjourned for this summer recess that Chamberlain read the whole of *Indian Currency*—when he wrote Keynes the following letter, dated 12 August, marked 'Private'.

My dear Keynes,

When you sent me the proofs of your book, I read the first two chapters as an initiation into the subject I was to help in investigating; but at that point I deliberately stopped, deciding that I would not fill my mind with your views till I had heard evidence and begun to form some opinions of my own which I might check and examine in the light of what you had written.

Now, since the Commission adjourned, I have read your book from cover to cover. It is if I may say so, admirably lucid, but I scarcely know whether to congratulate you on it or condole with myself! You will certainly be considered the author of the Commission's report whenever that document sees the light. I am amazed to see how largely the views of the Commission as disclosed by our informal discussions are a mere repetition of the arguments and conclusions to which your study had previously led you. At present I see no difference between us except possibly as to the terms in which we should write of a State Bank and I am hopeful that even if we should lay a rather different stress on the importance and feasibility of this proposal in future conditions, we shall be able to agree as to what should be said about it in the present.

There is just one incidental statement in your book (p. 88) [p. 62, JMK, vol. 1] which I don't follow, tho' I have noticed that more than one witness has agreed to it. You say:

'For purposes of export at times of depression, the 10 rupee piece would be worth less than 2/3rds of a sovereign.' Why?

Yours very truly

AUSTEN CHAMBERLAIN

A witness, secretary-treasurer of the Bank of Bengal, questioned by the Commission about the flow of capital between India and England, replied:

'It is all explained in Mr Keynes's book.'
'What have you got to say to that?' he was asked.
'I entirely agree with what Mr Keynes says.'

There is no doubt about Keynes's influence upon the Commission's report. As the published evidence clearly shows, the youngest member was in no way overwhelmed by his situation among the sages of the civil service and the lords of finance. One of his colleagues was his old chief, Sir Arthur Godley, now Lord Kilbracken; another was Sir Robert Chalmers, later to be his superior at the Treasury. Keynes took a conspicuous part in the proceedings from the start. He was one of ten commissioners and in hearing witnesses he asked approximately one-sixth of all the questions.

He must have been at an advantage from the beginning through his friendship with Lionel Abrahams who, as Assistant Under-Secretary of State for India and responsible for the system under scrutiny, was the first and most important of all the witnesses. In what was more like an urbane, rather academic conversation than any kind of cross-examination, Keynes was able to draw out and interpret the characteristic subtleties of Abrahams' thinking for his fellow-commissioners. Here is an excerpt from Keynes's examination of Abrahams on 5 July 1913 (Keynes's thirtieth birthday), from *Minutes of Evidence taken before the Royal Commission on Indian Finance and Currency, Volume I* (Cd. 7068):

FROM THE MINUTES OF EVIDENCE, 5 JUNE 1913

(MR KEYNES) In paragraph 7 of Appendix III (pp. 88–9) [*Appendices*, vol. I] you suggest that 5 millions sterling is a suitable amount to hold in gold in the gold standard reserve; is this amount contingent on the amount earmarked in the paper currency chest? (MR ABRAHAMS) *When I wrote that I was assuming that there would be gold held in the paper currency in London.*

Were you making any assumption as to how much? *No. We have for some years held sums varying between 5 millions and 7 millions; occasionally they have gone up a little; I had in my mind about 5 millions.*

Your view then is that you ought to hold about 5 millions in the gold standard reserve if you are holding from 5 to 7 millions in the paper currency? *I would not crystallise it too much. Supposing that at a particular time one had very little in the paper currency. I do not think that I should hold that one ought to increase the amount in the gold standard reserve, but still I should not seriously dissent from what you said.*

My point was how much gold you want to have in London altogether to whatever reserve it is credited; and I wanted to get at your notion as to what the proper figure for the total gold in London was; it does not seem to me that the particular way of crediting it is of such fundamental importance? *It is very indeterminate. One wants to have, I think, at least 5 millions, preferably more, which you can use almost at a moment's notice, which at any rate you have so much under your control that at the beginning of an exchange crisis you can offer to sell, say, a million of bills, of the kind that was sold in 1908, per week for several weeks, and feel that you are provided with the means to meet them.*

You will want to hold some gold, and I was wondering whether you had settled at all in your own mind what the amount should be in present circumstances? *No. I do not think that one can give anything more than one's own estimate of how much would make one feel quite comfortable with this responsibility of meeting an exchange crisis on one. I should say that if one were as low as 5 millions, one would not feel that one was ill-provided for, that if one had 10 millions one would feel that that was rather better but not a wasteful amount, and that if one had more than 10 millions I should feel at any rate that it was rather wasteful. I do not think I could put it more definitely than that.*

Are you of opinion that the amount in the gold standard reserve, which ought to be lent at short notice in London, is in any way contingent on the amount that is lent in this way from the general balances? *Only in this way, that if we were lending from our general balances as much as our approved borrowers would take it would be difficult to lend from the gold standard reserve as well, and certainly one ought not to be lending so much that approved borrowers of less than the very highest standing were accepted in order to find a clientele.*

You would argue in this way: that as long as it was your normal practice to have 5 millions or 6 millions lent at short notice from the general balances, then that 1 million lent in that way was enough from the gold standard reserve; and if your normal practice changed so that you only lent, perhaps, 2 millions from the general balances, then you ought to have more in the gold standard reserve lent in that form? *That, if I may put it in an almost primitive way, is not quite the way my mind works in these matters. I think what is behind your question is this: that the smaller your general balances at any given moment the larger your special reserves ought to be, if you are to be well equipped for meeting a sudden fall in exchange.*

Particularly, that the smaller your general balances, the larger your special reserves ought to be in the most liquid shape? *I think that the reason that I am not able to answer you quite as directly as I should like is that in preparing for an exchange crisis, or in considering how one will prepare for it, one has in mind that one will rely on certain special reserves, and one leaves the general balances out of consideration, thinking they will just be enough to pay the ordinary current expenses, and that they will be of no help for the exchange crisis. I realise that if at a time when our balances had risen as they have recently to a very unusual height, 18 or 19 millions, an exchange crisis had then come, those high balances would have been very helpful to us.*

I can understand your taking the view that the general total of the reserves ought not to be influenced by your temporary balances, but would you also hold that the form in which you ought to keep your permanent reserves is uninfluenced by the amount of temporary balances that you have? *Yes, because according to my view, and if I may so put it, our system rather stands or falls with its correctness, the various reserves that one holds can be realised when we want them. It is true that we cannot realise 4 millions of Consols advantageously in a week, but we have built up a system so that, if we saw the need for realising all our reserves, by the time we wanted our 4 millions of Consols we could have realised them, and our gold and our short-dated securities and so on would last us during the period required for the realisation of the Consols. I hope I have made it clear that that is why I do not attach, if you do not mind my putting it in that way, very much importance to the consideration that you were last mentioning.*

You would not feel at all that as long as it is the policy to hold 5 millions or more in the general balances at short notice, there is no need of holding a million as well in the gold standard reserve at very short notice? *No, because I feel that the general balance is hypothecated for quite different purposes. Also, just let me mention this to remove a possible misapprehension as regards fact: one speaks about our 5 millions or 6 millions as a standard for the general balance, that is to say, for the closing general balance on 31st March in each year; but that is a very fluctuating sum. As I mentioned previously, in the course of a few days we might be paying away 3 millions or 4 millions, and those occasions when we have very heavy payments recur at least four times a year, when the quarterly dividends have to be paid.*

You have suggested 25 millions as the proper limit of the gold standard reserve (see paragraph 19 of Appendix III, page 93 [*Appendices*, vol. I]; is the suitability of this particular sum in any way contingent upon the amount of sterling resources held otherwise? *I had in my mind that we should probably have 5 millions of gold in the paper currency reserve in England. That was the only special resource that I assumed. I assumed that our general balance would not be exceptionally high or exceptionally low, because it would serve the primary purposes that it is meant to serve.*

Your view is then that about 30 millions is the proper limit for all your sterling resources which are connected with the support of exchange? *Yes, I should call that a liberal limit.*

In calculating the proper amount of the gold standard reserve, are you considering merely the obligation under which the Government of India lies to support exchange and to be prepared to change into sterling all rupees and notes presented; or are you considering other possibilities as well? *Would you indicate the other possibilities that you have in mind?*

Are you considering the possibility that the Government of India would have to assist the Indian money market at a time of severe crisis, or merely that they should change into sterling such notes and rupees as the Indian money market should tender to them? *I have always assumed that if in a time of severe crisis the Government of India had to assist the Indian money market, it would assist it in India, and that the need for granting such assistance would not make any demand on the sterling resources which we have been considering.*

If the Indian money market were helped in India that would increase the amount of funds available in the hands of Indian bankers for tendering for sterling bills, would it not? *May I answer you in this way, that you are regarding, if I understand you rightly, the amount of the drain that may come on our sterling resources as a certain function of the currency which Indian bankers and the Indian public could tender for the purchase of bills on London; but I regard it as a function not of a certain quantum of currency but of a certain balance of foreign trade, and all my arguments and calculations are based on that.*

I am glad that point has been brought out. I myself should not say that it depended necessarily upon either of those, but it depends upon one or other of them according to the policy adopted; therefore I ask you which policy is adopted? Let me put it in this way: if the existing volume of the currency is the test then it seems to me that implies a policy of only giving sterling for rupees and notes; if the balance of trade is taken as the test then some other standard is applied. Would you agree with that? *I have always taken the balance of trade as the proper measure of the possible liabilities that would have to be met in a period of exchange crisis, and I have disregarded the quantum of currency altogether.*

With reference to a question which Sir Ernest Cable asked, do you think that when a certain point is reached in the accumulation of the gold standard reserve it is the profits on the further rupee coinage which ought to be diverted, or rather the interest on the former accumulations that should be diverted? *I do not think it matters very much, but I do not see how anyone could answer that with any definiteness. My feeling, as was brought out, I think, by the Chairman and other questioners, is that if you have worked up to a certain sum as being a suitable reserve at a given time you must let it go on increasing by moderate increments year by year, or decade by decade, so as to provide for the natural growth of trade; and whether it is better to let it grow by the accretion of interest or by the accretion of profits is a question to which I could scarcely give any useful answer.*

I put a more precise question than that. When you say after 25 millions has been reached further sums should not be credited to the gold standard reserve, do you mean that the interest of those 25 millions should not be credited, or that when further rupees are coined the profit on those rupees should not be credited? *I think I fully understood your question, and I am sorry if I did not make my answer clear. My answer was intended to be this: you must go on, or it is desirable to go on increasing your fund year by year; whether you increase it by adding the interest and diverting the profits or whether you increase it by adding the profits and diverting the interest is a matter on which I do not feel that I, or indeed anyone else, could give an opinion of any great value.*

I had not understood that the 25 millions you suggested was a figure which is only valid, as it were, for the moment? *In this as in many other things one is always in a state of flux. If 25 millions is valid now, then 25¼ millions will be valid next year, and 25½ millions the year after—I am taking, perhaps, rather large increases. As the business of India increases so ought your reserve to increase by an amount or in a ratio which it would be affectation to pretend to define with any exactness.*

I understood you to say that when the gold standard reserve had reached 25 millions no more ought to be accumulated. I understand now that what you are saying is that if the gold standard reserve were 25 millions now then no further accumulations ought to be made; is that right? *What I meant to say was this: Until we have 25 millions let us have the full profit and the full interest; when we have reached 25 millions then do not let us say the fund has reached its maximum, but let us provide for accretions on a smaller scale than hitherto; let us either add the interest but not the profit, or the profit but not the interest, or some proportion of the profit. I wish to be rather indefinite. I only wish to put forward the view that some accretion, but not so much as now, should take place when the 25 millions is reached.*

I wish only to elicit the precise nature of the indefiniteness, if I may put it in that way. Turning to the Indian branch of the gold standard reserve, is it not rather confusing to the public that the gold standard reserve should hold silver? *Yes, I think it is, more especially because the true explanation, or at least my view of the true explanation, has never been put before the public. What has been put before the public is rather the view that this Indian branch is a bulwark against hasty coinage, which does not very much commend itself to my mind. I think that what I regard as the true view is quite comprehensible, but I should agree that though comprehensible it is perhaps not easily comprehensible.*

Would you mind explaining what the reasons are against the book-keeping transaction by which 4 millions of gold would be transferred from the paper currency reserve to the gold standard reserve, and 4 millions of silver transferred from the gold standard reserve to the paper currency reserve; why should that not be done? *The difficulty is simply this: We may assume that the rest of the Paper Currency Act is going to stand as it is, because what I am going to say depends upon that assumption. If you wish at any moment to take out your 4 millions of rupees from the paper currency reserve you have to do one of two things; as I put it in answer to the Chairman, you have to apply one of two keys to the lock—you either cancel notes or you ear-mark gold. There are times when you would like to get at the rupees, but it is inconvenient to use either of these methods, and then, instead of these rupees being left in the paper currency reserve and in the gold standard reserve, you have a third and much easier method of getting at them, namely, you can either take a loan, which I do not think a good scheme, or you can make an investment in securities in England as against the rupees that you have taken out from the Indian branch.*

That is to say, more latitude is allowed as to the manner in which the resources of the gold standard reserve can be held? *Yes.*

So that if you have to make a sudden change, there are more ways in which you can do it? *That is so.*

But apart from that there would be no advantage in holding any silver in the gold standard reserve, would there? *No; that to my mind is the only advantage.*

Therefore, if the latitude which is allowed with regard to the gold standard reserve were allowed in the case of the paper currency reserve, you would then clear out the silver from the gold standard reserve altogether? *I am not sure that the Government of India would agree, but I am giving my opinion. My answer is yes; but I do not wish to commit anyone but myself to that answer.*

So that the explanation of a practice which is rather confusing to the public is that it is simply a detail of the machinery? *Yes.*

And has no real fundamental significance? *I do not think so. Of course, the general public who are accustomed to the Bank of England method of keeping a note reserve, which seems to me as unscientific a method as could be devised, would regard it as a very serious departure from orthodoxy that the greater latitude should be allowed in respect of the management of the Indian paper currency reserve. I do not think that there is anything in that view, but still it is widely held, or it would be widely held, if any change were proposed.*

The sympathetic questioner could also be needlingly provocative, unawed by eminence and authority. Here is an excerpt from his examination of Alfred Clayton Cole, who had been the Governor of the Bank of England until two months previously.

FROM THE MINUTES OF EVIDENCE, 17 JUNE 1913

(MR KEYNES) When you expressed the rather paradoxical opinion that the Indian cash balances in London were disadvantageous, were you speaking narrowly from the point of view of the Bank of England, or from the point of view of the whole of the London market? (MR COLE) *I was speaking from the point of view of the Bank of England, and I hope I made that clear.*

Your remarks would apply equally to all international banking on a large scale, would they not? *To all international banking on a large scale where a withdrawal of that money would affect the conditions of the money market.*

I can understand that if London were to cease to be an international money market the life of the directors of the Bank of England would be a less anxious one; and you are merely stating this as a particular application of that? *I am asked here to give the view of the Bank of England, and I am giving you the view of the Bank of England.*

And the view of the Bank of England is that any increase in the extent to which London is an international money market makes their time a more anxious one? *Any increase in the volume of transactions which pass through London for which the London money market is responsible, makes the maintenance of an adequate gold reserve here all the more important.*

But you would not deprecate the extension of England's liabilities in that way, would you? You would not wish London to be less an international money market, would you? *No: I want to see England maintained as the international money market, and that it should have the position it holds today.*

Then you would be sorry rather than glad if India was to give up holding its balances here? *From the point of view of the Bank of England I would rather they were what I call kept within more moderate limits; that is all.*

From the point of view of the position of the money market, you would be sorry? *I should not be sorry; it is merely a question of size.*

Would you be glad? *From the point of view of the Bank of England, from the point of view that London should not be liable to be drawn upon for very big amounts, I should be glad if the Indian balances were kept within more moderate limits. They rise to, I believe, 18 millions altogether. I am not clear what was done with the 18 millions.*

(CHAIRMAN) I think we have had it in evidence that the 18 millions, those very high figures, were due to what it is hoped may be found to have been rather exceptional circumstances, and partly also to under-estimating the revenue? *I quite agree, but I do not know what was done with that 18 millions here. As far as I can turn it up at the Bank, the loans through their broker have never much exceeded 11 millions; I suppose the balance all went to the banks, and there was no security for it.*

There were loans to the banks as well? *We check all the securities at the Bank for the India Office, and therefore, we know the amount of the securities. I know the maximum amount of securities deposited at any one time, and I know that the maximum amount of loans to what I call the market have not exceeded something between 11 millions and 12 millions: that is all.*

(MR KEYNES) I only wanted to get the point clear that there is nothing peculiar to India about this, and that in general you deprecate London doing international banking business on a very large scale? *No.*

(CHAIRMAN) I think you did not deprecate London doing international banking business on a very large scale, but you said there was a danger if these large amounts were suddenly withdrawn? *I say that that is a danger which, if it is possible to avoid it, it is well to avoid; but as long as London remains the international money market it has got to shoulder the burdens as well as the advantages of that. Mr Keynes's view apparently is that I deprecate London being an international money market; I absolutely correct that.*

(MR KEYNES) I understood there is a disadvantage, but I do want to have your opinion as to whether on the balance it is not an advantage to London to put itself into this position. It makes the problem of the reserves more difficult, but is it for that reason to be deprecated on the whole? *My answer to that is that you have got to shoulder your responsibilities, and on the whole, it is desirable that London should remain the international financial centre of the trade and commerce of the world. What you are dealing with on this Commission is the question of Indian finance, and you are not dealing with anything more.*

Your second reason for rather disliking these large balances was that they sometimes had the effect of forcing the market rate down; I suppose that is true of all large lenders in the market? *That is right.*

They have not had a different effect in that way from any other large lender? *No.*

So that there again, from the point of view of the market as a whole, you would not deprecate it? *No. It is quite desirable that London should have its lenders as well as its borrowers; it must have them.*

The Chairman asked you your opinion as to how far gold in circulation was available to meet a foreign drain, and I think you expressed the opinion that it was of some value? *Yes; I expressed the view that gold in circulation is of some value, because, if you get a famine, gold will not be so much wanted, and therefore it will come back to what I should call the bankers, and then it is available. What I stated was that it is better for India to hold gold which is taken, so to speak, at its face value, than to have it in rupees which have got to be melted and sold at their bullion value.*

When you gave that answer were you imagining a case in which India had hardly anything but gold, or in which gold was perhaps a fifth or a quarter of the circulation? *I was not imagining anything. I was only giving you the difference between having a gold circulation and a silver circulation.*

Do you mean by a gold circulation one in which nearly all the circulation is gold, or one in which about a fourth or fifth is gold? *My reply was quite independent of the proportion of the circulation.*

Then your answer applies even in the case where gold is a fourth or a fifth? *Certainly.*

Do you think that when money is returned from circulation it will be the gold rather than the rupees, even when the gold is only a small proportion? *They might come back in equal proportions; I cannot tell you. That is a question you must ask of somebody who has got Indian experience.*

Therefore, a certain proportion of the gold in circulation would not be available. The gold would not be available to anything like its full amount in a crisis, and you would not expect, if a fifth of the circulation was gold and a fifth of the currency came back in a time of crisis, that very much of that fifth would be gold? *I should imagine that if a fifth of the currency was in gold and four-fifths were in silver, it might be returned a fifth gold and four-fifths silver. I should say—but I do not know, as it is not a thing which I do know—that probably gold would come back quicker than silver, but that I cannot tell you. Gold is more used, I imagine, by those people who are European managers, and so on; but I really do not know, and it is not a question, I think, that I should answer. It is a question on which you should ask someone who has a knowledge of Indian conditions.*

You have not any opinion, therefore, as to whether in Indian conditions, gold, in circulation to the sort of extent I have suggested, would be available, and you did not intend to be expressing an opinion on that? *I only expressed the general opinion that if you have got a large amount of gold in circulation and bullion is required for export, gold is a better thing to export than silver, which has got to be melted down.*

With a large amount of gold in circulation, you say? *I am not troubling about the proportion of the amount in circulation.*

In the matter of the note issue, I understood that you are nervous about increasing the note issue lest at some not distant date a large number of the inhabitants of India should use cheques? *I am not nervous about anything, and 'nervous' is not quite the correct expression to use. I was asked my opinion as to an increase of the fiduciary issue, and I gave you the point that if cheques are largely introduced into the banking system in India, the note issue would not increase in future years as rapidly as it has done in the last twenty years.*

Then you did not mean to be expressing an opinion that that was likely to happen within the lifetime of those who are now alive? *I do not express any opinion on Indian matters, because I can only give you what is the experience here in London.*

The Chairman put the question to you that if cheques had not been developed in England as they have been, and if we had used notes as they do in some foreign countries, the system of note issue by the Bank of England would have had to be modified; I understood you to say no, and that we should have gone on just as they have in France? *Yes, that is my opinion.*

But you would not maintain that the method of regulating the note issue in France is the same as that in this country? *The conditions of the two countries are distinct, but the method of regulating the fiduciary issue of notes in France is under definite Acts of Parliament, just the same as ours. Of course, the two Acts of Parliament are quite distinct.*

And their provisions are of quite a different kind? *That is so; so they are in Germany.*

If in England notes were to be used on a large scale, and the Act were not altered, we should have to hold gold almost up to the full amount of the notes? *You have to hold gold today for every note issued above 18 millions-odd—I can give you the exact figure if you want it.*

But that is not the case in France? *That is not exactly the case in France, but I am not prepared to give the Commission any information on that without referring as to what the exact conditions of the note issue in France are.*

Is there any note-issuing country in the world which regulates its note issue on the same system as the Bank of England? *I think not.*

So that there is some experience for thinking that in a note-issuing country some different system is desirable? *Of course, I think ours is the best: therefore I do not think any different system is desirable.*

Do you think that the business of the world could be done if all banks adopted the Bank of England system? *The business of the world would be done. Whether it would be done on the present scale is another matter.*

One of the witnesses was a man whose articles and speeches had much to do in inspiring the inquiry—the Honourable Montagu de P. Webb, president of the Karachi Chamber of Commerce and an ardent propagandist of the back-to-Fowler school. Several of the commissioners, including Keynes, questioned him rather severely, but Keynes, who pressed hard on arguments which did not seem to be based on solid calculations or precise information, came the nearest to discomfiting him. [In Keynes's *Economic Journal* review of Webb's book *The Rupee Problem* (*JMK*, vol. XI), he had written: 'in his plea for the sale of Council bills...at a uniform price...Mr Webb does not appreciate the full effects of what he proposes.']

FROM THE MINUTES OF EVIDENCE, 11 JULY 1913

(MR KEYNES) Now I will turn to Part II of Appendix XXI ['Memorandum of Evidence Submitted by Mr M. de P. Webb, C.I.E., Chairman of the Karachi Chamber of Commerce' (Cd. 7071), *Appendices to the Interim Report of the Commissioners*, vol. II]. With regard to the remittances by sales of Council bills, I am not quite clear whether you criticise these remittances on the ground that they were made too soon, or on the ground that they should not have been made at all? (MR WEBB) *What remittances by sales of Council drafts do you refer to?*

I mean remittances by means of Council drafts in 1910, 1911, 1912, and 1913; do you argue that they were made too soon, or that they ought not to have been made at all? *I argue that no remittances over and above the requirements of the home charges should have been made at all. Of course the home charges must be provided for, but over and above the home charges I argue that no money should have been remitted at all, and that no Council drafts should, therefore, have been sold.*

That of the sums actually remitted a large part ought not to have been remitted at all? *Yes.*

You have probably noticed that on the 31st March 1913 the Secretary of State's balances were very nearly what they were on the same date in 1909, four years previously—they were just a trifle more. I think your memorandum does not give the figures for 1913? *I had not the Secretary of State's figures when I wrote that memorandum.*

The actual figures, I may add, were £8,372,900 on the 31st March 1913, therefore they were very nearly what they had been four years previously. I understand that of the sums remitted during that period, you hold that some part ought not to have been remitted? *I find that the balance four years previously (i.e., in 1910), held by the Secretary of State, was over 12 millions.*

1909 I am speaking of? *In 1909 it was £7,983,000.*

That is very nearly the same? *Yes, it is.*

Would you argue that during that period sums have been remitted which ought not to have been remitted? *Yes.*

They were all spent; which of the purposes on which they were spent do you think were improper? *I do not know in what direction they have been spent.*

I am putting on one side the sums credited to the gold standard reserve and to the paper currency reserve, to which I am coming later on; apart from those amounts all sums remitted have been spent? *I only know, so far as you have just this minute informed me, that the balance has been reduced to eight millions. That is all I know. But even if you tell me the balance has been reduced to eight millions I am still in the dark as to how it has been done and why it was not done a year or two before.*

I understood you to say that the remittances were not merely sent too soon, but that they ought not to have been sent at all? *So I thought.*

I am not now asking whether the Secretary of State remitted at the right date or not, but whether, at whatever date he remitted, he spent the money for improper purposes? *I cannot say that he spent it for improper purposes, because I am not aware where this money has gone.*

First of all, the home charges; you admit that they are all right? *Yes.*

Secondly, the purchase of silver, and I think you allow that? *Yes.*

Thirdly, there is the redemption of temporary debt; is that a proper purpose? *Yes.*

And fourthly, there is the expenditure on railway material? *Yes.*

Putting apart the gold standard reserve and the paper currency reserve, practically every penny remitted during the past four years has been spent on one of those four purposes? *If that is so, it has been spent on proper purposes, and the only criticism in that case that I should offer is, why was not the temporary debt paid off many years ago instead of only last year?*

Your criticism then comes down purely to this point, that the Secretary of State has done certain things at a later date than he ought? *That he has brought money to England several years in advance of his requirements.*

But it does not amount to any more than that? *That is one way of putting it. I can admit that in a sense the action of the Secretary of State resolves itself into bringing to this country several millions some years in advance of his own requirements. That appears to me to be very grave mismanagement.*

I only wanted to get exactly what your position was, because there are at least two different lines of criticism which to my mind are rather mixed up in your memorandum, namely, that through excess of precaution he postponed doing things which he could have done sooner, and the other point, that he was draining away money from India and doing various terrible things to India when he ought never to have brought the money from India at all; but now I understand that the second part is not your charge? *Yes, those are my charges—doing things that he ought not to have done.*

Then in regard to this money which he ought never to have brought at all, which are the ways in which he has used it that are improper; I come back to that? *I was not aware how it had been used before I received the information that you yourself have given me. If the money has been used simply for home charges, for the redemption of debt, for the purchase of silver, and for railway material, it has been used properly, except that the debt might have been redeemed a year or two earlier than it has been redeemed.*

If I am right that it has all been used for those purposes, then that part of your criticism falls to the ground? *I do not understand how it falls to the ground, because even if the money has eventually been correctly disposed of...*

I do not say that particular part of the proposition falls to the ground, only the part of your criticism that the money has been remitted in excess. I am not dealing now with your criticism that it has been remitted at the wrong time, but with that part of your criticism which says it ought never to have been remitted at all. That, I think, falls to the ground if the only purposes for which it has been spent are those I have named? *If all the* money has been properly disposed of, that portion of the criticism is in a sense disposed of.

If it has been spent on the purposes I have named, then it has been properly disposed of? *It has been properly disposed of in the end, eventually. I have never asserted for a moment that the Secretary of State has improperly disposed of the money. What has occurred is that he has accumulated vast sums for which he had no need, and then, under the effect of repeated criticisms, he has at length disposed of that money, but only under the stimulus of repeated criticisms.*

When you say improperly remitted, you mean remitted too soon? *Remitted years ahead of his requirements.*

Not remitted too much? *He has apparently disposed of it in the end.*

I come now to your proposal about fixing the price of Council bills. In your memorandum you have suggested that it should be fixed at $1s\ 4\frac{3}{32}d$ or $1s\ 4\frac{1}{8}d$; but in your evidence to the Chairman you suggested that it should be fixed at $1s\ 4\frac{1}{16}d$. Which of those figures do you wish to maintain? *The figure that I suggest for the home charges is one that shall be below the gold point. Of course, the gold point varies from month to month, and therefore it is impossible for me to give the exact figure; but I should think that about $1s\ 4\frac{1}{16}d$ would be a workable point for the home charges.*

I understood you to propose that the Secretary of State should put up a brass plate? *Yes.*

On which he should say that at all times of the year there should be a certain fixed rate for Council bills? *Yes. I think it should be $1s\ 4\frac{1}{16}d$.*

That $1s\ 4\frac{1}{16}d$ would be the fixed rate? *That rate should be a stable rate, but it would, of course, be liable to alteration.*

It would be maintained all the year? *Possibly, or at the end of six months there might be reasons for amending the rate. I should say that $1s\ 4\frac{1}{16}d$ would be about the correct figure to start with.*

That is your proposal, that there ought to be sales of bills at all times of the year at that rate? *Yes.*

Are you aware that the rate got for these bills between 1910 and 1913 was almost exactly $1s\ 4\frac{1}{16}d$? *Quite possibly.*

So that your proposal would have made no practical difference? *It would have made a great deal of practical difference in actual business.*

The Secretary of State would have undergone the risk and inconvenience of undertaking this liability to sell at a fixed rate without getting any more for his bills? *That I cannot say.*

I understood your line to be that the Secretary of State should not put himself out to help trade, but that he should get the most profitable rate for his bills? *Yes.*

If your policy had been followed, he would have undertaken certain risks, and would have got no more profitable rate than he actually got? *That I cannot say. I cannot see the risks.*

Taking my figures, if he did in fact get 1s $4\frac{1}{16}d$ that would be the case? *1s $4\frac{1}{16}d$ is about the specie point now, but a few years ago the specie point was considerably higher—it was 1s 4d and $1\frac{1}{2}$ annas, and there was a time when it was 2 annas, and there have been times when it was $2\frac{1}{2}$ annas—I am speaking in Indian phraseology; I should say $\frac{5}{32}$. If the Secretary of State has only got an average of 1 anna now, $\frac{1}{16}$ over 1s 4d, it is clear that he is doing right, but if 1 anna is an average which corresponds over a period of years, then he has got a poor rate.*

I am speaking of the period from 1910 to 1913? *I think from 1910 to 1913 the average rate ought to have been more than 1 anna, over 1s 4d, possibly $1\frac{1}{2}$ annas—$\frac{3}{32}$.*

Taking your figures, if he had put up his brass plate, he could not have got more than that? *He might have got $\frac{3}{32}$ four years ago; that is, his brass plate might have shown the rate of $\frac{3}{32}$. His brass plate, I suggest this year, should show 1 anna, but four years ago I think the gold specie point, the import point into India, was nearer $\frac{1}{8}$ than $\frac{1}{16}$.*

I was trying to argue it on your figure, but of course if you take a different figure, I shall have to use different arguments. I will pass from that to a further point connected with it. Suppose that the Secretary of State fixed some rate, which may be 1s $4\frac{3}{32}d$, or some other rate, and he does not sell enough bills to meet his various charges, how is he to make up the difference? *Ship home sovereigns.*

These sovereigns he has taken at the rate of 1s 4d, that is, he has issued rupees against them at the rate of 1s 4d? *He may not necessarily have issued any rupees against them at all. They may be sovereigns that the public have imported.*

How else have they got into his treasuries? *Through the collection of taxation.*

At the rate of 1s 4d? *I cannot tell what the rate is. The public import sovereigns when it pays them; sovereigns are paid to the Government in the form of taxation, and the Government then finds itself in possession of the sovereigns in its treasuries.*

The sovereign is legal tender for so many rupees at 1s 4d? *Yes.*

Therefore the Government could not receive it in payment of taxation at any other rate? *No.*

It therefore receives this gold at 1s 4d? *That is so as between the Government and the public, but the public would have imported the sovereigns at a different rate to the 1s 4d.*

I am speaking of the Government. The cost of bringing those sovereigns back would be $\frac{1}{8}d$, would it not? *Something like that.*

So the sovereigns that would have to be brought back to the Secretary of State would bring in money at the rate of 1s $3\frac{7}{8}d$? *Yes.*

You are proposing that he should stick out for 1s $4\frac{3}{32}d$, and then for the balance which he cannot get at that rate, he should bring sovereigns home at what works out at 1s $3\frac{7}{8}d$? *Yes.*

And you think that policy would lead to his getting a better average rate than his present policy? *Yes. My reason is that, roughly speaking, in four years out of five, the balance of trade is in India's favour, so I take it that in three years out of four, or in four years out of five, the rate of exchange would always stand at the gold import specie point, or in the neighbourhood of it, and that only on rare occasions, one year in five, would there be a risk of some small portion of the Secretary of State's home charges having to be shipped back in sovereigns. That is the risk.*

Suppose that seven-eighths were sold at 1s $4\frac{3}{32}d$, and one-eighth had to be brought back in the way I have described, will you take it from me that it would work out at about the same as if he had sold them at an average of 1s $4\frac{1}{16}d$, so that if only one-eighth had to be brought back in gold, he would be no better off than he is at present? *If the figures that you state are correct, that would be so; but it would be a much more correct procedure, in my opinion.*

It does not look, however, as if there is much in it from the public point of view of getting a better rate of exchange? *I have not worked out these figures that you tell me of.*

They are an important part of the argument, but you have advanced this proposal of yours without working them out? What I mean is this: You are suggesting to me that the Secretary of State remits home seven-eighths of his home charges at 1s $4\frac{3}{32}d$, and one-eighth of his home charges at 1s $3\frac{7}{8}d$? *This might happen only one year in five.*

In the case of one-eighth he has to bring home the sovereigns? *That is equivalent to bringing home one-eighth at 1s $3\frac{7}{8}d$, and you assure me that the average between one-eighth at 1s $3\frac{7}{8}d$, and seven-eighths at 1s $4\frac{3}{32}d$, is about 1s $4\frac{1}{16}d$; if that is so, then there is not much in it in the year in which it occurred.*

This calculation is the only sort of calculation that you can make, if you are wondering which of these two policies would pay best? *That is so.*

But, nevertheless, you have not examined it? *Assuming those figures to be correct, that state of affairs would arise on an average one year in five and only one year in five, because only one year in five would it be necessary to ship home gold in payment of a portion of the home charges. So one year in five* *he would be no better off, he would merely stand at 1s 4$\frac{1}{16}$d, but in the other years as a whole the exchange would be higher.*

You propose, therefore, that he should undertake this very serious liability of selling bills at all times of the year at a fixed rate, and run the risk of not being able to get his home charges back, for what would clearly be a mere tuppeny-ha'penny profit, even if he got it? *I cannot recognise the slightest risk whatever of any kind; on the contrary there is less risk than there is at present, because were this system in force, he would only withdraw from India the amount required for home charges—16, 17, or 18 millions, whereas at present the Secretary of State is withdrawing 25, 26, 27, or 29 millions wholly unnecessarily.*

But we have agreed that they are withdrawn for necessary purposes? *Not necessary purposes at the time they were withdrawn. They were subsequently made use of, but they were quite unnecessary at the time they were withdrawn.*

If less had been withdrawn in the earlier years more would have been withdrawn in the later years? *No, because the floating debt would never have been incurred, I take it, in London; and, therefore, there would have been no necessity to remit money home to pay off that floating debt.*

If it had not been incurred, then more money would have been required to meet the purposes for which it had to be spent? *Possibly, if the same balances had to be maintained, that is, if you hold that the level of the cash balances maintained by the Secretary of State is correct; but I assert that that balance was unduly heavy, and therefore that these loans were unnecessary.*

That is going back to another point, which we discussed earlier? *That is another point, I admit. May I state at this point that I cannot agree for one moment that the procedure of selling Councils at a fixed rate involves any risk on the part of the Secretary of State more than he is at present incurring? It does not involve the slightest risk.*

(SIR ROBERT CHALMERS) Is that so as regards the seasons? It might be that the season of demand for bills might not be the season at which the Government of India was in possession of rupees; you would admit that that would be the case, would you not? *Yes, that is a little additional risk.*

It might be a very important question? *That could be overcome.*

It would depend on a calculation of supply and demand? *Yes, but I imagine that would have to be overcome possibly by the shipment of gold.*

(MR KEYNES) Your proposal merely comes to this, that it is your opinion, not on the basis of any calculation, that if the Secretary of State brought over as much as he could at 1s 4$\frac{3}{32}$d, and the balance, whatever it might be, in gold, that would lead to a better average rate of exchange than what he now gets? *Yes.*

That is not based on any calculation or any minute investigation of any sort? *It is impossible to base it on any exact calculation, because there is no profit in working out imaginary instances on past experiences. There is no profit in going back three years, and saying that if 27 millions had not been remitted to England but only 16 millions had been remitted, and if exchange had been at such-and-such a point, and if this had occurred and that had occurred and the other had occurred, the result would be different. I do not think that is a profitable investigation.*

May I put to you one or two considerations that should be taken into account? Suppose you fix exchange at $1s\ 4\frac{3}{32}d$, then the Secretary of State would never sell any bills when there was gold available in Egypt or Australia, would he? *It depends on what the gold specie point was.*

When there is gold available there, I assume it would be below that? *Yes, quite possibly.*

In some years there is a very great deal available in Australia and Egypt, is there not? *Yes.*

An amount almost equal to India's balance of trade? *Quite possibly.*

In those years the Secretary of State would sell no bills? *I cannot say that.*

Or very few bills? *When you referred to the balance of trade, I thought you meant the balance of trade not taking the home charges into consideration, but over and above the home charges.*

Over and above the home charges the balance of trade is trifling, is it not? *I should not call it trifling.*

How much is it? *It varies between, I suppose, nothing up to as much as 10 millions or 12 millions.*

What is the average—about three millions or four millions; I think it is something small of that sort? *I should have thought, without looking into the figures, that the average would be nearer five millions in recent years. In recent years the balance has been very large, and in the years immediately following the closing of the mint the balance was very small.*

A great part of that balance is needed for payments of interest and so forth in England, and what you may call the available free balance is what the Secretary of State draws? *I think there is a much larger balance due to India than what the Secretary of State draws.*

How is that used? *It is liquidated by the shipment of sovereigns to India, and over 20 millions, I think, went in last year.*

That brings us to a point at which we can argue. I was thinking of the additional amounts available over what are now available. When there is a great deal of gold in Australia and in Egypt, all that gold would go and the Secretary of State would not sell bills? *Not if the Secretary of State's rate was fixed at too high a level.*

If fixed at $1s\ 4\frac{3}{32}d$ in such years, therefore, he would be in difficulties about selling the full amount? *If his rate was too high.*

He would be also in difficulties in those years in which there was an adverse balance? *Yes; he would be in difficulties in the sense that the rate would need revision.*

On the other hand, if you fix the rate at $1s\ 4\frac{1}{16}d$, gold would never flow to India from England in that case? *I should be very sorry to say never, but I do not think it would frequently flow.*

It would flow very seldom? *It would flow very seldom in present circumstances.*

Is he not driven therefore to a fluctuating rate, from the fact that sometimes gold is available in one place and the gold import point is at one figure, and sometimes gold is available elsewhere, and then the gold import point is a different figure, so the actual figure is not steady throughout the year? *It was for that reason I suggested that the rate of $1s\ 4\frac{1}{16}d$ would be a business-like rate to take to commence this method of selling Council drafts.*

Still you agree that if they took that rate gold would very seldom flow to India out of England? *Yes, I agree.*

But you have criticised the Secretary of State's policy precisely on the ground that the rate he has charged has had that effect? *I do not follow the question.*

I understand you have criticised the Secretary of State on the ground that he has sold bills at a rate which prevented gold from going to India? *Yes.*

And yet you have proposed a rate that shall have that effect? *Up to the extent of the home charges, certainly. I put the Secretary of State's requirements first. That is why I took the rate of $1s\ 4\frac{1}{16}d$, because that would enable the Secretary of State to make his remittances for a certainty before gold commences to flow.*

We then come back to the old point that you consider that he has remitted more than he needs in Great Britain? *Yes, at the time he made the remittances.*

If the gold had gone to India in the earlier years, it would have had to be brought back in the later years. Suppose over the four years he had to remit exactly what he did remit, and he remitted less in earlier years so that the gold flowed to India, he would have had to have brought all that gold back again? *I cannot agree to that straight away, because the fact of his not permitting the gold to be imported has been the occasion of a certain amount of silver coinage in recent years, the silver coinage affects prices, and prices affect the movement of trade. So I cannot say I should acquiesce altogether in that proposition; but, speaking generally, I say yes.*

I cannot see that the thing comes to much. All that would happen would be that the gold would have been taken out to India, the expense of which would have been borne by Indian traders, and then in a later year it would have been brought back to England, the expense of which would have been borne by the Secretary of State; and apart from those two items of expense, things would have been very much the same as they are? *Even assuming that things were very much as they are, assuming that the result so far as the Government books are concerned was the same, we should still have secured this important consideration—that the public would not have constantly had the rate of exchange jumped about, jumped up and jumped down, by the eccentric action of the Secretary of State.[1] Even assuming that there was no difference in the Government accounts, assuming that on the average at the end of three years the amount which the Secretary of State realised turned out the same, we should still have eliminated this disturbing influence of an official interference with the exchange, which makes it very difficult sometimes for the public to know what to do in the financing of their business.*

What do you mean by calling the Secretary of State's action eccentric; is it not dictated by well known rules? *I think not. I confess that at times I have been unable to conceive any rule by which it has been dictated at all. That is why I used the adjective 'eccentric'.*

The people most concerned in this question, you would agree, are the exchange banks? *They are the people who get most of the convenience out of the transactions.*

They have expressed themselves as entirely satisfied? *I quite understand that. I think they are perfectly satisfied. The bankers are the people who will take advantage of this convenience, and I should not expect any exchange bank to say otherwise than that it is a most excellent arrangement which ought not to be disturbed.*

I understand that the result of all this is that the one advantage which you claim for your proposals is that persons in India would have more certainty as to what the rate of exchange is? *Yes, that is one advantage.*

And there is no other important advantage? *I think there would be an advantage to the State; that is to say, I think the Secretary of State would have realised more for the rupees that he has sold than he actually has done. That point you question, but I do think he would have realised better myself. Those are the two advantages.*

[1] *See* note by Mr Webb...[quoting from the Indian press to illustrate how the Secretary of State had forced down the exchange, 'not...for the benefit of India, but solely for the benefit of a section of the London money market.'].

The role Keynes usually took, however, was simply that of a closely critical inquirer. An example was his questioning of the two representatives of the exchange banks doing business in India, J. A. Toomey and T. Fraser, who appeared before the Commission together and, each echoing the other, inevitably bring to mind Tweedledum and Tweedledee.

FROM THE MINUTES OF EVIDENCE, 26 JUNE 1913

(MR KEYNES) I come now to the question of the proposal for a state bank. You stated in your evidence that the establishment of such a bank would result in a banking monopoly: do you mean by that that the exchange banks would be almost driven out of existence? (MR TOOMEY) *They would.*

Would your objections be met to any appreciable extent if the state bank were precluded from accepting deposits in London—outside India? (MR FRASER) *That would not help.* (MR TOOMEY) *No, that would not help the situation at all.* (MR FRASER) *I do not think the central bank would ever come here for deposits. Our deposits in London are not such an all-important item in our business, and I do not think they would come here and compete.*

Am I to understand then that the exchange banks do not regard it as an important part of their business to attract funds in London and use them in India for financing trade? (MR TOOMEY) *We take deposits in London, and we certainly look upon that as an important factor in our business.*

That part of your business would be left untouched? *Yes, but it is not such a very large item.* (MR FRASER) *The question, of course, is a central bank with power to borrow in London. The assumption is that they would either offer the same rate as we do or a better rate, and the chances are that they would offer a better rate than the exchange banks in all probability, having regard to the fact that they have the backing of the Government.*

If the state bank were precluded from attracting deposits outside India would that remove your objection? (MR TOOMEY) *No, not at all.* (MR FRASER) *Certainly not.*

Your reason for this answer is that that part of your business, namely, attracting funds in London for financing Indian trade, is not an important part of your business; is that it? (MR TOOMEY) *We say that if the state bank had a London office and did exchange business we would be driven off the field.*

I understand you to say that, and I am trying to get at your reasons for saying it. I have pointed out one part of your business which would be unaffected, and I understand your answer to be that that is not an important part? *The London deposits are not so very important.*

(CHAIRMAN) In speaking of London deposits, do you mean English money or United Kingdom money? *Yes.*

(MR KEYNES) You would, therefore, lay no stress upon the claim which has sometimes been made by the exchange banks that they play a most important part in financing Indian trade by attracting funds in London for that purpose? *We do not make a point of that.*

[In the memorandum that Keynes later wrote on a state bank he took Toomey sharply to task for 'deliberately' minimising the importance to the exchange banks of this business.]

Suppose that the state bank were limited in its dealings in exchange to remitting about the amount the Secretary of State required, say, 25 millions a year, would that modify your objections? *It would not modify our objections in the slightest degree. If they were allowed to operate in exchange at all, the results to the exchange banks' business would be very serious.*

If they remitted merely the balance of trade, that would only be a fraction of the total trade—shall we say one-fifth? *If they were quoting rates of exchange, they would be able to quote much better rates than exchange banks could.*

Why should they wish to do so? They would probably wish to remit money to England at as favourable a rate to themselves as they could? *If they were to enter the exchange market it would be practically all up with our business.*

I do not understand why you assume that they would force the rate of exchange down? *They would have to quote better rates than the exchange banks, and we would have to sit out.*

Would they affect you more than the establishment of a new exchange bank, which attracted, say, one-fifth of the business? *We do not object to other banks starting, if they have got to start on the same footing as ourselves.*

Would you be wiped out by a bank which was restricted to doing no more than one-fifth of the business? *One-fifth of what business?*

One-fifth of the remittance business? *If a new bank were to start in the same way as we have had to start, they could only quote about the same rates as we do, and they could not cut under our rates; but a state bank could do business with no profit at all.* (MR FRASER) *We have a very good illustration of that in the Reichsbank in Germany. When the Reichsbank wants to influence exchange it is not a matter of profit or loss; they operate, and the other banks stand still and look on.*

That is, when they wish to attract gold? *It would be the same thing with a state bank in India. When the Secretary of State wanted remittances from the Government of India, the state bank would go on remitting to him, and we should not be able to enter the market and buy because it would not be a question of profit with the state bank.*

At present the Secretary of State stands out for as good a rate as he can get, does he not? *We do not admit that. He takes the market rate.*

He does not undercut the market rate; he does not ruin the market? *Certainly not.*

Why should a state bank act very differently, and have a very different effect on the market, from the Secretary of State, supposing it were remitting to the same amount? *The central bank would have to operate in India, and they would have to undercut and reduce rates until, we argue, there would be no profit left in exchange and we would have to go out, because there would be nothing left for us. You can only work an exchange business to make a small profit—the profit is small, and it is the turnover that makes the money. If that profit disappears, and you have not got anything to work for, you would naturally go.*

The state bank would have to offer a rate which would enable it to get 25 millions' worth of bills in the course of the year? *Yes.*

For getting those bills it would want as high a rate as it could get? (MR TOOMEY) *They would not bother about any particular profit.* (MR FRASER) *They are working with funds that cost them nothing to start with.*

Your view is that the state bank would not work for a profit and so would ruin your business? *Would ruin our business by undercutting.*

*   *   *   *

There is an important class of joint-stock banks that have grown up in India, and their deposits have increased even more than those of the exchange banks? (MR FRASER) *They have increased enormously.*

Those banks keep very small cash reserves against their deposits? (MR TOOMEY) *Very.*

So that apart from the Presidency banks the deposits in India are perhaps three times what they were ten years ago? *That may be. I accept those figures.*

With no corresponding increase of cash? (MR FRASER) *I should not like to make a definite statement on that point, not having any figures before me. I admit the enormous growth of these Swadeshi banks, as we call them, and the enormous growth in their deposits. It has been openly stated in some quarters, but I have not verified the facts, that their cash balances are not adequate.*

What is the relation of these banks to the Presidency banks; do they have sums on deposit with the Presidency banks to any important extent? (MR TOOMEY) *I should think not.* (MR FRASER) *I should think not too.*

Do they include in their cash sums left with the Presidency banks, or is it all free cash? *I should think the cash at the Presidency banks is taken as cash.*

Is that an important part? *I could not say.*

In the case of the exchange banks do they keep any appreciable sum with the Presidency banks? *Yes.*

Do they include that in their cash? *Yes.*

The position is, therefore, that to a quite important extent the Presidency banks act as bankers' banks? *That is so.*

And there is not much free banking money in India outside the Presidency banks? *Not in the busy season.*

I want to put to you whether you think that the Presidency banks, taking account of this great growth of deposit banking, are really in a strong enough position to act as bankers' banks? *Assuming they get the facilities from the Government that have been suggested, I think so.*

But under existing conditions? *If you can imagine a banking crisis when everyone was pulling on the Presidency banks, I should say they probably would not be able to meet the requirements of everybody.*

How do you feel in regard to these figures; in 1910 the total deposits, excluding public deposits, in India were about 55 millions? *What does that include?*

That includes the exchange banks, the private deposits with the Presidency banks, and those Indian joint-stock banks which have more than 5 lakhs of paid-up capital and reserve; the deposits were about 55 millions, and the cash in the Presidency banks was 7½ millions? (MR TOOMEY) *That is quite an ordinary average working balance.*

Supposing there were to be a banking crisis in India everybody would go to the Presidency banks for money? (MR FRASER) *The exchange banks would probably call upon London, I should think, and take Council telegraphic transfers.*

I wanted to get out that point: The exchange banks would rather rely in the next banking crisis on being able to remit large sums from London? *I do not say we would rely upon it, but if the necessity were forced upon us—* (MR TOOMEY) *We should have to ship sovereigns or take Councils.*

Suppose you had to ship sovereigns and to do this to a large amount, because your total deposits in India must be now something like 20 millions, do you think you would find it easy to rediscount your bills and to raise money in London? (MR FRASER) *We could always discount at a rate.*

If you wanted to take the money out in actual gold, not at an ordinary time but at a moment of crisis, do you think it would be easy for you to do that? (MR TOOMEY) *I see no difficulty about it.* (MR FRASER) *You must also assume that in those conditions the Secretary of State has no balances on the other side, and will not sell Council bills.*

I am taking this alternative first, that you had to send out sovereigns; do you think the exchange bankers would have no difficulty in raising in actual gold a very large sum in sovereigns in London at a time of crisis? *I should think not. If you assume they could not do it, then of course you stop the export of gold. If you are assuming that we cannot get sovereigns, you mean that we are no longer a free market for gold.*

I assume they could get gold if they had free resources, and you think there would be no difficulty in their obtaining free resources? *We are all constituents of the Bank of England, we know the bills the Bank of England takes, and the Bank of England always discounts bills for its customers. There is no reason to suppose they would not stand by us if we wanted accommodation.*

The other alternative would be that you should buy large sums in telegraphic transfers from the Secretary of State? *That is what we should naturally do assuming he had money on the other side, which he probably would have, because if he could not draw on his Treasury balances he would probably draw on his currency balances in an emergency.*

Then you are rather relying upon him to use his currency balances to relieve India's banking in a crisis? *We are not relying on that, but we are assuming that in these conditions he would have those means of meeting those drafts.*

Would you feel in a stronger position if the whole business were more centralised—if the Secretary of State's balances and the bankers' balances, instead of being kept in various places and by various authorities, were all kept in a state bank which would be under a certain responsibility to look after a situation of this kind? (MR TOOMEY) *I do not think a state bank would look after the situation any better than we can under existing circumstances.* (MR FRASER) *I should think the Presidency banks worked in conjunction with the Government would be quite as powerful and as good an influence as any state bank.*

Do you assume that they would have to work in conjunction with the Government? *They always have, and they always would, I think, in the event of a crisis, work in conjunction with the Government. Assuming such a crisis as you are picturing, which has never exactly come about, but assuming such a one ever did—we have not seen it, but of course we admit it might come —the danger is that India is going rather fast in the matter of banking, and new banks are springing up every day. I have only taken out fourteen of what you might call the leading Swadeshi banks—the figures are not all for the same date—and they show a capital of 2 crores 41 lakhs paid up, and deposits of 24 crores.*

The main point I am putting to you is this—that when the last banking crisis came in India, deposit banking was in its infancy there? (MR

TOOMEY) *There were very few local banks then.* (MR FRASER) *That is so—very few.*

There has been an enormous increase in their number, particularly in the last ten years? (MR TOOMEY) *Yes.*

More particularly in the last five years; and the increase is still going on? (MR FRASER) *Yes.*

So you have no experience as to what would happen if there was a banking crisis in a country where large deposits are now being made and which has not forgotten the habit of hoarding? *I should think that if a banking crisis such as that developed there would be a very serious run on some of the banks. The chances are probably that the old-established banks which have stood the storm and have got a reputation would not be run upon. I cannot say that I remember a run upon our own institution.*

You have a rapid growth of deposit banking, and a good deal of it in banks which have never stood a severe strain? *That is admitted, I think.*

And which have also no very high proportion of cash reserves? *I should think that some of what you might call the local banks do keep adequate reserves, but there are probably many of them that do not. I would not like to speak about that with absolute certainty. Such banks as the Alliance Bank of Simla, for example, and the Allahabad Bank have always stood very well, and been conducted, I think, on prudent lines; but there are others possibly that have not been.*

Further, there is no central banking reserve of any sort, such as the state banks of Europe have? *That is so, unless you accept the Presidency banks as occupying that position.*

And also there is no sort of mechanism whatever for any sort of emergency currency or for any expansion of the note issue? (MR TOOMEY) *Only the Gold Note Act.*

It can only be expanded against rupees or notes? (MR FRASER) *Against rupees or the deposit of gold. We can put down gold here and get notes issued in India, or rupees.*

All the Government can do is to exchange one form of currency for another: they cannot increase the amount of currency? *Except by fresh coinage.*

So that all the usual precautions which are taken by European countries that have deposit banking against a crisis are incompletely existent in India? *You mean in regard to such precautions as expanding the currency in the event of a crisis?*

And having a central reserve? *As regards expanding the currency in India, the people want cash, not notes.*

I am not saying that ought not to be given, but I mean that as that possibility does not at present exist, it is all the more important that the other sorts of precautions should be taken? *The other precaution being to centralise your reserves?*

Yes, and having some important authority which looks at the situation as a whole? *We would leave that to the Presidency banks working in conjunction with the Government.*

You do not think that a state institution, which was in the habit of working in conjunction with the Government, and did not have to fit up some patchwork arrangement in a moment of crisis, would be in a better position to deal with a situation of that sort than a state bank? *Has your state bank solely to deal with the crisis when it arises, or is it to have other functions?*

It would have other functions, but it would be practically in touch with the Government? *If we had a state bank which we could fall back upon in the event of a crisis, of course we should rather welcome it. But if we are to have a state bank which is going to take over the paper currency and to have a monopoly of Council bills and of all other Government business free of charge we should naturally oppose it.*

Might I put it like this, that while you feel a state-aided body with vast powers of that sort might be open to certain objections, still it is true that the banking position in India would be strengthened by such an institution at a time of crisis? *Granted that the bank exists for that purpose and that purpose only, of course it would relieve the strain.*

Allowing that for other purposes the bank were detrimental, if that were amongst its purposes would it be a good thing? *That is assuming an impracticable position.*

I am not saying there are not any disadvantages? *After all, if you did have a central institution, we all learn by experience, and you do not want banks to fall back too much upon any central institution. Each bank, properly speaking, should so conduct its business that so far as it possibly can be it is independent of these outside aids.*

But you would not maintain that that was the case in India at present, would you? As I understand, the banks keep a great part of their free money with the Presidency banks and keep no reserves of their own to any large amount? *I should not like to say what a number of those up-country banks do, because they are established at many points where the Presidency banks do not exist, so probably they do keep considerable balances. It is difficult to speak without actual knowledge, and I can only say that in the Presidency towns I think these banks keep their cash with the Presidency banks.*

I should like to know, if you can tell us, a little more about the relations of the exchange banks at present with the Presidency banks. I understand that you keep balances with them much in the way in which English joint stock banks keep balances with the Bank of England; is that so? *Much the same.*

Do you also borrow from them to any important extent? *In bygone days we did.* (MR TOOMEY) *But not now.* (MR FRASER) *Not much, anyhow.*

Not now? *Very little.* (MR TOOMEY) *Occasionally, possibly.* (MR FRASER) *I think in recent years the exchange banks have not been big borrowers from the Presidency banks.*

Apart from the question of competition in exchange, would your relations with a state bank be very different from your present relations with the Presidency banks? *Our present relations with the Presidency banks are most friendly. I should think with a state bank they would probably be the reverse.*

Is that a sentiment of yours, or have you definite arguments with which to support it? *I do not see how it could be very well otherwise, when we feel that the advent of a bank with all the privileges that have been suggested would naturally mean almost our extinction.*

I put aside for the moment the question of competition in exchange; apart from that, why should your relation to a state bank be unfriendly? *You are leaving out the question of exchange entirely?*

Yes? *Then they are there simply to benefit us, and exist to help us when we are in trouble.*

They are there to consolidate the existing system? *Then we could hardly regard them as enemies. Under those conditions we would not, I should think, feel they were enemies exactly.*

So that the central point of your opposition to the proposal for a state bank arises out of the possibility that they might deal in exchange? *That is one reason. Another reason is that we do not think the country on the whole would in any way benefit by a state bank. We cannot see that India as a country is suited for it. We have already given our reasons.* (MR TOOMEY) *We look upon a state bank in India as quite impracticable.* (MR FRASER) *We consider the existing machinery as it exists in the Presidency banks is ample for the country's needs.*

Do you think that for the Government to have a banker and for there to be a central institution is no advantage whatever, quite apart from other disadvantages? (MR TOOMEY) *I do not see how it would benefit trade.*

Assuming a lower bank rate, is not that a benefit to trade? *I do not think people in India are looking out for lower bank rates.* (MR FRASER) *You can have such a thing as too low a bank rate, especially in India. When you have a very low bank rate it always encourages speculation, and it would very probably bring about a state of affairs which you would rather wish to avoid.*

Chapter 3

AN INDIAN STATE BANK

The Commission had been appointed to study, explicitly, the management of the balances of the Government of India in India and the India Office in London; the sale of Council drafts by the Secretary of State in London; the gold standard reserve, the paper currency reserve, and the system by which the exchange value of the rupee was maintained; and the financial organisation and procedures of the India Office. But early in the investigation the commissioners realised that it was impossible to ignore two suggestions for reform: the provision of a gold mint in India, and the establishment of a central or State Bank.

The State Bank question arose in any discussion of the management of the note issue, the proper amount for Government balances, or the operation of the Government's remittance business. There was no general agreement, however, as to what was meant by a State Bank and the commissioners found themselves at a loss in examining witnesses whenever any of these topics was considered. To assist them Abrahams prepared a 'Memorandum on Proposals for the Establishment of a State Bank for India' (Appendix XIV [Cd. 7071], *Appendices to the Interim Report of the Commissioners*, vol. II).

Abrahams's memorandum related the history of previous discussions of the question—in 1867 after a disastrous capital loss by the Bank of Bombay, and in 1899–1901 at the time of the Fowler Committee—and called attention to the benefits expected by contemporary advocates of a State Bank scheme. The amalgamation of the three Presidency Banks, proposed in 1867, was abandoned because of the attitude of the shareholders of the Bank of Bombay, who opposed the move even though their own directors had approved of it. Abrahams took the opportunity of correcting Keynes's interpretation of the event in *Indian Currency and Finance* in a footnote.

Provincial jealousy, coupled with the difficulty of finding employment for the new capital to be provided, caused the discussion of a State Bank during 1899–1901 to be dropped.

'From the historical retrospect,' Abrahams observed, '...there has been a remarkable diversity of views, and no little vagueness, as to the duties that should be entrusted to a State Bank, and the advantages to be expected...'

Assuming, as had the proponents of previous schemes, that such a bank would be formed by an amalgamation of the three existing Presidency Banks, he stipulated three definite and inter-related duties:

(1) The Bank should be the custodian of the Government balances, those now accumulated in the Reserve Treasuries as well as those deposited with the Presidency Banks. From this change Abrahams anticipated a reduction in both the average rate of discount and its range of seasonal variation.

(2) The Bank should manage the paper currency reserve, since this reserve was currently managed jointly with the Treasury balances, a practice that facilitated the rapid transfer of Government funds from one place to another within India.

(3) The Bank should participate in the management of the sale in London of bills of exchange and telegraphic transfers on India for the financing of India Office disbursements, since the volume of such sales influenced the flow of sovereigns to India and hence the stock available for holding in the paper currency reserve.

Abrahams also listed duties or privileges that should not be imposed on or entrusted to the State Bank, all of which had been recommended in public discussion:

(1) It should not be responsible for the convertibility of the rupee in being obliged to provide sovereigns in exchange for rupees without limit, although it should continue the Government's current practice of doing so when convenient.

(2) It should not be obliged to support the exchange by the unlimited sale of bills on London at a fixed rate, except as the agent of the Government.

(3) As a corollary, it should not be responsible for managing the gold standard reserve, which should remain the duty of the Government, although the Bank might act as an agent of the Government.

(4) It should not be allowed to borrow in London for the financing of Indian trade, in order to avoid competition with the exchange banks.

(5) It should not be allowed to receive deposits in London for the purpose of financing Indian trade because of the serious inconvenience, both to the Bank and the trade, that would result from withdrawals of such funds.

(6) It should not be allowed any special privileges regarding coinage.

In discussing proposed methods of business, Abrahams emphasised the importance of safeguarding the interests of the Government, by ensuring that the Bank would be conducted on sound principles and that the Government would always be able to make withdrawals without delay. Abrahams held that security in these respects could be better achieved by the Government actively participating in the management of the Bank through the appointment of a representative as one of the directors, than by the alternative of relying on a code of rules imposed on the Bank. He particularly emphasised the necessity of having a Government representative in the London office of the Bank to ensure that the Secretary of State would always have sufficient funds in London.

Abrahams described the proposed duties of the London office and its relations with the India Office in the transfer of funds between India and London in considerable detail. Two activities, currently the responsibility of the Indian Government, were to be taken over by the London office and its exchange business was to be specifically limited to these: the sale of Council bills and telegraphic transfers on India, as laid down in the Bank's duties, and the sale, as the Government's agent, of bills on London for the support of exchange. Abrahams argued against allowing the Bank to undertake other kinds of exchange business, such as the buying of mercantile bills in either India or London and the sale of drafts on London on its own account, lest the competition be damaging to the existing exchange banks and hence to Indian trade. He also argued that the directors of the Bank, being chosen for their Indian experience, would not have the same wide knowledge of conditions outside India as the exchange banks.

With the establishment of a State Bank the Secretary of State would continue to obtain part of his funds for his disbursements in England from loans and from payments by other Government departments, paid in to his account at the Bank of England; for the remaining and larger part he would inform the Bank of his needs and the London office would sell drafts on India to meet them. If trade was favourable, causing a heavy demand for drafts on India, the Bank might transfer more funds than were needed by the Secretary of State and, subject to Government control, use the excess, which would be part of its general assets held against its liabilities to the Government and other depositors, to make loans to approved borrowers against security. If trade was unfavourable, other means might have to be adopted to supply the Secretary of State, such as the shipment of sovereigns from India to England, withdrawals from the gold standard reserve or the paper currency reserve against a corresponding payment to these reserves in India, the issue of loans by the Secretary of State, or borrowing by the Bank in London.

Abrahams concluded his outline of requirements for a State Bank with a discussion of the capitalisation and division of profits. In the past it had been assumed that an amalgamation of the Presidency Banks into one central bank would require an increase in capital; Abrahams gave figures showing the effect of increased Government deposits which indicated that this would be desirable. It might not be practicable, however, he pointed out, as the Presidency banks had found it difficult to employ the capital they already had. If this were so, Abrahams suggested, the Government might rely on an increase in its own control over the Bank as security for its increased deposits, rather than on an increase in the stockholders' capital.

Abrahams thought that the Government should share in the profits of the Bank. This share 'would naturally be a proportion of the profits corresponding roughly to the proportion between (a) the excess of its average deposits in each year over a fixed sum representing its normal deposits with the three Presidency Banks under existing conditions, and (b) the capital and reserve of the Bank'.

The final section of the memorandum was a summary of the advantages and disadvantages of a State Bank scheme. Abrahams saw the chief advantage in the deposit with the Bank of money now in the Reserve Treasuries which could be placed at the disposal of trade with a beneficial effect both on the rate of discount and on business generally. He recommended that a £1,000,000 emergency fund should be retained in reserve; the remaining funds in the Reserve Treasuries could be deposited with the Bank.

Abrahams saw other advantages in relieving the Indian Government of banking work outside of its proper sphere of operation. A State Bank with its close connection with the commercial community would be the best agent for lending from the paper currency reserve, if this practice was introduced. Similarly, it would be more efficient and proper for a Bank to undertake the sale of drafts in India and the handling of the cash balances. Instead of itself issuing loans, the Government could borrow from the Bank. The Government would have a share in the Bank's profits from the investment of now-idle balances.

Abrahams denied the probability of two advantages often argued to result from the establishment of a State Bank: economies obtainable by reducing Government establishments, and an increase in the popularity of the paper currency and the efficiency of its management. The latter was as likely to happen under the Government as under a State Bank, he thought.

Under disadvantages Abrahams first listed the possible difficulty and delay that the Government might encounter in realising its deposits, a difficulty which had figured earlier in his concern that the Government retain some control in the Bank's management. Lending either from the Reserve Treasuries or from the paper currency reserve, he pointed out, could also be accomplished by the Government depositing part of these funds with the Presidency Banks, although without the advantage of Government participation in the management. Another consideration was that amalgamation of the Presidency Banks into a State Bank with headquarters in Calcutta would mean a loss of the independence and the special local knowledge of the Banks of Bombay and Madras, with a resulting sacrifice of efficiency. Finally, in the sale of remittances in India, he foresaw that conflict might arise between the Secretary of State's representative in the London office of the Bank and the Bank's head office in India.

There was no reason to believe, Abrahams said, that the establishment of a State Bank would have any effect on the flow of gold, either in the direction of India or away from it; on the maintenance of the exchange value of the rupee; or on the stability and development of the currency system.

Both the Secretary of State and the Government of India were favourably disposed towards the establishment of a State Bank. It would rest with the Presidency Banks to decide whether the prospective advantage to the commerce of India as a whole would outweigh the provincial jealousies encountered in 1901, he concluded.

Abrahams sent an advance copy of his memorandum to Keynes, who returned his comments with the following note:

To LIONEL ABRAHAMS, *1 July 1913*

Dear Abrahams,

Many thanks for letting me see your memorandum. I enclose my comments. I recommend you to type them before attempting to read them—I have no typist here.

I think your document will be *most valuable*. It brings things to a head and gives the mind something to bite on, if I may mix my metaphors a little. There is very little of importance, as you will see, on which I don't agree. But there are one or two additional things I should have said, if I had been writing the memorandum myself. (I think at a somewhat later stage it may be useful if I do write a memorandum for the Commission on this subject.)

Do you know if we are to hear you on this matter before the recess? I daresay not.

Yours sincerely,

J. M. KEYNES

(The Commission did not hear Abrahams again until the end of the second round of witnesses in November.)

Keynes's comments, which follow, show the lines along which he was thinking between the writing of the brief section on the need for a State Bank in *Indian Currency and Finance* and the production of his own memorandum for the Commission. His arguments in *Indian Currency* related mainly to the undesirability of the Government's being responsible for the note issue but having no responsibility for banking in general. At the time of reading Abrahams's memorandum, with the Commission half-way through the hearings, he seemed mainly concerned with two practical questions: (1) the advantage (already introduced in *Indian Currency*) of the Bank buying sterling bills in India, which would serve as a liquid reserve against the note issue and act as an aid to trade, and (2) the opposition of the exchange banks to the scheme. In Keynes's State Bank memorandum these concerns are fully elaborated in Section V on 'Regulation of the Note Issue' and Section VI on 'The London Office and Remittance'.

The comments are given here in the form in which Keynes jotted them down, the headings corresponding to headings used in Abrahams's memorandum. There is no copy among Keynes's papers of the early version of the memorandum that these comments refer to, but it is evident that Abrahams took some of his criticisms into account in the published version. For example, Abrahams made it entirely clear under 'Duties' that the Bank would be acting as the agent of the Government in supporting the exchange. He was also quite explicit in describing the exchange business of the Bank under 'Relations with the India Office'.

COMMENT ON ABRAHAMS'S STATE BANK MEMORANDUM

Duties to be entrusted to the Bank

I am in very general agreement.

I agree that the ultimate responsibility for 'the convertibility of the rupee' and the ultimate ownership of the gold standard reserve should remain with Government. But I think the Government should act *through* the Bank in dealing with these matters— e.g., if sterling drafts have to be sold on London, they should be sold by the Bank under the instructions of Government, i.e., the Government would put the London branch in funds from the gold standard reserve and the Bank would then sell bills in India against these funds.

The Bank should have nothing to do with coinage; but if, by

any chance, there be a gold mint, then the Bank should have in relation to it the same privileges that the Bank of England has here.

The Bank might be responsible, in a semi-underwriting capacity, for the issue of rupee loans.

Methods of Business

The Bank should be controlled, I agree, rather by Government direction than by legislative enactment.

Relations with the India Office

When we heard representatives of the exchange banks in evidence, they expressed determined hostility to a State Bank, because, it seemed to me, they imputed to it functions it is unlikely to be given. This part of the proposal ought, therefore, to be put very explicitly. I understand that you would prohibit the Bank from buying sterling bills in India and would entirely limit them to those methods of remittance now open to the S/S [Secretary of State].

Presumably you would also prohibit the Bank from accepting deposits in London; but you do not say so. On the other hand, it is not quite clear whether you do not contemplate the Bank's sometimes borrowing in London.

I should like your intentions in these respects made a little plainer.

[In his published memorandum Abrahams listed the acceptance of deposits in London as a duty not to be entrusted to the Bank because of the possible inconvenience to Indian trade from withdrawals. As regards borrowing, he was against allowing the Bank to borrow in London on the security of its own investments in order to send money to India; he thought that this kind of business could not be profitable, particularly under the conditions necessary to avoid unfair competition with the exchange banks. He did, however, in discussing relations with the India Office, consider borrowing by the Bank in London as a possible means of furnishing the Secretary of State with funds when the Bank's London balances were not sufficient.]

134

The possible prohibitions in regard to London business are the following:

(1) Prohibition against buying sterling bills in India.

(2) Prohibition against buying bills on India in London.

(3) Prohibition against receiving deposits in London.

(4) Prohibition against all forms of borrowing in London.

I am in favour of prohibitions (2) and (3) and, on the whole, of (4)—I expect all London borrowing had better be left to the S/S. But I feel very doubtful about prohibition (1).

The kind of reasons which influence me are to be found in §§6–10 of chapter II of my book. For the Bank to keep a portfolio of sterling bills seems to me by far the best and cheapest method by which to keep the semi-liquid part of the reserves. It is a better way than to sell Councils and lend the proceeds at short notice in London. Recent continental experience is pointing very decidedly in this direction. At any rate I should not like the Bank to be entirely cut off from this expedient. It might be an admirable plan for the Bank to hold in normal times five to eight millions in sterling bills of various maturities up to three months. They would mainly be bought in the busy season in India as a partial alternative to selling Councils, and later on as they matured they would be used to meet the S/S's disbursements in London.

Provided that, except in a crisis, the Bank never rediscounted its sterling bills, never bought bills in London, and raised no loans or deposits in London whatever, I do not think that the exchange banks, to whom the bulk of the exchange business would still be left, would have any real substantial grievance. (In evidence they alleged that they would be ruined if the new Bank were to do *any* exchange business whatever—because, so they said, a State Bank would do it at cut-throat rates and would thus abolish profit even from that part of the business which the Bank itself did not touch. But I do not myself see that there is force in this or understand why the new Bank should not be as anxious as anyone else to do exchange business at the best rates obtainable.)

Capital, Division of Profits, etc.

You do not, apparently, contemplate the Government's putting any capital into the Bank. Why, if necessary, shouldn't they? Hasn't the German Government (I am not sure) put up some of the capital of the Reichsbank?

[It had not. When Keynes came to write his own State Bank memorandum two months later he decided that continental experience suggested that it was probably inadvisable for the Government to subscribe any part of the Bank's capital.]

I do not like your method of dividing the profits; and I do not think it would be very easy to determine the net profits of the note issue. I think the shareholders should have the profit up to a certain percentage and that the surplus profit should be divided between them and the Government on some fixed proportion subject to decennial revision. I am not much taken, at first sight, by your principles of determining the proportion to go to each party.

Advantages and Disadvantages of the Scheme

The following are, in my mind, the governing considerations:

(*a*) The Government could bank.

(*b*) The note issue could be covered to some extent by bills. As the discussions of the Commission have proceeded, I have been much impressed by the evident impossibility of this *unless* there is a State Bank. If the present system goes on, loans can only be made from the balances and the P.C.R. to the Presidency Banks and on the security of Government paper etc. The amount which can be put out in this way is very limited. I do not think, therefore, that the paper currency can possibly in the future take its proper place in the system if it continues to be divorced from banking. The evils of too close a connection between the elasticity of the note issue and the extent to which the banks find it worth their while to invest in Government paper have been amply demonstrated in U.S.A.

I attach great importance to this consideration.

(c) There would be a strong bank to deal with the next banking crisis. As you know, my opinion is that the present banking position is very weak. The Government in effect keeps a part of the banking reserves, but there is no machinery for bringing its resources into normal connection with banking. The arrangements which would be patched up to meet an emergency might not be very satisfactory.

The evidence we have heard has made it plainer to me than it was before that the Presidency Banks are already to an important extent bankers' banks. But I do not think they are strong enough to support the whole burden.

I attach great importance to the establishment of a strong banking authority.

(d) At present there is apt to be unprofitable haggling between Government and Presidency Banks about (e.g.) the interest payable on loans or the subsidy required to support a branch bank where there is now a sub-treasury. It would pay Government to give any subsidy which was short of the expense of maintaining the sub-treasury; but not unnaturally they will not do this. If in such matters the interests of the two parties were joint instead of opposed, some real economy might result. But this is, relatively, a minor point.

Now in regard to these you do (a) full justice; but to (b) and (c) not, I think, full justice.

Disadvantages

(i) This, of course, is the commonplace criticism [the objection that amalgamation of the Presidency banks would sacrifice local knowledge and on-the-spot efficiency].

How much is there really in it? Not very much, I believe. But I don't at present see the best way to answer it.   J.M.K.

1.7.13

137

Apart from Abrahams (who maintained an official neutrality) only two of the many witnesses who appeared before the Commission were in favour of a State Bank—the rest preferred the *status quo*. But Keynes persisted with many questions on points of detail and practice, as, for example, in the following cross-examination of F. C. Le Marchant, a former member of the India Council and former chairman of its Finance Committee, on his objections to the proposal:

FROM THE MINUTES OF EVIDENCE, 31 JULY 1913

(MR KEYNES) With regard to the establishment of a State Bank, you say there are a number of practical difficulties in setting it up. Some witnesses have spoken of the practical difficulties rather, if I may say so, in the abstract, and I think it is important to bring them to a head and to know exactly what they are. Even at the expense of some recapitulation of what you said in answer to the chairman, would you enumerate what appear to you the most significant of them? (MR LE MARCHANT) *I think the first difficulty is the risk of interfering with existing institutions, which conduct the trade of India with very great success. It is difficult for a State Bank, if it has sufficient funds provided by Government, to limit its transactions. Of course, there are different ideas of a State Bank; some are that it should practically confine itself to internal business in India, but on the other hand there is an idea that it should do a business on this side and control exchange.*

Are the other institutions you are thinking of exchange banks? *Mainly.*

You are not thinking of a case in which the State Bank is additional to the Presidency Banks? *I think it would be very difficult for it to be additional if it did precisely the same work. I believe that the exchange banks give liberal advances in India to their clients; how far the Government would be prepared to do the same business, I do not know. Then again it would be an important question on this side, what sort of representation the bank had; for instance, in the case of the state banks abroad, their representatives in London are the leading financial houses. It would make a great difference whether the State Bank in India had as its representative one or two of the leading houses in London, or whether it had an office and a staff and business in London.*

Which would be the right way of doing it, in your opinion? *If you have an eminent London house as a correspondent, you have the advantage of their knowledge and their experience. It is difficult to compare different advantages together.*

If the State Bank took over in London some of the work now done by the Secretary of State, that would really mean having an office, would it not? *Certainly; but if it did nothing more than that, I do not think there would be any advantage in conducting that which is not already enjoyed by the India Office. I should have assumed that in most of the original ideas of a State Bank there was to be a large capital and business on this side, which would put the bank in more direct communication with the banking community and trade of London.*

These are your first two difficulties—the possible interference with the exchange banks, and the difficulty of finding the right way of representing the Bank in London: what further points are there? *I attach a great deal of importance to the cost of having a sufficient number of branches in India to develop any business beyond the business now conducted by the Presidency Banks.*

It has come out to us in evidence that the number of Government Treasuries is much greater than the number of Presidency Bank branches—I mean five or six times as great, perhaps? *It is some 270-odd against 35, I think.*

Would there be great expense, do you think, if the branches transacted the business now done at the Government Treasuries in so far as related to holding the balances and the management of the paper currency? *Do you mean if the bank took over all the Treasuries?*

Yes? *I have the impression that the officers in the Treasuries are officers of Government, with pay and retirement, and whatever promotion Government may offer. If they become entirely officials of the bank it would be a very material change in their status, and an expensive one to the bank, I should think. I do not know whether it would be contemplated that the officers should remain officials of the Government and yet do the work of the bank.*

I am not trying to get solutions of the difficulties from you, for that would not be reasonable; what I am trying to discover are your prima facie objections. That, I understand, is the third one—the possible expense of setting up the numerous branches such as are contemplated. Is there any further difficulty? *I think all the incidents attaching to banking on a large scale have to be taken into account. There is, for instance, the question of advances; if they are conducted on a very strict scale I do not know that the bank would enter sufficiently into the commerce of the country to be of much use; if, on the other hand, they are on a very free scale, then there are all the attendant risks to the Government of being identified with business.*

I suppose you would agree that the Presidency Banks at present are on a very strict scale? *I believe them to be so.*

Is there any further point that occurs to you at the moment on that head? *No.*

(CHAIRMAN) I think, in answering questions of mine, you did say that you thought there was a danger of the bank becoming merely another Government department? *I think, in view of the responsibility of the Government for its actions and the probable presence of representatives on it, that, looking at the extent to which the railways have become Government property, there would always be some possibility of the bank becoming a Government branch.*

Did I rightly understand you to express the view that, even if it did not go so far as that, the responsibility of the Government would be still so much involved that they really would get no relief or little relief? *I think they might get some relief in the ordinary transaction of business, but still no doubt much attention would be required. It would mean Government officers and Government work.*

In the last resort, if anything went wrong with the bank, how would its failure be regarded? Who would be blamed? *I think it is customary to blame the Government whenever a case can be made out, and they would have to accept the blame, probably.*

You do not think it would be possible for them to wash their hands of the responsibility? *No, I do not.*

(LORD KILBRACKEN) That responsibility would come ultimately on the Secretary of State in Council, would it not? *Yes, I think it would.*

And he would have to be responsible to Parliament for any part of the operations of the bank of which individual Members of Parliament might disapprove? *I expect so.*

(MR KEYNES) I do not propose to take you in any detail over this question of the State Bank so far as its positive advantages go; but suppose there were strong positive advantages, do you think the kind of objections which you have been outlining are insuperable ones? Is not your point of view rather, here are these difficulties, and I see no great positive advantage in the thing, and therefore there is not much to be said for it? *It is very difficult to contemplate the exact working of an institution which is in the air. It is difficult to give a conclusive opinion on what one might call a project.*

Do you regard the sort of difficulties that you have been mentioning as of a very far-reaching kind? *I think, taken in the aggregate, they are.*

When it came to a sympathetic witness, William Bernard Hunter, the secretary and treasurer of the Presidency Bank of Madras, who had recommended a central bank in his written evidence, Keynes carefully questioned him to bring out the objections that he would have to any alternative.

AN INDIAN STATE BANK

FROM THE MINUTES OF EVIDENCE, 17 JULY 1913

(MR. KEYNES) I think I understand clearly the great advantages which, as you maintain, would accrue from the existence of a State Bank, but I would like to question you as to how far you think those advantages might possibly be obtained without a State Bank. First of all with regard to the paper currency, I understand that you think that the bank could use methods of popularising it which absolutely could not be open to the Government? (MR HUNTER) *I think that they would have means. I would not go so far as to say that the Government could not do the same if they would, but it would be more difficult for them than it would for the bank. We have direct dealings with the trading public and the Government have not, and we can induce our constituents to take notes by offering them more favourable rates than they could obtain by taking silver, which would cost us a lot of money to transfer.*

You suggested that against the paper currency a certain amount could be held in the form of bills? *Yes.*

Do you think that if there were no State Bank the Government could possibly enter into the business of buying bills? *No, I should think it probably could not.*

So that part of your proposal is really contingent upon the State Bank being established? *Yes, that is so.*

Would it be possible for the Government to lend to Presidency Banks against the security of bills? *They might do it in that way.*

But you think that the use of the balances for discounting bills is essentially a banking operation? *I think it is. It could be carried out better by the bank, and more promptly.*

Then there is the point about the Government balances, which for various reasons which have been explained to us, are very big in India. Do you think that Government could possibly lend anything like all those balances to the existing Presidency Banks? *No, I do not think they could use them—not the balances that they have at present of something like 20 crores. I do not think that would be a business proposition at present under present circumstances.*

So that your proposal for putting Government money at the disposal of trade is contingent on the establishment of a State Bank? *Yes—the whole of their balances.*

There might be some increase even in the absence of a State Bank? *I think under existing conditions very much more of the balance could be put at the disposal of the Presidency Banks temporarily during the busy season.*

141

About how much more, do you think? *Of course, it would depend upon the season. It seems to me they could meet the requirements of the Presidency Banks out of their funds which are doing nothing.*

Could they, do you think, lend enough of their balances to the Presidency banks really to meet your criticism, or could they only lend enough to meet your criticism if there were a State Bank established? *I think that under existing circumstances they could lend us enough.*

So that that part of your proposal is not absolutely contingent on the establishment of a State Bank? *It is not absolutely contingent on that.*

It would be more efficient though if there were one? *It would be more efficient if there were one.*

I come back to another point about which I think you have not said anything, or, at any rate, have not said much, in your memorandum, and that is the banking resources of the country. Do you think that there will be any substantial advantage in having the banking resources amalgamated, from the point of view of security? *Do you mean of the three Presidency Banks?*

Yes, having their cash resources amalgamated? *It certainly would strengthen the position to a certain extent, in so far as the demand varies in point of time. In Bengal the demand arises earlier than it does in Madras. Our season continues longer. Therefore the amalgamation of banks in that way would strengthen the position. Do you mean whether it would make a stronger bank?*

I was thinking rather of the case of a crisis? *Yes, I think decidedly in the case of a crisis, if there were an amalgamation of the three banks the credit of the three banks would be stronger than the credit of an individual bank. A bank such as I have outlined would be able to command credit in London.*

Do you think that the present position is so safe that these are rather minor considerations, or do you think that the present position is not as good as it might be in the matter of meeting a crisis? *I think there are dangers about the present position.*

You would not feel perfectly happy in a severe banking crisis in India? *Certainly most unhappy. Unfortunately I went through a very serious crisis in Madras, and there was no outlet, absolutely none. I refer to the failure of Arbuthnot and Co.*

What do you mean by no outlet? *There was no outlet for obtaining resources. We were tied up in the Presidency practically. We have no recourse to London, and no possibility of raising money elsewhere; we depend upon our own cash balance.*

Could you not even draft in money from Bengal? *If Bengal happened to be easy at the time you could borrow money up to a certain point, but then you have your Bank Act, which comes in and provides that you can only borrow against certain securities. The Bank Act precludes a Presidency Bank from lending to another Presidency Bank without specified security.*

I think in answer to a question earlier today you discriminated between the effects of the sale of Council bills and of lending money in India in this way, that if Government released funds by the sale of Council bills that helps shippers rather than producers? *The Council bills are not applied for until the produce has been brought down for shipment.*

But if the Government money were available in numerous branches all over the country, you think that would strengthen the financial position of producers as against that of shippers? *I think so; they would be enabled to get financed more cheaply, and would be able to hold their produce if the market were unfavourable.*

That is to say, the money market in India is a very imperfect one? *Yes.*

Funds which are available to one class of borrower are not at all available to another class? *That is so. The producer has got to pay his kist, that is, the Government revenue, at a certain time, and, in order to pay that, he must either be able to sell his produce or to borrow on it. If the rates are high it practically means that the money is not available to lend, and, therefore, he has to sell; he sells to the exporting merchant, and the exporting merchant sells his bills to the exchange bank, and they obtain Council bills.*

Abrahams had not been sanguine about the reception of his State Bank memorandum; 'You are my chief hope', he had written to Keynes. But when the Commission adjourned in August for a summer recess, some sort of agreement had been reached that two of their number should draw up a definite, detailed State Bank scheme for consideration—even though one or two members strongly endorsed the testimony of witnesses that there was no public demand for it. The two chosen were Sir Ernest Cable, the owner of a big jute business in India and a former president of the Bengal Chamber of Commerce, and Keynes. Cable produced a skeleton memorandum which dealt mainly with the Bank's capitalisation, leaving Keynes to fill in its functions and methods of operation. Keynes was invited to stay with Cable in Devonshire from 27 August to 3 September to discuss it and have 'a day or so at the partridges'. (Cable wrote a breezy letter in a bold and breezy hand.) In the course of the visit they consulted on practical questions with Hunter, who had already given the Commission his own written recommendations.

Keynes wrote the final memorandum—a scheme 'which ought to make

143

any banker's mouth water', he described it—and in the end it became his plan, signed with his name and published as an Annexe to the Royal Commission's Report. Cable's written comments on the first draft consist mostly of suggested changes in wording in order not to 'parade red rags' (his phrase) in front of fearful Presidency Bank shareholders, and such remarks as 'Don't admit complexity?! This will be used as an admission!' Keynes followed his advice. Of Section VI, on the London Office and Remittance, Cable observed: 'Thin ice all through this section well glided over!'

One of the first members of the Commission to see the memorandum was R. W. Gillan, Finance Secretary to the Government of India and a former Comptroller of Currency, with whom Keynes had corresponded when he was learning about India in Cambridge. Although Gillan had some serious practical objections, he wrote of the memorandum as a whole (9 October 1913):

> It clears things up immensely. In the past one had not a single proposition but a number of phantom shapes melting into one another and had really to meet the criticism directed against all or any of them. You have brought out in the most definite way how irrelevant much of this criticism is, and at any rate we have now a straight issue.

Basil P. Blackett (later Sir Basil Blackett and Finance Member of the Government of India 1922–8) had been borrowed from the Treasury to fill the post of Secretary to the Commission originally proposed for Keynes and was now grappling with the draft report. He reacted enthusiastically: 'Your memorandum on the Bank provides the only really satisfactory starting point for the report, and enables the other questions as to gold standard and paper currency reserves and the balances to be grouped around the State Bank in proper proportion...'

But in the same letter, dated 8 October 1913, Blackett expressed a fear 'that the Commission may be put into the position of having the thing forced on them by one of their colleagues and that the public may see too clearly that this is very much what has been happening when the memorandum is eventually published'. Also, he warned, the memorandum necessarily anticipated so many decisions as yet unmade, that the Commission might feel that the word was being taken out of their mouths.

He suggested a tactful introduction to remind the Commission of the origin of the memorandum and forestall these possible objections. Keynes followed his outline of what might be said rather closely and yet produced a very characteristic covering note.

AN INDIAN STATE BANK

To the Members of the Royal Commission

This memorandum is the outcome of a request made to me by members of the Commission at our last meeting in the summer, that, in consultation with Sir Ernest Cable, I should draft a State Bank scheme. It is probably a longer document than members of the Commission expected. This is due to my having found it unsatisfactory to make proposals without explaining the reasons for them at the same time.

The project of a State Bank has everything to lose from *vagueness* on the part either of its friends or its critics. I have made the scheme, therefore, as 'cut and dried' as I can, not because I suppose that it is really possible at the present stage to settle on details, but in order to bring to a head all specific objections.

Many of the ideas expressed in regard to the reserves and other points represent, I believe, very much the kind of conclusions which the Commission have been moving towards, and are in some cases simply the formulation of decisions tentatively arrived at in discussion. I have endeavoured to show how well these ideas fit in to the State Bank scheme and how much better they harmonise with it than with alternative proposals. But I do not intend to suggest that the underlying principles stand or fall in every case with the State Bank.

I have worked in close collaboration with Sir Ernest Cable, to whom I owe a great number of valuable criticisms and suggestions, especially on practical points. In some parts it is primarily his scheme, in others primarily mine. I have also had the advantage of very full discussions with Mr W. B. Hunter of the Bank of Madras.

19.11.1913   J. M. KEYNES

Not all of the commissioners had moved so far towards the same kind of conclusions. There is no doubt that Keynes was anxious to convert the reluctant; an example is his careful letter (pp. 212–14) to Sir James Begbie, a colleague whose support he wanted. Another is the following note that he circulated to reinforce his argument. It is undated but obviously relates to some time after the memorandum had been distributed.

SOME ASPECTS OF RECENT EVENTS

With reference to my State Bank memorandum, I wish to direct the attention of members of the Commission to some aspects of recent events.

The Government of India, feeling that it would be unwise to lock up their balances through the coming winter, have applied to the Secretary of State for leave to lend up to £3,000,000 to the Presidency Banks at rates $1\frac{1}{2}$ to 2 per cent below bank rate. They did not state whether these loans were to be for definite periods or whether security against them was to be provided.

The point to which I wish to call attention is the following. The Secretary of State sanctioned this proposal, subject to the alteration, that the Government should require from the banks payment at a rate not more than one per cent below bank rate. Sir James Begbie has pointed out to me that the Presidency Banks would not feel it prudent to lend up to the hilt the whole of the sums put at their disposal by Government. As the scale of their transactions would be somewhat increased, they would feel it necessary to retain a certain proportion of the new resources in reserve. Thus the assumption that they could earn a rate not below bank rate on the *whole* of the sums placed at their disposal by the Government is an erroneous one. If they had to pay on the whole amount at a rate within one per cent of bank rate, they might very well, therefore, be losers on the transaction taken as a whole. This is a consideration which leapt immediately to the mind of a practical banker. But it was a consideration not at all unnaturally overlooked by a civil servant.

The incident also illustrates the hindrance to the transaction of business which must arise when there is a haggling between the Government and the banks over every transaction, and the Government feels it necessary to assure itself that the banks will make no more profit than is absolutely required in order to induce them to enter on the business at all.

These difficulties seem to me to be characteristic of the

sort of thing that is bound to arise in the absence of a State Bank.

Two other points may be mentioned also. In the first place it is not improbable that the coming season in India may be a somewhat anxious one. This makes it undesirable, as the Government themselves feel, that their balances should be locked up out of the money market's reach. But it also means that great discretion ought to be used in the extent and in the rates at which this money is put at the market's disposal. In the second place, bank rate is a very inadequate index of how much the banks ought to pay—though it is certainly difficult to think of a better one. The bank rate in India is not for three months' loans, but is a rate charged *de die in diem* for outstanding loans. It does not regulate the amount charged for all classes of business. The bank authorities should feel free to keep the bank rate at the most desirable level in the general interests of the banking community. But they would hardly be free to do this if the amounts payable by them to Government were largely dependent on the nominal level of the bank rate. This method of regulating the amount of the payment due to the Government might very easily make it the interest of the Presidency Banks to lower their published bank rates sooner than they would have felt it wise if they had been left to themselves.

Keynes's enthusiasm made him over-optimistic with respect to Sir Shapurji Broacha, the most ardent anti-State-Bank man on the Commission. He wrote to Cable in October that he thought that Sir Shapurji had 'come round'—but Blackett later reported that Sir Shapurji had arrived back after an absence in India 'under the impression that it will still be possible to get a majority report damning a State Bank and [had] evidently quite misunderstood the concordat arrived at...' (11 December 1913).

The 'concordat' seems to have been a compromise reached while the commissioners were studying the first draft of the Report. The draft incorporated Keynes's revision of Blackett's introduction to the memorandum (in another version than the one above); it was used as 'Section V—State or Central Bank', which came immediately before the summing up of the Commission's conclusions. This treatment dissatisfied Keynes who, from the evidence of a conciliatory letter from Chamberlain (28 November 1913), appeared to have hoped that the whole Report would lead up to a discussion of the State Bank. On the other hand, Sir Shapurji Broacha reacted with a vigorous statement of reservation:

> ...I feel constrained to place on record my strong disapproval of the manner in which the Report again and again reverts to the theme of a State Bank as the great solution of India's financial problems. In some mysterious way, the State Bank becomes almost the central theme of the Report, and recurs time after time in the most unexpected places. There is nothing in the evidence to justify the Commission in pressing this impracticable proposal...

The compromise made was to assume the continuance of existing banking conditions in India and the absence of any central bank in making recommendations in the main body of the Report, and to publish Keynes's memorandum as an annexe. Sir Shapurji Broacha withdrew his reservation. Section V of the Report (in a third and final revision by Keynes) explained the reasons for the commissioners' decision, directing attention to the memorandum—with the effect of giving it considerable prominence. The early appointment of a small expert committee to study the question was advised. Here is section V of the published Report:

STATE OR CENTRAL BANK

We have made no reference to the State Bank question in the earlier passages of our Report, in spite of its frequent relevance, because we were unwilling to introduce, in passing, remarks which might appear to prejudge, one way or the other, a question which we were not prepared to discuss in detail. Many of our recommendations, notably those which relate to the maintenance of exchange, the position of gold in the currency, the system of budgetting, and the raising of loans by Government, are not appreciably affected by any decision which may be arrived at on the bank question. But others, especially those which relate to the elasticity and fiduciary portion of the note issue, to the custody, employment, and proper amount of the Government balances in India and London, and to remittance, are somewhat intimately bound up with the presence or absence of a State Bank. The Bank question has also a close connection with subjects not directly falling within the terms of our reference, such as the absence of a final banking reserve in India and the question of giving the Presidency Banks access to London, the extension of co-operative credit in India, the improvement of banking facilities and the encouragement of sound banking in that country.

It has been represented to us that, under several of these heads, the difficulties and inconveniences which arise are largely contingent on the absence of a strong central banking institution, competent to manage the note issue, and so constituted as to be in a position to hold and manage the whole of the Government balances and to transact for Government other business naturally falling within the province of the Government's banker, such as remittance. In the lack of such an institution the Government of India's position, while not unexampled, is unusual. So long as the Government remain aloof from banking, so long as they maintain (to any important extent) an independent treasury system, and so long as the management of the note issue is kept outside banking, some features of the present system, which may be regarded as anomalous, will remain. We have endeavoured in the preceding parts of our Report to make such recommendations as will permit the continuance of these features with as little general inconvenience as possible. But those which relate to the note issue and to the employment of balances may be regarded, from one point of view, as palliatives rather than cures.

We have been naturally led, therefore, to give some consideration to the possibility of such more radical changes as are contingent on the establishment of a State Bank—a proposal which presents at the same time some attractive features and some obvious practical difficulties. But we found from the outset in examining witnesses upon the subject of a State or Central Bank that the absence of anything in the nature of concrete proposals and even of any general agreement as to what was implied by the phrase 'a State or Central Bank' made such examination difficult and unsatisfactory. It was arranged, therefore, before we adjourned for the summer holiday in August, that two of our number, Sir Ernest Cable and Mr J. M. Keynes, should prepare a detailed scheme for their colleagues' consideration. We annex to our Report the memorandum submitted to us by Mr Keynes, after collaboration with Sir Ernest Cable, in accordance with this decision.

We had previously received the memorandum on the subject of a State Bank or Central Bank submitted to us by Mr L. Abrahams, C.B., with the concurrence of the Secretary of State. This memorandum was printed as Appendix No. XIV to our Interim Report. The memoranda in question indicate most of the advantages and disadvantages attaching to the proposal on general grounds and the considerations to be borne in mind in dealing with it. It is unnecessary for us to recapitulate them here.

A study of these two memoranda makes much clearer the nature of the questions at issue; and the schemes proposed in them present prima facie several attractive features. But most of the witnesses whom we have examined had not been in a position to consider or pronounce upon the specific proposals therein contained. It was not possible for us, therefore, to submit these schemes to a sufficiently searching examination without much delay in the presentation of our Report. We recognised, further, that such an examination would probably involve a visit to India and a careful study of the conditions on the spot, and we came to the conclusion that we were not fitted as a body to undertake this task. We do not feel ourselves, therefore, in a position to make recommendations, one way or the other, on the question of a State Bank.

But we regard the question, whatever decision may ultimately be arrived at upon it, as one of great importance to India, which deserves the careful and early consideration of the Secretary of State and the Government of India. We think, therefore, that they would do well to hold an inquiry into it without delay, and to appoint for this purpose a small expert body, representative both of official and non-official experience, with directions to study the whole question in India in consultation with the persons and bodies primarily interested, such as the Presidency Banks, and either to pronounce definitely against the desirability of the establishment of a State or Central Bank in India at the present time, or to submit to the authorities a concrete scheme for the establishment of such a bank fully worked out in all its details and capable of immediate application.

The war of 1914–18 put to one side all of the Commission's recommendations. India did not get a central bank until 1935—one currency committee, one more Royal Commission and one White Paper on constitutional reform later.

Keynes's memorandum is printed here as it appeared with the Report, 2 March 1914. It carries the date on which he finished it, 6 October 1913.

MEMORANDUM ON PROPOSALS FOR THE ESTABLISHMENT OF A STATE BANK IN INDIA

Introductory

A central bank must necessarily stand in a somewhat close relation to Government. If the bank is to be useful, it must have the management of the Government balances and of the note issue. It would be contrary to experience elsewhere and to what seems reasonable for India to hand over these functions to a purely private institution. If Government is to interfere at all, it cannot help involving itself in ultimate responsibility for the bank, and if it is thus to involve itself, its powers must be sufficient to permit an effective supervision. From a Government with feeble powers and placed in the position of interested but irresponsible critics, there would be a greater likelihood of vexatious interference; while too great a dependence on the terms of the bank's charter must tend to make these terms too rigid and narrow for practice.

The constitutions of the principal state banks of Europe and of the Bank of Japan are briefly outlined in an appendix to this memorandum. Their general character points overwhelmingly to the conclusion that the higher executive officers responsible for the policy and administration of the bank must be appointed by Government and rest under its ultimate authority. In all state banks of importance the influence of the shareholders is chiefly consultative and advisory.

If these preliminary points are granted, we are at once faced with a somewhat different proposal from that which the Government had before them in 1900–2. The position at that time seems to have been that, if the Presidency Banks would amalgamate on their own initiative and also increase their capital by a substantial amount, the Government would seriously consider the handing over to them, on terms to be discussed later, of the management of the paper currency and the use of a large portion of the public balances. The advantages to be gained by the Presidency Banks were insufficiently certain or precise, and the proposals fell through. Several of the difficulties which have appeared serious to some of our witnesses are more relevant, I think, to the proposals of 1900–2 and to the popular idea of a State Bank thus fostered than to the proposals to be developed below.

The question why anyone should wish to set up a State Bank and the advantages to be got from it are treated in section VIII. Section II is devoted solely to the problem whether it is feasible to devise for such a bank a working constitution.

The main difficulties to be faced are the following:

(i) To combine ultimate Government responsibility with a high degree of day-to-day independence for the authorities of the Bank.

(ii) To preserve unimpaired authority in the executive officers of the Bank, whose duty it would be to take a broad and not always a purely commercial view of policy, and at the same time to make use of the commercial instincts and commercial knowledge of representatives of the shareholders.

(iii) To maintain in the day-to-day management of the Bank the high degree of decentralisation to which great importance is rightly attached in the case of so large a country as India.[1]

Further points, such as the *status* of the Bank in London, the

---

[1] As the Government of India wrote to the Secretary of State when advocating the establishment of a central bank (18 January, 1900): 'Nothing would be more unwise than to discard the valuable local knowledge, skill and experience of the existing directorates and managements of the Presidency Banks.'

method of regulation of the note issue, the division of profits between the shareholders and the Government, no doubt present difficulties. But these must certainly be capable of some solution. Fundamental objections to the proposed bank must arise out of its failure to satisfy the three main conditions set out above.

An outline constitution so far as affects these three fundamental points is given below.

Outline constitution, so far as concerns the relation of the bank to government, the powers of the shareholders, and decentralisation

1. The supreme direction of the Imperial Bank of India shall be vested in a Central Board of three members, consisting of the Governor of the Bank (who shall be chairman), the Deputy Governor, and a representative of Government, together with three or more Assessors.

2. The Governor shall be appointed for periods of five years (subject to age limit) by the King on the recommendation of the Secretary of State, and shall be removable in like manner. He shall be eligible for reappointment. The salary of the Governor shall be Rs. 100,000 per annum.[1]

3. The representative of Government shall be appointed by the Viceroy, and shall be, in general, the Financial Member of the Viceroy's Council, the Member for Commerce and Industry, or the Secretary from the Department of one of them.[2]

4. The Assessors shall be the managers of the three Presidency head offices (see below) and of such other head offices as may be created hereafter, or their deputies. The Assessors shall have the right to attend any meeting of the Central Board and to lay their views before it, but shall not vote. The Central Board shall also have the right to summon any of the Assessors to attendance.

---

[1] These figures are put forward very tentatively, to suggest the status of the officers affected.

[2] Or the Comptroller of Currency, the proposed appointment of whom has been lately announced.

5. The Deputy Governor of the Bank, and managers of the Presidency head offices, who shall all be of the same status and receive salaries of Rs. 60,000[1] shall be appointed by the Viceroy on the nomination of the Governor of the Bank and of the Government representative on the Central Board. But the appointment of a manager to a Presidency head office shall be subject to the approval of the Presidency Board (including representatives of the shareholders) of the head office in question.

6. Within the limits of the Bank Act, the Central Board shall have absolute authority, and the signature of the Governor supported by a majority vote of the Board shall be legally binding upon the Bank; save that the representative of the Government shall have discretionary power (for use in emergencies only) to suspend the carrying into effect of any decision until it has been reported to the Viceroy, with whom shall lie an ultimate right of veto.

7. The Central Board, which will have no direct dealings with the public, shall have its offices and establishment located at Delhi (or Calcutta). Its members will keep in touch with the chief commercial centres of the country, partly by the attendance from time to time of the Assessors, and partly by touring on the part of the Governor or his Deputy.

8. All transactions between the Bank and the public in India shall be under the authority of one or other of the head offices. In the first instance, Presidency head offices shall be established at Calcutta, Bombay and Madras, and the spheres of influence of these head offices shall be the same as those of the existing Presidency Banks.[2]

9. Each head office shall be under the direction of a Presidency Board, consisting of the manager (who shall be chairman and have the casting vote), the deputy manager, a representative of the local government, and three (or four) unofficial members.

10. The unofficial members shall be elected by the share-

[1] See n. 1, p. 153.
[2] Including Ceylon, as at present in the case of the Madras head office.

holders on the local register of each Presidency from amongst their own number.

11. Any business, within the limits of the Bank Act, and not contrary to the express instructions of the Central Board, entered into by a Presidency Board, shall be legally binding on the Bank.

12. Although the Central Board shall have authority to issue instructions, to which the Presidency Boards shall be subject, on all matters, nevertheless in general, and failing special prior instructions to the contrary, a Presidency Board shall have entire discretion to transact on its own authority all business of the following descriptions:

(1) To discount Indian (rupee) trade bills, maturing within a maximum period of six months, subject to a minimum rate arranged from time to time in consultation with the Central Board.

(2) To rediscount sterling trade bills, bearing the endorsement of another bank, subject to minimum rate arranged from time to time in consultation with the Central Board, and subject to daily report to the Central Board.

(3) To make interest-bearing loans (subject to a minimum rate, etc.), for periods not exceeding six months against such kind of security as is permitted by the Bank Act.

(4) To buy and sell in India, subject to daily report to the Central Board, gold bullion and such bonds and securities as may be dealt in according to the provisions of the Bank Act.

(5) To provide trade remittance for customers to all parts of India, and private remittance to London subject to certain conditions.

(6) To accept interest and non-interest-bearing deposits, subject to a maximum rate, etc.

(7) To accept valuable goods for safe keeping.

(8) To open, staff, and control branch banks at any place within the Presidency Board's sphere of influence.

13. A general report on all such transactions shall be forwarded to the Central Board weekly, and more frequently when the Presidency Board think it desirable, or the Central Board request it.

14. In regard to the rates charged for discounts and loans, and allowed on deposits, the Presidency Boards shall be free to vary the rate charged in individual transactions and at their different branches, subject to minimum (or maximum) rates, fixed weekly (or in emergency more frequently) in consultation with the Central Board.

Discussion of the outline constitution

The object of the above draft proposals is merely to indicate in a more precise way than is otherwise possible the kind of relations which are contemplated between the Government, the Central Board, the Presidency Boards, and the shareholders. It will be worth while to discuss these points more fully and to consider also how far such proposals satisfy the three fundamental conditions which were laid down in the introductory section.

1. First, as regards the relation of the Bank to the Government. The creation of such a bank as is here proposed certainly increases in a sense the responsibilities of Government. But there are two senses of the term 'responsibility'. The Government may be said to be responsible if, in the last resort, it is the Government that has to come to the rescue. Or it may be held that it can only be called responsible if, in addition to this, it is the proper object of criticism or blame if anything goes wrong. Those acquainted with the present banking position in India would maintain, I think, that the Government already possesses responsibility in the first and more important sense. So long as they manage the note issue, and maintain large cash balances outside the ordinary banking system, they are bound to come to the rescue of the Presidency Banks in the event of a widespread crisis involving the banks generally.

The prevention of occurrences contrary to the public interest, rather than the avoidance of responsibility, ought in general to be the first object of Government. The only good reason for avoiding responsibility in the first sense is in the case of kinds of action which governments are not competent or have not the machinery to perform well; and the only good reason for avoiding it in the second sense, when it already exists in the first, is in cases where explicit responsibility would involve them in such unpopularity or criticism as might impair their general efficiency. It cannot be maintained that some responsibility for banking, seeing that it is in fact undertaken by nearly all civilised governments, is inherently undesirable. The undesirable features in the Government's present degree of responsibility for these things in India are rather due to the lack of a suitable machinery. I need not enlarge on this. There is an absence of trained experience and specialised knowledge on the part of those responsible, so that financial duties are apt to be thrown on officers concerned, during the greater part of their careers, with quite other things. The business is of a kind where immediate action and undivided responsibility in regard to details is essential, whereas, if it is dealt with in the ordinary mills of Government, this is nearly impossible. But given a suitable machinery I do not see why anyone should wish to divest Government of the duties in question. That the solution lies in the provision of a more suitable machinery, rather than in the getting rid of existing functions, has been strongly impressed on me in the course of the Commission's deliberations. This more suitable machinery the creation of a State Bank affords.

It seems clear that Government cannot entrust any of its existing duties to private hands. It has also become plain that, whether a State Bank is established or not, Government, so far from relinquishing old duties, must bend itself to new ones. The functions of the note issue, it is generally agreed, must be extended, and an element of discretion must be introduced where there was previously rule of thumb. As in the case of the note issue, so in the case of the cash balances, there must be less rule of thumb and more discretion. Now, with a State Bank all this would be easy, and there are plenty of precedents to look to; but as soon as an attempt is made to work out precisely by what sort of procedure these objects are to be attained in the absence of a State Bank, it becomes apparent that it is not altogether through chance or obtuseness that such desirable changes have not been made long ago. The existing system has been deeply conditioned by the absence of a State Bank. The history of the management of the cash balances, for example, bears witness to this. At no time has anyone supposed the existing system to be perfectly satisfactory. It has established itself because it is the only system which frees the officials from the exercise of a discretion for which they do not feel themselves competent and from which they therefore shrink. The evidence is that actual practice has always tended to be more rigid than the actual letter of the rule laid down by the Secretary of State; and naturally enough. Similarly in regard to the paper currency. In the first instance, no doubt, the system was set up in uncritical imitation of the Bank of England's, and under the influence of the theory that it was a positive advantage for note issue to be separated from banking; but for thirty years at least this theory has lacked vitality or offspring, and note issue in India has remained divorced from banking because there has been no bank to join it to, and because, for a rule-of-thumb system, it is a fairly good one.

The choice lies between a good deal of responsibility *without* thoroughly satisfactory machinery for the discharge of it; and a little more responsibility *with* such a machinery. The balance of advantage is with the second alternative.

As regards the Secretary of State's exposure to pressure or parliamentary criticism of an undesirable kind, the creation of a State Bank would, without question, improve and strengthen his position. Recent experience shows that he cannot, under the present system, resist cross-examination on minute details of financial management. If arrangements are introduced for loans from the cash balances and for some degree of regulation of the currency reserve by discretion, will he not be liable to all kinds of questions in Parliament on details of executive policy? If the Government of India is lending three crores from the cash balances and some business men think they would like four crores, what will there be to prevent the working up of a strong agitation by means of the Press, daily fed and inflamed by questions in the House, for lending on a larger scale? I do not see how the Secretary of State could be more exposed than he is to what may really be a most undesirable thing, namely, cross-examination on actions which are, in truth, none of his business.

The State Bank, on the other hand, would have a high degree of independence; and there would be numerous questions to which the Secretary of State's proper answer would be that it was entirely a matter for the Bank. He would never admit, for example, the faintest degree of responsibility for the precise level of the bank rate at a particular moment. The Secretary of State would be behind the Bank, but his authority would only come into play on rare and important occasions. On important changes of policy and on alterations of clauses in the Bank Act, the Secretary of State would have the last word and with it the responsibility. If over a period of time there were a widespread feeling that the regular administration of the Bank was ill-conducted, it would be his duty to grant an inquiry and to act in the light of its report. But for the ordinary daily work of the Bank he would necessarily disclaim responsibility to a far completer extent than is at present possible in the case of any of the financial business now conducted by the Government. The method of appointment suggested above of the Governor and Deputy Governor is intended not to make them Government officials, but to place them in a position of considerable independence. A State Bank would certainly act as a buffer of no little importance between the Secretary of State and external pressure.

This day-to-day independence of the Bank, which would incidentally prove a relief to the Secretary of State, would be absolutely essential from the Bank's own point of view. It is not likely that the commercial community would acquiesce in any proposal where it was absent. Banking business must be outside the regular Government machine, ignorant of 'proper channels', and free of the official hierarchy where action cannot be taken until reference has been made to a higher authority. The officials of the Bank should have precisely the same powers for the prompt transaction of business that the officials of the Presidency Banks have now.

The presence of private capital is probably a considerable bulwark against some kinds of political pressure. Continental experience shows that private ownership of the Bank's capital, even although the shareholders have no more than advisory powers, is an important safeguard of the Bank's independence; and continental writers have laid great stress on this.[1]

The outline constitution given above has been designed with a view to these conditions. The Bank, though ultimately dependent on the State, would lie altogether outside the ordinary Government machine; and its executive officers would be free, on the one hand, from the administrative interference of Government and free also, on the other hand, from too much pressure on the part of the shareholders, in cases where this might run counter to the general interest.

A State Bank of the kind proposed might really get the best of both worlds. It is difficult to predict how a new institution will work out in practice. But the advantages of a state and of a private institution may be, partly at any rate, combined. Representatives of the public interest must have the ultimate control, because a State Bank is given powerful monopolistic rights; and the public interest may not invariably be at one with the interests of shareholders, though on the whole and generally speaking the shareholders must benefit largely by their connection with the State. On the other hand the alliance of the State with private shareholders serves to keep the executive of the Bank in close touch with commercial opinion, and introduces that element of

[1] See Appendix B.

commercial self-interest, from which, in the present economic arrangement of affairs, a State Bank, as well as private institutions, may derive a real advantage.[1]

It may be added in this connection that the Governor and Deputy Governor of the Bank should invariably be persons of commercial or banking, not of administrative or official, experience, and should be appointed, so far as may be possible or convenient, from the staffs of the Presidency offices. Though it would not be wise to lay down any rule or principle on the matter, and while it might be an advantageous thing to introduce from time to time officers whose banking experience had lain elsewhere, the governorship of the Bank should be a position to which the leading officials of the Presidency offices could reasonably look forward as a possible prize. It might, perhaps, increase public confidence in the non-official character of the Bank's management and in the Government's intentions, if it were definitely laid down that members of the English or the Indian Civil Service were ineligible for appointment as officers of the Bank.

2. Second, as regards the relation of the Central Board to the Presidency Boards, and the arrangements for decentralisation. We are here presented with a problem which is largely peculiar to India; but a little may be learnt from the organisation of the head offices of the Reichsbank described in Appendix A, and the establishment of local committees or directorates is fairly familiar in the case of many important banks doing business partly in London and partly abroad.

It is clear that the organism of the Central Board must be quite distinct from that of any of the Presidency head offices. It would

---

[1] The same point is emphasised in the following quotation from the official history of the Reichsbank: 'Through the co-operation of the Reichsbank authorities, who are not interested in the financial profits of the bank, with the representatives of the shareholders, who are practical business men, the bank management is safeguarded, since it takes into consideration the interest of the public; and at the same time the experience and business knowledge of the shareholders, who are financially interested in the success of the bank, are utilised in the guidance of the bank. This bank organisation, which strikes the mean between a purely state bank and a purely private one, has proved to be the best system according to the experience of most European countries.'

be undesirable, e.g., that the Calcutta office should be superior in any way to the Bombay office. The Presidency Boards and Presidency offices must all be on a complete equality and stand in the same relation to the Central Board. Even if it proved convenient for the offices of the Central Board to be located in Calcutta, this board would be quite distinct from the Bengal Presidency Board, just as the Imperial Government has been distinct from the local government of Bengal. This has not been a feature of earlier schemes, and the suggestion that one of the Presidency offices would be in effect the head office of the whole bank has been responsible for setting up local jealousies which the present scheme ought to avoid.

In the outline constitution given above, Delhi (or alternatively Calcutta) has been suggested as the headquarters of the Central Board. Delhi is open to a good deal of obvious criticism, but has, on the other hand, some advantages. To place the Central Board at Calcutta might lead to an undue overshadowing of the Bengal Presidency Board, as well as to a confusion in the public mind regarding the relation of the two boards to one another. The suggestion of making the Calcutta office the head office would no doubt commend itself to Calcutta interests. But there is no question of this; and it is doubtful whether local Calcutta interests would welcome a Central Board, on which Calcutta shareholders would not be directly represented, in immediate proximity and with superior powers to their own Presidency Board on which local interests have ample representation. To fix the Central Board at Delhi safeguards, on the one hand, its own impartiality and, on the other hand, the complete locol independence of the Presidency Boards. This location would also facilitate the attendance of the Government representative,[1] and would be geographically convenient both for touring on the part of the officers of the Central Board, and for attendance at meetings on the part of the assessors from the local boards.

[1] It is understood, however, that the new Comptroller of Currency is to have his headquarters at Calcutta.

The chief objections to Delhi are, first, that this location would place the Bank too much under the direct influence of Government, and second, that the officers of the Bank would be too little in touch with commercial opinion. The first objection is obviously not capable of a precise answer and will appeal with varying force to different persons. But it may be pointed out that there is little reason for supposing that high authorities will wish to interest themselves in the Bank's daily transactions of which they will not, apart from the Government's representative on the Central Board, have any official cognisance at all; and that the Bank's independence is considerably safeguarded by its constitution, and by the complete absence of connection with the Civil Service on the part of the Governor and Deputy Governor. The second objection is partly met by the following considerations. In the first place, the Central Board is to have no direct dealings whatever with the public, to whom, therefore, so far as the transaction of business is concerned, its location will be a matter of indifference. In the second place, the Central Board would rely for its knowledge of the commercial situation partly on the not infrequent touring of the Governor or Deputy Governor, and partly on the attendance at its meetings of the managers of the Presidency head offices. Their knowledge of the *general* position would probably be more complete in this way than if they were permanently fixed at some one Presidency town. The fact that the busy seasons in different parts of India are to some extent distinct, emphasises the convenience of touring on the part of the Bank's highest executive officers.

The duties of the Central Board would be chiefly concerned with bank rate, with the remittance of funds from one Presidency to another, and between India and London, and with questions of general policy. But it might be advisable that they should also have directly under them an Inspection and Audit Department, not for the purpose of controlling the Presidency Boards and the various branches of the Bank, but as an independent check, after the event, on the nature of the business done, and as a means of rendering more actual the ultimate responsibility of the Central Board for all the Bank's transactions.

The position of the Presidency managers in their capacity of Assessors to the Central Board requires further explanation. It would not be practicable to make them complete members of the Central Board, since this would imply more regular attendance at the Board's meetings than would be compatible with their duties at their own head offices. At the same time, it is desirable that they should be in close touch with the Central Board in person and not only by correspondence. The proposed scheme is intended to make it possible for them to attend the Central Board on occasions when they can conveniently be absent from their own office, and when they specially desire to place their views or proposals before the Central Board in person. The Central Board, on their part, would be able to convene from time to time meetings at which all the Presidency managers would be, if possible, present. While the Central Board's offices and establishment must be fixed, there is no reason why the Board itself should not meet from time to time if it should be found convenient, at various centres.

One of the main points to be emphasised regarding the relation of the Presidency Boards to the Central Board is that all questions of *individual* credit would be ordinarily within the discretion of the Presidency Boards. The general magnitude of the transactions of any kind must come within the cognisance and ultimate control of the Central Board. But the nature of the individual transactions making up the total, in general, should not. The local boards would thus possess substantial autonomy in the discount of inland bills and in the granting of advances. In all matters relating to individual credit they would possess the same independence as each Presidency Bank has now. They would also control the movement of funds within their own Presidency. They would, therefore, be able to conduct all ordinary business with members of the public with exactly the same degree of despatch as at present and without reference to higher authority.

3. Third, as regards the relation of the Bank to its shareholders. The chief points to be considered are the fair treatment of the shareholders in regard to their share of profits, the utilisation of the commercial knowledge and the commercial instincts of the shareholders' representatives, and the maintenance of the supreme authority of the Bank in the hands of officers who are not open to pressure on matters affecting public policy and the general good of the commercial and banking community.

The question of profits is treated in the next section of this memorandum. The other two considerations are dealt with in the proposed scheme, on the one hand by constituting half (or, perhaps, a majority) of each of the Presidency Boards from representatives of the shareholders and by requiring the approval of these representatives to the appointment of the managers of the Presidency head offices; and on the other hand by giving the shareholders no direct representation on the Central Board, though allowing them full opportunity of access to this board and of laying their views before it through their local managers. It might also be proper, as in the case of the Reichsbank, to distinguish certain questions, such as the drawing up of the annual balance sheet, on which special attention should be paid to the views of their representatives.

Such limitation of the powers of the shareholders as is proposed in this scheme may appear to Indian opinion a somewhat novel feature which is open to criticism. But it is, I think, an unavoidable consequence of the great privileges and responsibilities of a State Bank, and does not go so far as in most of the state banks of Europe and elsewhere.

Capitalisation of the Bank and division of profits

There is no question but that the nucleus of the new Bank is to be obtained by the amalgamation of the capital and reserves of the three Presidency Banks.

Continental experience suggests (see Appendix A) that it is

probably inadvisable for the Government to subscribe any part of the capital of the Bank itself. Subscriptions from the Government are not necessary (see what is said below in regard to proposals for an increase of capital), and would complicate rather than simplify the relations between the Government and the shareholders.

It is proposed that the assets of the three existing banks be taken over in the following manner:

(1) The existing assets of the banks to be accurately valued.[1]
(2) The reserves of each to be levelled, so as to bear the same ratio to their respective capitals, by reducing reserves and paying away the excess to the shareholders, or by increasing the reserves out of earnings as may be determined hereafter.[2]
(3) One share in the State Bank to be issued to shareholders for each share held in the Presidency Banks.

When this has been carried out, is any further increase of capital desirable? Earlier proposals for a central bank have attached a good deal of importance to an increase of capital. But this has probably been the case because these proposals have approached the question from a somewhat different point of view. The Government have often in the past given the low capitalisation of the Presidency Banks as a reason why they did not care to deposit a large part of their free balances with these banks. This objection was applicable in hardly less degree to a central bank which was merely an amalgamation of the existing Presidency Banks. Proposals for such a central bank were coupled, therefore, with proposals for an increase of capital. But the relation of the Government to the proposed State Bank will be such, that the additional guarantee which would be afforded by the subscription of further capital by the shareholders seems scarcely necessary. The advantage of the additional capital to

[1] As they stand at present in the books of the banks, the assets are almost certainly undervalued.
[2] This will present no practical difficulty, as the ratios of reserves to capital in the three banks happen to be very nearly equal as it is.

Government would only arise in the case of the Bank's failure. In the event of so extreme a calamity, the loss by Government of £1,000,000 more or less would be, relatively, of small consequence—the other results of such an occurrence would be so far more serious. The constitution of the Bank ought to ensure its being worked on such lines that the contingency of failure in the sense of insufficiency of assets to meet liabilities, is almost inconceivable. Moreover, if failure were to result, it must be admitted, I think, that the responsibility of Government would be so great that they could scarcely remove the whole of their balances intact, leaving to the shareholders the whole burden of the loss.

The only other reason for an increase of capital is lest the Bank should suffer from an insufficiency of working capital in its daily business. I doubt if this is likely to be the case. The capital and reserves under the above scheme would amount to £5,000,000, and with the control of the paper currency and of the Government's cash balances the resources of the Bank would be very great.

If, however, it were held for any reason that some increase of capital was desirable, it would not be difficult to raise it. For example, new capital might be issued for $3\frac{3}{4}$ crores (doubling the existing capital) of which only 20 per cent would be called up. The offer of such shares to the existing shareholders *pro rata* at a premium of (say) 100 per cent[1] would be a valuable concession to them, or the issue may even be made at par if it is considered politic to offer great inducements. It may be assumed in either case that the shares would be taken up. While some such method as this might be advantageous if the object were to afford some additional guarantee for the deposits, an insufficiency of working capital might be best met by an issue of preference shares. Power could be taken in the Bank Act to issue 5 per cent preference shares to a considerable amount, only to be issued by degrees,

[1] The existing shares of the Presidency Banks stand at a premium of more than 200 per cent.

if and when required. Although the issue of preference shares may appear unusual to English bankers,[1] and is thrown out merely as a suggestion, I do not see that it is open to objection.

It would probably be wiser not to add the reserves of the existing banks to the capital and distribute them by way of a new issue of shares. Although this would mean, in effect, no more than a change in book-keeping, it is open to the objection that it would weaken, in appearance, the balance-sheet of the new bank and create an unwieldy nominal capital on which to pay dividends.

It may be objected that the proposed scheme takes no account of the fact that the market values of the shares of the three banks are not all at quite the same level.[2] It is not likely, however, that, when the assets have been revalued, the actual earning power of the banks in recent years ascertained, and the necessary readjustments made by payment of cash bonuses or otherwise, so as to bring the ratio of surplus assets to capital to the same proportion for each bank, that any appreciable difference between the position of the three banks will be apparent. If on investigation it were to appear that the real earning powers of the banks or the ratios of surplus assets to capital are substantially different, it would be proper to make allowance for this. But everything points to the reasonability of taking a broad view and treating all the banks on a uniform plan.

The question of the division of profits between the shareholders and the Government raises a problem of a good deal of difficulty. Apart from the question of prestige, the management of the note issue and of the Government balances will provide the Bank with a considerable source of revenue, likely to grow in the future, in the fruits of which the Government must obviously share.

One method would be for the Bank to pay for the prestige

---

[1] Nevertheless the 'A' shares, created this year by Barclays Bank, are not very different from preference shares.

[2] Market quotations, August 1913: Bank of Bengal, Rs. 1,700; Bank of Bombay, Rs. 1,670; Bank of Madras, Rs. 1,440. In each case the quotation is for Rs. 500 shares.

by performing certain Government services without remuneration, and for the use of the public balances by a sum dependent
on their amount and the bank rate; and for the Government to
retain the estimated profits of note issue. This method would not
be satisfactory. There is no certainty that the arrangement would
work out equitably as between the shareholders and the Government. And the chief objection to it is in the inherent difficulty
of separating the business of the Bank into compartments, and
of deciding how much of its net profit it has derived from each
source. Such a method of division of profits runs counter to
what ought to be an important principle of a central bank—the
regarding of the Bank's operations *as a whole*.

In the case of the Bank of France, the Government receives
no direct share of the profits of the Bank, but gets its benefit in
a rather complicated way by a number of indirect services and
payments. But the normal continental arrangement is one in
which the Government receives its advantage partly by the free
performance of services on the part of the Bank, partly by a tax
on the note issue, and partly by a share in the profits. The
arrangements which govern the distribution of the profits of the
Reichsbank are given, as the leading example, in Appendix C.
The details of the German plan are not suited to the Indian
conditions; but the general idea running through it is, I think,
a good one.

In the case of the Imperial Bank of India, I suggest something
of the following kind:

1. The Bank shall perform without special remuneration the
following duties:

(*a*) To purchase gold bullion at a notified rate, to issue (but
not mint) gold and silver, to manage the note issue and the
custody of the paper currency reserve.

(*b*) To accept payments and make disbursements on behalf
of the Government (Imperial and local) at all places where
the Bank has set up a branch.

(*c*) To manage the Government debt in India.

2. The Bank shall pay to the Government annually a sum equal to the present income from the *sterling*[1] investments now in the paper currency reserve, and from such investments as may be transferred from the gold standard reserve in exchange for gold (see pp. 181–2 below). The Bank shall also pay over the proceeds of any tax chargeable on excess issues of paper currency (see Regulation of Note Issue, below).

3. The annual net profit of the Bank, after due allowance for depreciation, preference dividend (if any), etc., and after deducting payments to the Government under (2) above, shall be dealt with in the following manner:

(*a*) A regular dividend of 10 per cent on the capital to be distributed among the shareholders, being made up to this amount from the reserve, if the net profits fall short of 10 per cent.

(*b*) Of the remainder, after payment of 10 per cent, two-fifths to be transferred to the reserve when this remainder is not more than 20 per cent of the capital, and one-third when it exceeds 20 per cent.

(*c*) The divisible surplus, after deductions (*a*) and (*b*), shall accrue to the shareholders up to an additional 5 per cent of their capital, and thereafter to the shareholders in the proportion one-third, and to the Government in the proportion two-thirds.[2]

The effect of these provisions is shown, in percentages of the capital, in the table on page 171.

At present the net profits are approximately 17 per cent, of which 14 per cent is divided and 3 per cent placed to reserve. Under the above scheme the Government receives no share until 15 per cent is being divided amongst the shareholders and nearly 4 per cent placed to reserve. Thus, the position of the share-

[1] For the treatment of the *rupee* investments now in the paper currency reserve, see pp. 181–2 below.

[2] Provision should probably be made for an increased proportion to Government and diminished proportions to the shareholders, and to reserve in the event of the net profits not exceeding 30 per cent.

Net profits (percentage)	Percentage to Shareholders	Percentage to Reserve	Percentage to Government
8	10	-2	—
10	10	—	—
12	$11\frac{1}{5}$	$\frac{4}{5}$	—
15	13	2	—
16	$13\frac{3}{5}$	$2\frac{2}{5}$	—
18	$14\frac{4}{5}$	$3\frac{1}{5}$	—
20	$15\frac{1}{3}$	4	$\frac{2}{3}$
22	$15\frac{11}{15}$	$4\frac{4}{5}$	$1\frac{7}{15}$
25	$16\frac{1}{3}$	6	2
28	$16\frac{14}{15}$	$7\frac{1}{5}$	$3\frac{13}{15}$
30	$17\frac{1}{3}$	8	$4\frac{2}{3}$

holders is almost certainly improved, and the Government take no appreciable part of the profits unless the control of the paper currency, the custody of the Government balances, and the prestige attaching to a state bank have the effect of raising the profits very greatly above their present level. Those who believe that the establishment of a state bank may have a very beneficial effect on Indian commerce and banking, will think it wise to facilitate such a course by a fairly generous offer to the existing shareholders.

One or two points may be added.

There has been a wise provision in the successive arrangements between the State and the Bank of France, by which the Bank is bound to open a certain number of additional branches within a given period of years. This undertaking is reckoned, as it were, as part of the payment made by the Bank for its privileges. In the case of the Bank of India, I suggest that while the Presidency Boards shall have discretion to open branches wherever they wish, they shall also be required to open them at the request of the Central Board, and that it shall be the declared policy of the Central Board to open branches, as rapidly as opportunity offers, and the necessary staff and organisation become available at most places where there is now a District Treasury.[1]

[1] These are 271 in number, while the Presidency Banks have at present only 35 branches between them. It will naturally take some time, therefore, to complete this policy of expansion.

There must also be conditions, as in the constitution of the Reichsbank, providing for the revision of relations between the shareholders and the Government.

1. The Bank Act shall be reviewed at intervals of ten years, and shall be subject to equitable revision at the option of Government or at shorter intervals with the concurrence of the shareholders.

2. At each decennial revision the Government shall be free to take over the whole goodwill and assets (including the reserve) of the Bank at 25 years' purchase of the average of the sums payable to the shareholders in the five years preceding.

The first provision may seem to place the shareholders somewhat at the mercy of the future good faith of the Government. But it is difficult to limit the authority of a sovereign power. Every institution, however purely private, is ultimately dependent on the Government's equitable regard for existing interests. From a Government which was deliberately prepared to revise the charter *inequitably*, even a Presidency Bank would hardly be safe.

The profits of an Indian bank are likely to be very fluctuating. It might be advantageous, therefore, if the shareholders were competent to form a reserve for the equalisation of dividends, which should remain wholly their own property in all circumstances. This might be invested in Government paper, or held by the Bank on payment of interest at a rate equal to the average bank rate during the year.

Regulation of the note issue

The chief object of the principles set up in 1844 to govern the Bank of England's note issue was the certain avoidance of those evils attendant on an inconvertible and inflated paper currency, of which the history of the previous half century had contained notorious instances. In attaining this object by too rigorous a set of rules the utility of the note issue was destroyed. The main function of the Bank of England's notes at the present time, apart from a very few special types of transaction, is to supply the joint stock banks with a convenient form of bullion certificate more easily handled than bullion itself. The inconveniences which would otherwise have arisen have been avoided, however, by the great development of the cheque system.

Abroad the Bank of England's principles have found no imitators. But in India they were adopted in 1860 and still persist. The effect of their rigour is not moderated by any widespread use of cheques. Many authorities are now agreed that some development of elasticity in the note issue is, therefore, required.

When we look to the experience of other countries, of which much has now accumulated, as to how this elasticity can be best obtained, the following alternatives are before us:

(i) A fiduciary issue fixed in *amount*, as in the case of the Bank of England, but with power to exceed it (until the cash falls to a certain minimum *proportion*) on payment of a tax. This is the system in Germany and elsewhere.

(ii) A fiduciary issue fixed in *proportion* to the note issue.

(iii) As in (ii), but with power to exceed the proportion on payment of a tax.

(iv) No rules but the discretion of the bank of issue to govern the amount of the reserve, but a limitation to the aggregate issue of notes. This is the system in France, where the maximum placed on the aggregate issue has been raised from time to time whenever the actual issue showed signs of approaching it.

In the choice of a system for India, the fourth of these alternatives can be put on one side. The second ought to be neglected also. For on this system, when once the prescribed proportion has been reached, not a single additional note can be encashed without a breach of the Bank Act; for if one note is cashed, the fiduciary issue, being the same as before while the cash is less, must exceed the prescribed proportion.

Our choice lies, therefore, between (i) and (iii). Between these two there is not really any very substantial difference. For when the *amount* is fixed from time to time, it is naturally fixed so as to be some reasonable *proportion* of the total. In the case of a country with a rapidly growing note issue, the advantage lies, I think, with (iii); otherwise frequent legislative changes will be required. Germany adopted (i) in the first instance, because it seemed less of a break with the Bank of England's system; but, as their note issue has developed, frequent legislative changes have been necessary to raise the amount of the untaxed fiduciary total, so as to make it a reasonable proportion of the whole circulation.

In what follows, therefore, I propose for India a variety of (iii):

Proposed rules to govern the Indian note issue

1. Up to 40 per cent of the gross[1] circulation of notes may be held in a fiduciary[2] form without payment of tax, the balance being held in cash (gold or rupees).

2. Up to 60 per cent may be held in a fiduciary form, on payment of a tax to the Government at the rate of 5 per cent per annum on the excess of the fiduciary issue above 40 per cent of the total circulation.

3. The proportion, in a fiduciary form, shall *never* exceed 60 per cent, i.e., the proportion of cash shall never fall below 40 per cent, save that the Secretary of State in Council shall have authority, in emergency, to suspend the provision of the Bank Act which enjoins this.

The propriety of the particular percentages here proposed is, of course, a separate question from the propriety of the principle. In judging of it, we must bear in mind that, while the percentage given in (i), i.e., 40 per cent, is what one would expect the Bank to work up to not infrequently, the percentage given in (2), i.e., 60 per cent, is an outside limit, which the Bank would never

[1] This is interpreted below to include the notes held by the Bank itself in reserve, as well as the 'active' circulation.
[2] *What* fiduciary form, is discussed below.

work near to except, possibly, on occasions of dangerous crisis. For if it ever worked near to 60 per cent, the encashment of a few notes would put it in danger of having to apply for a suspension of the Bank Act. Thus, if the absolute maximum is fixed in the form of a *proportion*, plenty of margin must be allowed, and the maximum proportion must be fixed well above what would be thought the highest reasonable proportion for normal times. If comparisons are to be made, this figure is considerably more cautious than the corresponding figure for the Reichsbank. The legal maximum proportion for their fiduciary issue is 67 per cent, but as the so-called 'cash' includes some items which are not cash at all, the corresponding figure may be put at 70 per cent. In September 1911 the Reichsbank actually worked up to 57 per cent, holding only 43 per cent in cash at the end of that month. In September 1912 they worked up to 50 per cent. This year the authorities have felt that to work up to such a figure in comparatively normal circumstances may be incautious, and they have somewhat strengthened their position. But no one has suggested that they should lower the proportion up to which they are *legally entitled* to work. I am clear, therefore, that it would be unwise, in the case of India, to fix the legal maximum below 60 per cent (i.e., to fix the legal minimum of cash above 40 per cent). Plenty of 'play' ought to be allowed for occasions of emergency, when any suggestion, even, of a suspension of the Bank Act might provoke panic. But it is equally clear that the *normal* maximum ought to be well below this amount. For this, reliance must inevitably be placed on the judgment of those in authority at the Bank, and not on legal safeguards.

The propriety of the figure, namely 40 per cent, fixed in (1) is much more open to question. It partly depends on how much tax is to be paid on excess issues. I believe that it would be safe to allow the Bank to work up to this amount before any pressure need be put on the authorities, other than their own judgment, to raise the bank rate beyond 5 per cent. But no principle is involved in the choice of this particular figure.

The existing fiduciary issue was 24 per cent of the *average* gross and 26 per cent of the *minimum* gross circulation in 1911–12; and the corresponding figures (estimated) in 1912–13 were 21 per cent and 24 per cent. Precise comparison with the Reichsbank is not possible, because at any given date their fiduciary issue is a fixed amount and not a fixed proportion, but a study of the figures suggests that 40 per cent is about the equivalent of German practice.

We may take the present normal minimum gross circulation at about 60 crores of which from 42 to 45 crores is active (i.e., excluding Government Treasuries and Presidency Banks); of this 14 crores is now held invested. The notes now held in Government Treasuries, as well as those now held in the Presidency banks, would be held in the reserve of the new bank, although, presumably, the former would not be maintained at their present magnitude. We may assume that the Bank would hold its whole cash reserve, apart from till money, in notes (see below, pp. 181–2).

Now, if in the slack season there were 40 crores in circulation and 20 crores in the Bank's own reserve, the fiduciary portion could rise without payment of any tax to 24 crores.

If in the busy season the active circulation rose to 45 crores and the reserve fell to 15 crores, the fiduciary portion could rise, as before, to 24 crores without payment of tax, and 4 crores higher on payment of a 5 per cent tax on the excess 4 crores, a safe margin being still preserved below the permissible maximum of

(In Crores of Rupees)

Active circulation	Notes in reserve	Fiduciary issue	Cash	Percentage of cash to active circulation
40	20	24	36	90
45	15	24	36	80
45	15	28	32	71
50	20	28	42	84
50	20	30	40	80

36 crores. Recent experience shows that the circulation would frequently rise higher than this.

This scheme would, therefore, put very large funds at the disposal of the Bank. Nor would any risk be run of inability to encash the notes, as is shown in the table above, which gives the percentage of cash to active circulation in each of the hypothetical cases instanced above and in some others also.

Further, probably 10 to 15 crores of the reserve held against the fiduciary issue (see below), would be held in sterling securities or sterling bills, capable of being realised in London. Thus more than 100 per cent of the active circulation would be held in cash or in a sterling form.

Finally the existence, quite apart from the paper currency reserve, of £20,000,000 in gold coin (if proposals to this effect are adopted) in the gold standard reserve must be borne in mind when the possibility of grave emergencies is in question. In all ordinary times the existence of the gold standard reserve should be treated as irrelevant to the proper magnitude of the paper currency reserve; but against very grave emergencies, when the Government's guarantee of the note issue (see below) may possibly be required, the coin in the gold standard reserve would provide a temporary bulwark, pending the realisation of the sterling securities.

It would hardly be reasonable, I think, to criticise the above scheme on the ground of insecurity to the holders of notes.[1] These figures also bring out the essential wastefulness of the present system. More than 100 per cent of the *active* circulation is now held in cash.

So far merely the amount of the fiduciary issue has been discussed, and not the form of the securities to be held against it. At present 10 crores are held in rupee paper and 4 crores in Consols. It is suggested below that 6 crores in Consols should be transferred, in exchange for sovereigns, from the gold standard

---

[1] The normal proportion of cash to active circulation would be higher than in most European systems of note issue, higher even than in the case of the Bank of France.

reserve. This would make 20 crores in all of permanent investment, and this is certainly the highest figure at which the permanent investment ought to stand at present; perhaps it is too high.

The security for the fiduciary issue, beyond the 20 crores of permanent investment, should consist of approved securities (Government paper and possibly a few others) temporarily transferred from those held by the Bank on its own account or pledged with it by its customers, and of bills of exchange, both sterling and rupee. The securities, pledged with the reserve, should be taken at a safe margin below their market value.

For the fluctuating part of the fiduciary reserve, bills of exchange having two good names to them are far preferable to securities, if they can be obtained. They come into existence precisely at the moment when there is most need for additional currency and are liquidated when this need comes to an end. Securities, on the other hand, must be carried by somebody all the year round. Moreover the amount of securities forthcoming is likely to be limited. Suppose a bank or a firm can get money at 5 per cent on the security of government paper and use it at 6 per cent for three months in the year, then on the average of the year they make about $4 + \frac{1}{4}$ ($6 - 5$) per cent, i.e., $4\frac{1}{4}$ per cent. It suits a bank to hold some government paper. But the above calculation shows that a point would soon come when this would not pay. Bills, on the other hand, do not lock up money all the year round. To discount at 6 per cent and rediscount at 5 is a much more profitable transaction for a bank than the transaction outlined above.

Experience elsewhere shows that the elasticity of notes based on government paper is very limited, and that bills are the essentially suitable backing to that part of the note issue which is fluctuating and called into existence in the busy season only. The amount of government paper which it suits the banks to hold, since it must be held all the year round, is not suddenly expansible; nor is it easy for them suddenly to liquidate their holdings, or, from the Government's point of view, desirable that they should. The American note issue, which is based on government paper, has proved hopelessly inelastic, and it is one of the principal objects of the projected reforms in that country to introduce an elasticity based on the discount of trade bills.[1] In all European countries bills are the pivot on which the whole meaning and utility of the note issue essentially turns.

The only question is how far bills of a kind suitable to the portfolio of a State Bank would be forthcoming in India. It might be a matter of time before they would be available to the full extent which is desirable.

This leads us to the question of the relations of the State Bank to other banking institutions. The State Bank ought to aim, I think, to the greatest possible extent at *rediscount* business. So far as possible, that is to say, it should aim at filling its portfolio with trade bills which have passed through the hands of another bank or shroff or marwari of high standing and have received their endorsements. This seems to me to be the right channel through which the accommodation newly available should filter down to the great mass of Indian traders. The State Bank would have on its list certain banks and private native financiers of high standing who would be amongst its regular customers and for whom in general it would be prepared to rediscount freely.

The power of rediscount might prove a powerful aid to the development of Indian joint stock banks on sounder lines than

[1] The following quotation from a recent communication to *The Standard* about the less well-known experience of Cape Colony is instructive: 'The Cape legal tender issue represents the only attempt to establish a scientific system in South Africa, but it becomes increasingly clear that this system is not suited to satisfy the larger requirements of the Union. The application of this system to the Union would necessitate, on the part of the banks of issue, the investment of additional funds in Government securities as cover, which fact, in its turn, would narrow the already small margin between deposits and advances, and thus lessen the bank's power to grant facilities. This system has already proved inelastic, despite its limited range, a fact in itself proving its unsuitability for adoption as the note currency of the Union. Despite the demand for currency by trade during the last few years, the Cape circulation has rarely exceeded £1,200,000, although as long ago as 1891 experts placed its natural level at £2,000,000...In short, the banks are finding more profitable means of investment for their funds than Government securities, and the Cape note circulation consequently does not expand.'

hitherto, and involve at the same time a valuable check on them. For, on admitting a bank to the rediscount list, the local manager of the Presidency branch would require, from time to time, to examine somewhat carefully, in confidence, the bank's position; and the risk of losing its position on the rediscount list might act, to some extent, as a deterrent to rash banking.

Apart from this check, the creation of a rediscount market would render such banks most vital assistance. Indeed I am doubtful how far it is possible for them to develop on really sound lines without it. The smaller the bank, the larger the number of its branches, and the less developed in banking habits the country in which it acts, the higher in proportion to its resources ought its free cash reserves to be. If a newly founded Indian joint stock bank were to keep sufficiently large cash reserves to provide against all reasonable contingencies, it could scarcely hope to earn adequate dividends. At present, apart from cash, such a bank is very short of modes of so employing its resources as to keep them fairly liquid. There is no one to whom they can safely lend at call. A bank which pays from 4 to 6 per cent to its depositors cannot be expected to hold large quantities of high-class investments yielding barely 4 per cent. Such bills as they may get hold of must probably be held until maturity. Inevitably they tend to lock up in industrial enterprise a higher proportion of their resources than is wise. Some recent failures seem to be due to a different cause, not so much to the locking up resources as to advances against *worthless* security. But in really bad times comparatively well conducted institutions may find themselves in difficulty, not because their security is worthless, but because it is temporarily unrealisable.

If a State Bank were to encourage the transaction of business by means of trade bills, through making bills easy things against which to obtain advances, native banks might hope in time to obtain more of them for their portfolios and would have something which they could turn into cash at need by rediscount.

In this matter of the development of the use of trade bills, however, I am looking not so much to the immediate future as to the ultimate development of Indian banking practice on sound and well-tried principles.

Two further points in regard to the note issue remain for discussion.

The notes must, I think, remain Government notes in the sense that the Government, in addition to the Bank, guarantees them. In this case they could preserve their present form and appearance unchanged, i.e., they could remain, as they are at present, Government promissory notes payable on demand at certain places in legal tender money.[1]

This should allay suspicion without laying on the Government any real additional burden. For if the Bank were, by a violent chance, to get into difficulties, there cannot be the least doubt that the Government would have to maintain the solvency of the note issue whether they had formally promised to do so or not.

The remote contingency of the Government's having to give temporary effect to this guarantee could be properly laid on the gold standard reserve. For, although an exchange crisis changes the form of the gold standard reserve, it in no way affects the total amount of legal tender money held there.

The Government's guarantee carries with it as a necessary consequence—probably desirable on general grounds anyhow—the allocation of specific assets as cover for the note issue and a division in the Bank's published accounts between the issue and banking departments. Rather oddly, this feature of the Bank of England's arrangements has not been generally imitated abroad.

[1] In 1900 the Government of India in a despatch (18 January 1900) to the Secretary of State regarding proposals for the transfer of the note issue to a central bank, wrote: 'As any change in the form of the note might involve temporary contraction in the paper circulation, as change in such matters is peculiarly undesirable in India, and as the reserve would be under the supervision and control of Government, we should have no objection to the notes continuing in their present form, with the possible addition of the name of the bank and the counter signature of the officer employed to supervise the reserve. We are of opinion, though not forgetting the objections that have been previously raised to such a course in India, and indeed recently adverted upon by so high an authority as Lord Northbrook, that there is nothing in the peculiar circumstances of India to prevent the note issue being transferred to a bank. We are, moreover, disposed to believe that it is through the agency of a bank that the note issue may have a larger development in India.'

In the normal continental type, no distinction is made between the reserve held against the note issue and the reserve held against other banking liabilities. Legally, the whole cash reserve is treated as being cover for the notes; and no notes are held by the Bank itself, so that there is no distinction between total and active circulation. Among its assets the Bank must hold a sufficient quantity of security of a kind which is legal backing for the fiduciary part of the circulation; but no part of the Bank's securities is specifically allocated to the note issue.

In this respect the Bank of England provides India with the better model. In the published accounts a distinction should be made between the issue and the banking departments thus (with hypothetical figures):[1]

Issue department

	Crores		Crores
Gross circulation of notes		Government book debt	10
outstanding	65	Consols	10
		Security pledged with issue department:	
		Approved securities } Bills of exchange }	6
		Gold	15
		Rupees	24
			65

Banking department

		Crores
Capital, etc.	Notes in reserve	20
Deposits, etc.	Investments	
	Bills	
	Advances, etc.	

Several details in this require explanation:

1. The 'Government book debt' corresponds to the 10 crores of Government rupee paper now held in the paper currency

---

[1] In a continental bank these two accounts would be merged; the circulation of notes would appear as 45; no notes would appear on the asset side of the banking account; and the investments and bills in the two departments would be lumped together. This would make the proportion of cash to circulation appear to be 87 per cent, instead of 60 per cent as in the above. This difference in account-keeping, which makes the position in continental banks appear stronger than it really is, must be kept in mind in making comparisons.

reserve. I propose that this rupee paper should be cancelled, and be replaced by a Government book debt bearing no interest. This corresponds to the Government book debt due to the Bank of England, and avoids fluctuations in accordance with the market value of rupee paper.

2. The Consols (four crores from the existing paper currency reserve and six crores from the gold standard reserve in exchange for gold) would be taken over at market value. The initial book value should, in the event of subsequent depreciation, be written down to market value annually, but should not be written up, in the event of appreciation, until market value exceeds book value by 10 per cent, and then only by the excess beyond 10 per cent.

3. The approved securities pledged with the issue department should show a margin of 5 per cent; the bills of exchange should be taken at par, less rebate.

4. So long as the fiduciary issue does not exceed the untaxed maximum, it will make no difference to the Bank's profits whether they make up the gross circulation to the untaxed maximum by transfer of securities to the issue department and increase the notes in reserve correspondingly, or let the gross circulation fall below the untaxed maximum by a reduction of the notes in reserve. When the untaxed maximum is passed it will pay the Bank better to let the notes in reserve fall somewhat, as they will avoid payment of tax by the amount of the fall. This circumstance is, no doubt, the explanation of the continental method of account-keeping. But, provided the Bank is governed by caution, the extent to which they will feel willing to reduce their notes in reserve in order to avoid payment of tax will be no more than is reasonable. And even if the notes in reserve sank to zero, the position, measured by percentage of cash to note issue, would still be as strong as in a continental bank.

5. As the Government guarantees the note issue, the securities and cash belonging or pledged to the issue department will become their property, so far as required for meeting liability

on the notes, in the event of difficulties. But apart from the interest on the 10 crores of Consols, the annual profits of the note issue (and any excess in the value of the assets of the issue department over its liabilities) are the property of the Bank.

In concluding this section, a word may be said about the circle system. There seems no reason why it should not be abolished. There should be a legal right of encashment of notes of all denominations at a small number of prescribed offices of the Bank; and all other offices, though under no legal obligation, should be authorised to encash notes whenever they can do so without embarrassment. It is to be hoped that, as time goes on, the occasions when they would not find it convenient to encash them would become increasingly rare. The notes are, of course, legal tender, and must be accepted *in payment* by all branches of the Bank.[1]

The London office and remittance

With this section we enter on a debatable part of the subject, which is largely independent of the rest.

No important object would be served by allowing the Bank to compete with the exchange banks in attracting deposits in London. Nor is there any clear advantage (sufficient to counterbalance the opposition which would be aroused) in allowing it to enter into the regular business of trade remittance by buying trade bills in both directions. Such competition with the exchange banks is in no way necessary to the prime objects of a state bank.

But it is desirable that the Bank should be free to carry out the Secretary of State's remittance in the most satisfactory and economical way, and to hold balances in London and use them in the London market. It is also desirable that the Bank should not be unduly fettered in providing private remittance on London for its Indian customers. If at some up-country branch of the

[1] Cf. §18 of the German Bank Act:
The Reichsbank is required to redeem its notes to bearers in German currency (N.B., in silver or gold at the option of the Bank): (*a*) At the main office in Berlin, and (*b*) at its branch offices *as far as the cash and money exigencies of the latter permit.*

State Bank a customer wished to buy a draft on London for £50, it would be absurd if the Bank had to refuse to do this business for him.

The London office of the State Bank would be, therefore, a comparatively small affair. It would have no direct dealings with the public, only with the Secretary of State, the money market, and other banks. The Secretary of State would continue to do his ordinary banking business with the Bank of England and to maintain a balance there; and it would be the business of the London office of the State Bank to keep him in funds. The main point for discussion is as to what the best machinery will be for carrying out the remittance transactions wherewith to keep the Secretary of State in funds.

The methods of effecting remittance are two: by selling drafts on India in London, as at present, and by buying sterling bills in India. There will be great advantages in leaving both these methods open to the Bank. The due safeguarding of the interests of existing banks is not incompatible with this. The State Bank should be precluded from buying sterling bills in India, *except from other banks*; its dealing in sterling bills, that is to say, should be entirely a rediscount business of bills bearing the endorsement of another bank. The sale of rupee drafts in London might be by tender as at present, but it would probably be a better plan for the London office of the State Bank to quote rates for bills and transfers to applicants. In this matter, also, the State Bank should be confined to dealing with other banks and not direct with the trading public, or (as an alternative, if this proposal should be deemed a hardship to certain important houses which tender direct for Council bills at present and do not, as it is, do their business through an exchange bank) should sell for not less than a lakh at a time.[1]

The exchange banks would thus have two ways of putting themselves in funds in India, corresponding to the two ways

[1] At present, however, 'specials' are often sold by the Council for much less sums than this.

open to the State Bank of providing themselves with funds in London. They could rediscount sterling bills in India or buy (as at present) rupee drafts in London. The existence of the first method, as well as the second, might sometimes prove a real advantage to them. The State Bank would naturally quote rates for rediscount in India and for the sale of drafts in London which would make it worth the while of the exchange banks to take the course most convenient at the moment to the State Bank. If at a season when the exchange banks were wanting funds in India, the Secretary of State was also in need of additional cash in London, inducement would be offered to the exchange banks to buy drafts; and if the Secretary of State's needs were mainly in the future, inducement would be offered to the exchange banks to rediscount sterling bills in India, which could be held by the State Bank until the Secretary of State wanted the money.

The price which would be paid for sterling bills in India by this State Bank would necessarily be governed by the London rate of discount for such bills taken in conjunction with the rate of exchange, not by the local rate for rupee bills. Thus, if the London rate of discount for three months' sterling bills of this type were $4\frac{1}{2}$ per cent and exchange stood at $1s\ 4\frac{1}{16}d$, the corresponding rupee price for three months' sterling bills offered in India would be approximately $1s\ 4\frac{1}{4}d$ per rupee. Any concession on this price offered by the State Bank in India, so long as its London office was able to enforce $1s\ 4\frac{1}{16}d$ as the rate for telegraphic transfers on India, would be an inducement to the exchange banks to rediscount in London and then buy telegraphic transfers there. At the same time, such a policy might be advantageous to the State Bank itself. As the London rate of discount is frequently below the India rate, this policy would sometimes involve rediscounting sterling bills at what would be, in effect, a lower rate than was being allowed on rupee bills. But this could afford no reasonable ground of complaint to Indian merchants. For the money thus employed would not have been available in any case for rupee advances. The alternative to the use of these funds for the rediscount of sterling bills would be the remittance of them to London through the encashment of telegraphic transfers and their employment on the London market.

There can be no question that the method outlined above is the most perfect method of effecting remittance from the purely financial point of view, and also that it will be more easy of favourable explanation to the public, for the following reasons. At present the train of events is a very complicated one. The exchange banks buy sterling bills in India, which they bring to London and rediscount, in part, in the London money market. With the proceeds of rediscounting they buy Council drafts or transfers from the Secretary of State, which, when encashed in India, replace the funds which the banks have paid out in originally buying the sterling bills. The Secretary of State lends the proceeds of selling Councils, until such time as he has need of them for his disbursements, either to the exchange banks themselves or to other constituents of the London money market, by whom the money is largely used for rediscounting bills either for the Indian exchange banks or for similar institutions working in other countries. If, on the other hand, as is proposed above, the State Bank were to rediscount sterling bills for the exchange banks in India and hold the bills until the money was actually wanted by the Secretary of State, the whole (or nearly the whole) of the floating sterling resources would be directly employed in the assistance of India's foreign trade, instead of assisting it in a very slight and indirect way through general help given to the London money market. No one could justly maintain that money was being diverted away to purposes wholly unconnected with India. In the second place the floating sterling resources would earn a higher rate of interest than at present, partly through the elimination of an intermediate profit and risk, and partly because three-month bills could safely be taken in many cases in which money is now lent by the broker for only six weeks.[1] And, in the

---

[1] Because, if it turned out that the money was wanted after six weeks, the bills could be rediscounted at the Bank of England. At present money is not lent for more than six

third place, these advantages would not be counterbalanced by any increase of risk. Whenever it turned out that the Secretary of State was in need of funds somewhat sooner than had been anticipated, it would always be possible to rediscount at the Bank of England on favourable terms sterling bills, domiciled in London, and bearing the endorsements both of the State Bank of India and an exchange bank. Apart from the ease of rediscount, such bills would afford the finest possible security, and the Bank could only suffer loss in the event of the simultaneous insolvency of the Indian drawer, the London acceptor, and the exchange bank through which the bill had been negotiated.[1]

This proposal is in no sense novel, and is merely an adaptation to Indian conditions of the practice most usually followed by foreign countries. A foreign bank or government, which wishes to keep floating resources in a sterling form, generally utilises for the purpose so far as it can its portfolio of sterling bills negotiated in its own country.

The exchange banks might be further guaranteed against ordinary trade competition by restricting the State Bank in its London rediscount business to the Bank of England.

The above proposals together with a few further points of detail can be summarised as follows:

1. The Indian offices of the State Bank shall be permitted to supply their own customers with sterling remittance, but in the purchase of sterling *trade* bills they shall be confined to the rediscount of such bills for other banks.

weeks and seldom for so long, because of the remote contingency, which always exists, that it might be wanted by them. In giving evidence, the Secretary of State's broker seemed to be unaware that the *average* rate for three months' money is higher than the *average* rate for six weeks' money (i.e., that a man who always lent for three months would make more on the average than a man who always lent for six weeks); but this is a well-known fact, or, if not well known, easily ascertained by reference to the records of recent years.

[1] The smallness of the risk involved is well illustrated by some figures which have been calculated for the Reichsbank. They estimate that since their foundation in 1875 their average loss on bills is well under one-3,000th part. Many of these bills are for small amounts, and without the extra guarantee of rediscount, both drawer and acceptor are in the same country and subject to similar contingencies, and the period in question is long enough to include several occasions of crisis. The average loss on rediscounted sterling bills could hardly amount to as much as one-10,000th part.

2. The London office of the State Bank shall have no direct dealings as a banker with the general public. Its business shall be confined to:

(*a*) the sale to other banks[1] of drafts and telegraphic transfers payable at its Indian offices; (*b*) the rediscount of sterling bills at the Bank of England; (*c*) borrowing for short periods from the Bank of England; (*d*) the loan of funds on the London money market; (*e*) the replenishment of the Secretary of State's funds at the Bank of England; (*f*) the flotation of sterling loans on behalf of the Secretary of State.

To these functions another might possibly be added, namely, the management of the Secretary of State's sterling and rupee debt in London. But there are considerable advantages in leaving this with the Bank of England if that institution is prepared to abate its now somewhat excessive charges.

It remains to discuss the management of the London office.

There is some slight danger that through its close connection with the Secretary of State and the weight of authority on its Board, this office might tend to become too influential and important. This is sufficiently guarded against perhaps by the close limitations of its functions. It will have authority, of course, in regard to purely London questions, such as the employment of balances in London and advice as to the issue of sterling loans, but the only Indian question in regard to which it will be in a position to give authoritative advice will be the purchase in India of sterling bills.

The London Board will to a certain extent take the place of the present Finance Committee of the Secretary of State's Council, and may be expected to be in much closer touch with the India Office than is likely or desirable as between the Central Board and the Government of India. Its creation will fit in very well with Lord Crewe's recent proposals for a reorganisation of his Council, on which it will not be easy in future, as I understand his scheme, to find room for more than one financier. Room can

---

[1] See also the alternative proposal, above.

be found on the London Board for those other financial advisers, the addition of whom to the Finance Committee has been advocated by several witnesses.

The London Board, which would not include the manager of the London office, might consist of the Financial Secretary at the India Office (or the Permanent Under-Secretary or Assistant Under-Secretary when either of these is possessed of financial experience), the Member of the Secretary of State's Council specially attached (under Lord Crewe's scheme) to the Financial Department, a representative of one of the larger mercantile houses concerned in the India trade, and two other members of financial or banking experience (one of whom perhaps might be, in general, primarily of Indian experience and the other of London experience).

Other functions of the Bank

Some of the functions already discussed, together with one or two others, may be summarised:

1. The Bank will perform the same functions that the Presidency banks perform now, with relaxation, in some particulars, of the existing restrictions.

2. It will hold as Government banker, without payment of interest, the balances now held in the Reserve Treasuries and in London, with the exception of an emergency reserve of £1,000,000 which would be retained by Government in India (as proposed by Mr Abrahams), and of that part of the London balances held directly in the name of the Secretary of State at the Bank of England. It will also hold the Government balances at all places where the Bank sets up a branch.

3. It will manage the note issue on terms outlined above, and, with the exception of certain payments to Government, will enjoy its profits.

4. It will manage the Government debt in India; and it would probably prove advantageous to entrust it with the issue of new rupee loans.

5. Its functions in regard to remittance and the duties of the London office have been discussed above.

The following duties should *not* be entrusted to it:

(i) The management of the mint;

(ii) The custody of the gold standard reserve.

But when the gold standard reserve is brought into play for the support of exchange, the Bank should act, under the Government's orders, as the Government's agent in the matter.

Something may be said in this connection about the position of the gold standard reserve in the event of the establishment of a State Bank.

In the immediate past the stability of the rupee has been supported both by the gold standard reserve and by the paper currency reserve. This has been necessary because the former reserve has not been quite strong enough to bear the burden by itself. But as a permanent arrangement it ought not to be necessary; or, at any rate, the paper currency reserve ought to be used for this purpose to only a limited degree. The ideal to be worked up to is a state of affairs in which the gold standard reserve is held by the Secretary of State for the *main* purpose of supporting exchange and is adequate to this purpose, and in which the paper currency reserve is held by the Bank and is controlled *mainly* with an eye to the internal affairs of India. The gold standard reserve, in this case, should be governed by ultra-conservative methods, being held in gold to a far greater extent than at present; while the paper currency reserve should be ruled by more commercial considerations, and a much smaller proportion than at present held in actual cash.

Although the custody of the gold standard reserve and the ultimate responsibility for the maintenance of exchange must remain, in the most direct manner, with the Secretary of State, he should use the Bank as his agent in the actual sale in India of sterling drafts on London on the occasions in which the gold standard reserve is brought into play for the purpose for which it exists.

The moment at which this reserve is brought into play ought

not to depend, I think, upon anyone's discretion, but should be governed by rule. There should be a notification, that is to say, that the Government will at all times sell, through the Bank as its agent, sterling bills on London at $1s\ 3\frac{15}{16}d$.[1] When advantage is taken of this it will be the business of the Secretary of State to put the London office of the Bank into funds wherewith to encash the bills thus sold.

The gold standard reserve, while primarily held for the support of exchange, should not be legally ear-marked for this sole purpose. It can properly be regarded (see above, p. 177) as constituting, under certain conditions, an ultimate safeguard and guarantee of the convertibility of the note issue.[2]

General advantages of a State Bank

The outline of the proposed Bank's functions and of its draft constitution is now complete. A number of the advantages which are claimed for it have been developed in passing. It will be useful to summarise these, and to dwell on certain other points, not less important, which do not so naturally arise when it is the Bank's constitution which is the matter in hand.

There are first of all the direct advantages to Government. These affect questions which have been the special business of the Commission. The chief of them may be enumerated:

(i) The existing 'Independent Treasury System', by which, whenever the Government balances are swollen, deliberately or not, large sums are taken off the money market, is done away by the removal of the cause of this system, namely, the absence of a large public or semi-public institution with which large balances could be safely and properly deposited, together with the difficulty of employing civil servants in a policy of discretionary loans out of the balances.

---

[1] This is $\frac{1}{32}d$ higher than the present figure, and would diminish by that amount the possible fluctuation in the rupee. I think it would be safe and desirable to meet to this extent the proposals of several witnesses.

[2] The propriety of this might be brought out further by showing that in a future crisis the convertibility of the note issue and the support of exchange may not always prove to be entirely distinct problems.

(ii) The objections to holding large sums at loan for short periods in the London money market are avoided by the method of dealing with sterling resources proposed in Part VI [*The London Office and remittance*].

(iii) A bank, responsible for the management of the note issue, has greater opportunities than are open to Government for pushing the circulation of notes and for popularising them by an increase in the facilities available for convertibility.

(iv) The responsibility of Government officials for a variety of financial and semi-financial business is greatly reduced by handing over to a bank all questions of balances, note issue, remittance, and loans on the London market.

(v) The Government has at its command the services of officers of the highest position, trained in financial and banking business, instead of civil servants who, however full of adaptability and intelligence, have been selected and trained mainly for other purposes.

(vi) A buffer is placed between the Secretary of State and vexatious criticism on small details of financial business.

Next come the immediate advantages to the business world:

(i) In addition to the partial release of Government balances through their deposit in a central institution, a considerable amount of funds is made available by the reform of the note issue.

(ii) The present wide fluctuations of the bank rate and its normal high level in the busy season may be somewhat moderated.

(iii) The increase of branches, which the union of Government and banking business should promote, would gradually bring sound banking facilities to many parts of India, where they are now almost entirely wanting, both directly and by supplying a basis, in reliance on which private and co-operative banking could be built up.

(iv) The introduction of the rediscount facilities, while probably not of the first importance in the immediate future, might greatly aid the eventual development of Indian banking on the most desirable lines which European experience has evolved.

At this point something may be said about the bank rate question, and the possibility of obtaining substantially the same results without the interposition of a state bank.

India suffers not from a high *average* bank rate, but from a wide range of fluctuation and a high *maximum* bank rate. If the *average* bank rate were high, this would mean that the normal return to capital under conditions of least risk was high; and this could not possibly be cured by any monetary device. But a high temporary bank rate, due to the increased volume of cash temporarily required for moving the crops, ought to be capable of amelioration by introducing an elasticity into the credit currency. It is important, however, not to underestimate the magnitude of the problem. Several witnesses have maintained that a loan of three crores made by the Government from its balances or from the paper currency reserve would be a sufficient cure for high bank rates. I am convinced that this is a serious misapprehension of the facts. What is true is that at any moment an unexpected and sudden loan of three crores by the Government would break the current bank rate. If borrowers and lenders had adjusted themselves to an expectation of 8 per cent it would be reasonable to hold that a sudden offer by the Government of three crores would bring the rate down to 6 per cent or less. But this is not the standpoint from which to consider proposals for permanent policy. What present sources of supply would fail and what new sources of demand would spring up, if there were a reasonable expectation beforehand of borrowing in the busy season at 6 per cent?[1] Three crores is a very small percentage of the present transactions; it is not $1\frac{1}{2}$ per cent of the value of the exports; it is barely half of the normal *annual* addition to India's banking resources; and to expect great consequences from the loan of it is to take a short-sighted and

[1] The rate for money is largely determined by the *fringe* of borrowers and lenders who are specially sensitive to any change of conditions. If, for example, the normal maximum rate for money in India was to fall, some up-country traders could afford to pay the cultivator a little more and might hold the goods a little longer, since they would not be forced by high rates for money to hurry the goods forward to a place where they could form a basis for sterling credit.

superficial view of the causes which really determine the value of money. The proposals made above in regard to a fiduciary issue of notes would have a more substantial effect; but I think it would be optimistic to expect even from them a normal maximum of 6 per cent. Their eventual efficacy is largely bound up with the future development of the use of notes.

This leads us to compare proposals, contingent on the establishment of a State Bank, with proposals for the loan of Government funds to the existing Presidency Banks. If the loans contemplated are comparatively small, there need be no difficulty in lending them on the security of government paper, and the problem of the terms on which they should be lent, while not quite easy of solution, ought not to prove insuperable. But small loans could not, of course, have large consequences. Though they would, *pro tanto*, be useful and employ funds which are now wastefully idle, to offer them as a cure of high bank rate or of the existing faults in the Indian financial system is to trifle with the problem. If, on the other hand, fairly *large* loans are contemplated, other objections rise to importance. It is uncertain (for reasons given in Section V [*Regulation of the note issue*]) whether government paper would be forthcoming in large quantities as security for temporary loans, and even more uncertain whether it is desirable to encourage the holding of a large amount of government paper in this way. The Government could only get their funds back as a lender, by spoiling their market as a borrower. Yet there are great difficulties in lending by a Government department against the really desirable security, namely trade bills. It would take them to a wholly unfamiliar region, and require them to exercise an unaccustomed discretion.

The most serious objection still remains. It would be a perilous policy for the Government to lend on a scale sufficient to influence the bank rate, and for it to remain nevertheless wholly without responsibility for the bank rate policy. The ultimate lender and the ultimate controller of the credit currency cannot safely remain aloof from the control of the bank rate. So long as the

Government do not lend and there is virtually no credit currency, the Government can maintain this aloofness from banking. As I have said already, existing arrangements are deeply conditioned by the fact of this aloofness. But if the Government are to lend their balances and to introduce, under their own control and discretion, a proper elasticity into the credit currency, and if they are to do these things on a sufficient scale to make any real difference, then they cannot ignore considerations of bank rate policy. Such a scheme involves an exercise of judgment on the part of Government officials in high matters of banking policy, without these officials having access to any first-hand banking experience. The Government is driven, therefore, to call in the assistance of a State Bank to do these things for them and to be responsible at the same time for the bank rate.

These considerations were apprehended by the Government of India when they put forward proposals for a central bank in 1900. After mentioning the suggestion of a note issue on the German model, they add:

> Theoretically we admit that the system might be grafted upon the present management of the paper currency by Government. But a bank would be able to measure the need and extent of accommodation much better than a Government could hope to do, and we believe that in all countries where it has been adopted, the agency of a bank has been chosen for working this system. Moreover, in India recourse in any form to a currency reserve in the hands of Government would encourage the tendency to look to and rely upon Government exclusively. From this point of view there would be particular objections to applying the system to the currency reserve while it remained under Government control.

The last point seems to be a very sound one. Whenever the bank rate was high, there would be a clamour that the Government were not lending all they might.

Proposals for direct loans to the Presidency Banks, on a very moderate scale, from the Government balances and the paper currency reserve may serve to meet certain of the more superficial criticisms. The Government will have an answer to the charge that they keep their whole surplus in a barren form. Indeed, so far, the proposals are good; and for every reason they will commend themselves to the lovers of appearance. But as an attempt to solve the real problems of the Indian financial situation, I do not think they are to be regarded seriously. They are incapable of future development, since they depend for their justification on the trifling and innocuous character of their consequences. And they are right off the line of banking evolution. They do nothing towards extending to India the advantages of civilised experience.

Something has been said of the advantages of a State Bank to the Government and of its direct advantages to the commercial world. I will turn in conclusion to some wider and more general issues; but must treat them briefly.

I attach great importance to the increased stability which a State Bank would introduce into the Indian banking system. India is not well placed at present to meet a banking crisis. The Presidency Banks are already banker's banks to an important extent, but they are not strong enough to support the whole burden. In effect the Government keeps a part of the banking reserves, but there is no machinery for bringing its reserves into normal connection with banking. With no central reserve, no elasticity of credit currency, hardly a rediscount market, and hardly a bank rate policy, with the growth of small and daring banks, great increase of deposits and a community unhabituated to banking and ready at the least alarm to revert to hoarding, even where it had been seemingly abandoned, there are to be found most elements of weakness and few elements of strength.

A recent article by Mr H. M. Ross in *Capital* (4 September 1913) brings out these points very plainly. This article contains much which deserves reference, but the following passage is, in the present connection, the most important:

India and the United States of America are now practically alone among the great trading countries of the world in possessing no central bank. In view of the American banking crisis of 1907 the relation is an ominous one. The vast monetary resources of the United States, badly handled and selfishly hoarded when they should have been freely used where most required through the medium of a great central institution, were of no avail to avert wholesale bankruptcy and a general suspension of payment by the banks. In a similar crisis it would be the policy, nay, it would be the duty of each Presidency Bank to conserve its resources for the benefit of its particular area. In the general interests of the country this should not be.

Mr Ross might have added that India and the United States are also alone in having no rediscount market, no elasticity in the note issue, no bank rate policy, and an 'Independent Treasury System' in place of a Government banker. In America the 1907 crisis served to demonstrate that such a system is indefensible, and the country is now engaged in remedying these defects so far as is possible in the very difficult circumstances which arise out of the presence of innumerable small banks, on the one hand, all with vested interests and a terror of anything which might conceivably diminish their profits, and of a public, deeply suspicious of all moneyed interests and of anything which might strengthen their power, on the other.[1] In India the obstacles are

[1] Since the above was written, a new Currency Law for the United States has been carried. It is interesting to notice that, while decentralisation is secured by the establishment of from 8 to 12 regional banks, the cohesion and strength of the new system will depend on the central Federal Board to be established at Washington (not New York). This Federal Board seems from the available account to have some slight analogy with the Central Board for India proposed above. 'The Federal Board will consist of the Secretary of the Treasury, the Comptroller of the Currency, and five members appointed by the President with the consent of the Senate. Its powers are enormous. A vote of five of its members can require a regional bank to discount the paper of other regional banks. It can fix the rate of discount. It can temporarily suspend the reserve requirements. It can borrow or refuse requests for notes from the regional banks and has other important supervisory functions.' The Government will bank with the new regional banks, and a principal object of the new organisation is to encourage the practice of rediscount.

far less to the introduction of the recognised preventives for the diseases of the financial body.

I have already pointed out the importance of a strong central institution in relation to the development on sound lines of native joint stock banks. The encouragement of rediscount should be an encouragement to these banks to use their funds, as they ought, in the assistance of trade, instead of in speculation or in fixed enterprises.

The great increase of branches in country districts may lead to the State Bank's playing an important part in the development of co-operative banking amongst agriculturists. The local branches should always aim at being the Co-operative Bank's bank and at helping them by judicious loans.

This increase of branches will be much facilitated when a single institution is in control of banking, the Government's balances, and the currency chest in country districts. At present there is apt to be unprofitable discussion between Government and Presidency Banks about (e.g.) the interest payable on loans or the subsidy required to support a branch bank where there is now a District Treasury. It would pay Government to give any subsidy short of the expense of maintaining the Treasury. But they are naturally unwilling to hand over too much profit to private persons and yet are not in a good position to gauge how much this profit would be. So long also as the district currency chests are not handed over to the branch bank, some economies are open to the Government Treasury which are not open to the bank. A system of haggling between the Government and Presidency Banks as to the opening of branches, in which both parties have to be convinced that they are certainly making a good bargain, must be worse than one in which the interests of the two parties are joint instead of opposed and the only consideration is whether a branch is worth opening *on the whole*.

In conclusion it is worth while to recall the Government of India's latest pronouncement on the subject, when in June 1901, they were 'regretfully compelled' to 'hold the scheme in abeyance': 'We desire at the same time to record our deliberate opinion that it would be distinctly advisable, if practicable, to establish a central bank in India, so as to relieve Government of its present heavy responsibilities and to secure the advantages arising from the control of the banking system of a country by a solid and powerful central institution.'

Some adverse criticisms

The chief criticisms of proposals for a State Bank which I remember to have heard are the following:

1. that there is no popular clamour for it;
2. that it would increase the responsibilities of the Secretary of State and expose him to vexatious questions in Parliament;
3. that India is too large and too various in local custom to be worked by a single bank;
4. that the local jealousies of Bombay and Calcutta are too strong;
5. that the former Bank of Bombay suspended payment in 1866;
6. that talent is not available in India to staff the Bank's directorate;
7. that it would not be fair on the exchange banks.

It is not quite just to these criticisms to give so bare a catalogue of them. Some of them become more imposing when they are enlarged on. In regard to several it is possible for each individual to judge for himself how much weight ought to be given them. An admirable summary of the views expressed by witnesses can be gathered from pages 16 and 17 of the index to the evidence received in the summer.

(2), (3), (4) and (6) are, in my own opinion, the more substantial. With (2) I have already dealt. The particular constitution proposed for the Bank is designed, in part, to mitigate the force of objections (3), (4) and (6). Of these (3) has, I think, very little force provided that reasonable autonomy is allowed to the local boards. I pressed all the witnesses, who raised this objection, to particularise the difficulties, arising out of the size and variety of India, which they chiefly had in mind; but without success. With regard to (6) it must not be forgotten that at least as much talent will be available as at present.

The 'vested interests' question is turning out much less serious than might have been expected. The Presidency Banks of Bengal, Bombay and Madras show no pronounced signs of hostility, and the authorities of the two latter have declared themselves, subject to certain conditions, definitely favourable. The present system is so wasteful that a change will provide a wide margin of profit for the shareholders of these banks to participate in.

The exchange banks seem likely to oppose any substantial change in the present position. Their legitimate trading interests, however, are very fully safeguarded in the above proposals; and, as they will share in the advantage of increased stability in the Indian financial system, opposition will probably be mistaken even in their own interests. They will be but repeating the mistake which they made in 1892 in opposing the closure of the mints. It might have been expected that they would have welcomed a measure intended to introduce stability into their business, and which has in fact made the fortunes of all of them. But they held at that time that it was on the fluctuations of exchange and on the supposed bounty given to exports by a depreciating currency that they chiefly depended for their profits.

In 1900–1 the amount of consideration which should be paid to the exclusive claims of the exchange banks was the subject of some difference of opinion between the Government of India and the Secretary of State. The former wrote: 'We cannot see that the exchange banks make out a strong claim for protection, and a suggestion which has been made that a central bank should be bound to make any and all remittances through their agency is out of the question.' And, later, in answer to the exchange banks' protest against 'state-aided competition': 'We could have wished that this contention of the banks, which appears to us to be untenable, had been supported by some clearer indication of the actual manner in which the competition they deprecate may be expected to prove unfair and injurious.' This comment is equally applicable to the evidence given to ourselves by Mr Toomey and Mr Fraser. As arising out of this evidence, it may be pointed out that the exchange banks have absolutely unrestricted opportunities for purely Indian business, that this side of their activities has very greatly increased, and that Mr Toomey deliberately depreciated the importance to them of the business of attracting deposits in London for use in India, a part of their business on which they used greatly to pride themselves and which was at one time no small part of the ground on which they claimed special consideration.

The memory of the business world is short. Apart from vested interest, the main difficulty in the way of the above proposals is the great *vis inertiae*, engendered by an experience of good times and only to be dispelled, perhaps, by something disastrous. Nor do I believe that opposition to these proposals will chiefly depend upon the kind of detailed criticisms enumerated above, or that the *essential parts* of them are open to specific and detailed attack. The real ground of objection is at the same time more vague and better founded. The proposed scheme is a large one, and all of its consequences cannot possibly be predicted with certainty. Such a scheme must naturally provoke a doubt as to whether it is worth while to embark for a *terra incognita* which may, for all one knows, contain something hazardous in it. But the land must not be thought more unknown than it really is. The above proposals contain nothing more than an adaptation to Indian conditions of methods which have been tried successfully in a great many places.

6 October 1913   J. M. KEYNES

APPENDIX A

The relation of state banks to their governments

The existing arrangements in various continental countries and in Japan are given below in outline. I describe the Reichsbank and the Bank of France in a certain amount of detail, and the rest very briefly indeed, because these two are the prototypes of several others, the constitutions of which contain few original ideas.

Reichsbank

No part of the capital is owned by the State.[1]

The authorities of the Bank are:

1. The *Bank-Kuratorium*, consisting of the Imperial Chancellor as chairman and four members, one appointed by the Emperor and three by the Bundesrat. This is of the nature of a board of trustees and meets only four times a year to receive a general account of the Bank's operations.

2. The *Bank-Direktorium*, consisting at present of a president, vice-president and six members, all appointed for life by the Emperor on the nomination of the Bundesrat. This board (to quote the Bank Act) is 'the managing and executive authority of the Reichsbank...Its orders are to be sanctioned by a majority vote, and subjected to the instructions and directions of the Imperial Chancellor.'

The *Direktorium* is 'endowed with special independent powers, even though these can be checked by higher officials; it acts in its own name as the central managing body of the Reichsbank, forms its resolutions on its own responsibility by majority vote, and has the rights of a "supreme imperial board"'.[2]

3. The Central Committee of Shareholders (*Zentralausschuss*) consisting of fifteen members elected by the general meeting of shareholders. This committee must meet at least once a month. Reports must be presented to them, relating to most of the more important weekly items in the Bank's transactions, and containing a statement of the *Direktorium*'s views as to general policy. The committee's powers are purely advisory.[3] But the Bank Act enumerates a number of questions in regard to which 'the

[1] When in 1876 the Bank of Prussia was converted into the Reichsbank, the capital previously held by the Prussian Government was repaid.

[2] See the official history of the Reichsbank, 1876–1900.

[3] Except on one or two minor points, not deserving of reference here, in regard to which they can veto change.

suggestions of the Central Committee should receive special consideration'. Amongst these may be mentioned the filling up of vacancies in the *Direktorium*; the drawing up of the annual balance sheet; the maximum amount to be loaned by the Bank in advances against collateral; the discount rate and the loan interest rate, as well as changes in the principles and the terms on which credit is to be given. The interests of the shareholders are further safeguarded by the annual appointment by the Central Committee of three of their number as deputies having the right to attend with advisory powers all sittings of the *Direktorium* and to examine the books of the Bank.

The salaries and pensions of the members of the *Direktorium* are fixed annually in the Imperial Budget.

The ordinary officials of the Reichsbank 'have the rights and duties of imperial functionaries', and are precluded from holding shares in the Bank.

The members of the Central Committee of Shareholders draw no stipend.

The rules governing the management of the local head offices (*Reichsbank Hauptstellen*) also deserve notice. The Reichsbank now has 486 branches[1] (as compared with 569 of the Bank of France), of which twenty are head offices. Each of these offices is under the supervision of a local board of at least two members and of a commissioner (*Bank-Kommissarius*) appointed by the Emperor. The executive authority is in the hands of two managing officials. There is also for each such office a district committee, appointed by the Imperial Chancellor from amongst the shareholders of the Bank resident in the city where the local head office is located. The powers of the local committee are similar to those of the Central Committee, and they also have the right to appoint two or three deputies for purposes of closer supervision.

These local head offices have a high degree of independence. They are empowered to carry on independently in the district assigned to them by the *Direktorium* all forms of transactions

---

[1] It originally opened in 1876 with 201 branches.

permitted by the Bank Act. The signatures of the two managing officials of a local head office are legally binding on the Reichsbank.

Besides the twenty head offices, there are seventy-seven offices which have nearly as much independence as the head offices. All the rest of the branches are sub-offices directly dependent on offices or head offices, and requiring approval for their transactions by the higher office. According to the strict rule 'no bill may be purchased by them which has not been previously laid before the higher office'. But this rule has gradually been mitigated so that the higher branch can name to the sub-office those persons and business houses from whom, without inquiry in each case, bills may be purchased within the fixed limits of credit, with the reservation, however, that sanction may subsequently be refused.[1] In other respects the powers of sub-offices have been gradually developed. The chief obstacles, according to the official history, which have retarded the free development of sub-offices, are especially relevant to Indian conditions. In the first place the keeping of large balances at the sub-offices, or alternatively the too frequent remittance of money backwards and forwards, would have been involved. Sub-offices have not been allowed, therefore, on their own authority to accept fixed deposits on the one hand or to make advances against collateral on the other. In the second place 'at the creation of the Reichsbank most of the directors of sub-offices were not officials trained in banking, but agents some of whom performed the duties of the office only as incidental work and received for it no fixed salary, but only a percentage of the profits'. In the course of its development the Reichsbank has tried two different lines of advance, the grant of increased powers to sub-offices in places where the amount of business was important, and the transformation of such sub-offices into offices. On the whole the second line of advance seems to have been the more successful.

[1] See Official History of the Reichsbank.

Bank of France

No part of the capital is owned by the State.

The authorities of the Bank are:

The Governor.

Two Deputy Governors.

A General Council (*Conseil Général*) of fifteen *Régents* and three *Censeurs*.

The Governor and Deputy Governors have always (since 1806) been appointed and removable at will by the Minister of Finance. The *Régents* and *Censeurs* are appointed by the 200 amongst the shareholders who hold the largest number of shares.[1] Three of the *Régents* must be treasury disbursing agents (*Trésorier-Payeurs général*), i.e., officials, and five must come from the business portion of the shareholders, from amongst whom the *Censeurs* also must be chosen. The *Censeurs* are inspectors or auditors. They attend meetings of the *Conseil Général*, have access to the records of the Bank, and are entrusted with the duty of reporting any irregularities to the shareholders.

The *Régents* and *Censeurs* divide themselves up into five committees to deal with special departments, e.g., the *Comité d'escompte*, the *Comité des billets*, etc.

The managers of the branches are appointed by the Minister of Finance from amongst three candidates nominated by the Governor of the Bank, who has also the power of dismissal. The names are considered, as well, by the *Conseil Général*.

It will be noticed that, so far as the letter of the law goes, the power of the representatives of the shareholders is very much greater than is the case with the Reichsbank. This is much modified, in practice, by the following considerations. In the first place the Governor has the right of veto. This right, though the occasions of its use in the last hundred years have been very rare indeed, preserves the ultimate authority of the State over changes in policy or regulation unimpaired. In the second place the

[1] This provision is quite peculiar to the Bank of France. A shareholder has at present to hold about £20,000 worth in order to participate.

official element on the *Conseil Général*, made up of the Governor, the two Deputy Governors and the three *Trésorier-Payeurs Général* amongst the *Régents*, commands six votes out of a total of eighteen. Since the Governor has a casting vote, if only three of the twelve unofficial members vote with the officials, the latter have an assured majority. The practical effect of this has been, in the words of M. Rouland who was governor in 1865, that 'nothing of any description which concerns the great interest of the public, or the larger duties which the Bank has to perform towards commerce and industry, is left to the discretion of what is called the interested party (i.e., the shareholders)'.

The Imperial Bank of Russia

This Bank stands by itself (so far as the larger countries are concerned) in being wholly owned, as well as managed, by the Government. It is under the direct control of the Minister of Finance.

The Bank of Belgium[1]

No part of the capital is owned by the State.

The Governor is appointed by the King for five years, and may be re-appointed. The active administrative council consists of the Governor and six directors appointed by the shareholders. The shareholders also elect a council of seven censors to audit and supervise. The Government exercises further supervision through a Special Commissioner, and Article XXIV of the Bank Act runs: 'The Government has the right to control all operations. It shall have the power to prevent the execution of any measure which shall be contrary to the law, to the statutes, or to the interests of the State.'

The Bank of the Netherlands

Closely similar to the Bank of Belgium.

---

[1] See *The National Bank of Belgium*, by Charles A. Conant.

The Austro-Hungarian Bank

No part of the capital is owned by the State.

The Governor and two Deputy Governors of the Bank are appointed by the State.

The Bank of Italy

The capital is privately owned, but the nomination of the Director-General must be approved by the Government; and the Ministers of Agriculture, Commerce, and the Treasury form a board with powers of supervision and inspection.

The Bank of Spain

This is a private institution, but privileged and standing in very close relations to the Government.

The Bank of Japan

Baron Sakatami, ex-Minister of Finance, writes as follows:

'When the Bank was first established, the Government was a very large shareholder, but these shares were afterwards transferred to the Imperial Household Department... The Government's supervision is very strict. It appoints the Governor and the Deputy Governor; the directors are also appointed by the Government from among candidates elected by the shareholders; the Government appoints official inspectors from among the officials of the Department of Finance...'

APPENDIX B

State banks and private capital

On the occasion of the last renewal of the Reichsbank Charter in 1909, many people urged that the private shareholders ought to be bought out by the Government on the avowed ground that these were making profits which ought to accrue to the State. The following quotation from an article written by Professor Lexis in the course of this controversy is instructive:

The officials of a pure state bank have merely to adapt themselves to the regulations coming to them from above; but a bank of issue with private capital, even when entirely managed by the State, has a sort of independence as regards the State—an independence which protects it against interference with the vital conditions of its existence. For the former, indeed, the interference of legislation is always needed; but the latter must never forget that a great private capital is in its charge. The Central Committee of the Reichsbank has undoubtedly only a very moderate authority, but its influence, nevertheless, is far greater than that of the advisory board of a State railroad company, because it represents the owners of the bank capital.

It was noticeable that the demand for the suppression of the private capital of the Reichsbank came, not from the socialists, but from the agrarians. 'The agrarians', it has been said, 'wish to render the State master of the Bank, because they are today masters of the State. If the State becomes master of the Bank of the Empire, the agrarians hope that nothing can any longer prevent them from compelling the State to employ the funds of the Bank in the execution of their programme.'

There was a similar controversy in Belgium in 1900. The following arguments against the abolition of private capital may be quoted from the *Documents Parlementaires*:[1]

There is, first, the confusion of public and private credit, to the great damage of each; for they ought to remain distinct, for their respective good and for the mutual assistance which they are at times called upon to lend to each other. Further, there is the acceptance by the State of a task—the task of discounting—which is not within its competence, and of which, even with the best of will, it will acquit itself badly. It is neither wise nor practicable to suppress the legitimate stimulus of private interest in such affairs as discount. It must not be

[1] See Conant, *History of the National Bank of Belgium*.

believed that in such a matter disinterestedness alone suffices or can afford a better guide than the foresight of those who run the risks and reap the benefits of such operations.

The division of the profits of the Reichsbank

The duties to be performed by the Reichsbank without remuneration and the rules governing the proportion of the profits which accrues to the shareholders are as follows:

(1) The Reichsbank must purchase gold bullion tendered to it at a fixed rate. It is required to accept payments for the account of the Empire and to make disbursements without compensation. It bears the whole expense of management of the note issue.

(2) The Reichsbank must pay a tax of 5 per cent to the Government on the excess of the fiduciary issue beyond a certain amount.

(3) The net annual profit of the Reichsbank is to be divided at the close of each year in the following manner:

1. In the first place, a regular dividend of $3\frac{1}{2}$ per cent of the capital is to be distributed among the shareholders.

2. Of the remainder, 10 per cent is to be transferred to the reserve fund, 20 per cent to the shareholders, and 70 per cent to the Imperial Treasury.

3. If the net earnings are less than $3\frac{1}{2}$ per cent of the capital, the difference is to be made up from the reserve fund.

These arrangements, however, have been altered at every decennial revision of the Bank Act. Originally (1875) the guaranteed dividend was $4\frac{1}{2}$ per cent (instead of $3\frac{1}{2}$ per cent), 20 per cent of the balance went to reserve, and of the rest the State took a quarter when the total dividends of the shareholders exceeded 8 per cent. In 1891 $3\frac{1}{2}$ per cent was substituted for $4\frac{1}{2}$ per cent, and the one-fourth share began to accrue to the State when the shareholders' total dividend exceeded 6 per cent. After 1901 the share of the State began as soon as the 3½ per cent dividend and the transfer to reserve had been made, and the shareholders received 25 per cent of the surplus. The present arrangement dates from 1911.

The actual dividends of the shareholders in recent years have averaged about 7 per cent:

1907	9·89 per cent
1908	7·77 per cent
1909	5·83 per cent
1910	6·48 per cent
1911	5·86 per cent
1912	6·95 per cent

In 1912 the State received £1,088,732 as its share of profits and £231,374 as note tax, £1,320,106 altogether; as compared with £879,881 in 1911, £1,001,139 in 1910, £822,409 in 1909, and £1,280,838 in 1907.

The agreement between the shareholders and the State is subject to revision every ten years. And, further, 'the Empire reserves the right of option on January 1, 1891, and thereafter at the expiration of every ten-year period: (*a*) of discontinuing the Reichsbank established by this Act, and acquiring its property on the basis of the book values, or (*b*) of acquiring the total stock of the Reichsbank at valuation... In either case the reserve fund, in so far as it is not required to defray losses, is to be equally divided between the shareholders of the Empire.'

If at any of the decennial periods the Government had taken full advantage of this provision, it would have been much more disadvantageous to the shareholders than the new arrangements for division of profits actually made.

Sir James Begbie, secretary and treasurer of the Bank of Bombay, was an individualist who finally parted company with the rest of the Commission on the question of a gold currency and wrote a dissenting note to the Report. In his 'Notes on Some of Mr Keynes's Proposals for the Establishment of a State Bank' he found several difficulties—all, however, in connection with the section on 'The London Office and Remittance', which, as Keynes had remarked, was 'a debatable subject...largely independent of the rest'. Summarised, with reference to the numbered sections of Keynes's reply which follows, the difficulties were:

(1) Keynes's use of the word 'rediscount' as opposed to 'purchase' in writing of the power to be given to the Bank to rediscount sterling trade bills bearing the endorsement of another bank. Begbie objected that the cost of remitting the money back to the place of discount, i.e. India, including the rate of exchange, must be taken into account. He did not believe that the Bank would be able to compete with the London discount market rates. But Keynes had explained the mechanics of this, and probably Begbie was simply asserting that he did not think it would work.

(2) His doubts, for the same reasons, that the Bank would be able to rediscount sterling bills held by the exchange banks.

(3) His opinion, while 'in full accord with the proposals for an elastic expansion of the note issue covered preferably by bills', that it would be unwise to encourage many of the new banks to rediscount bills to the State Bank too often, lest they be tempted to take on too many risks.

(4) Keynes's expectation that 'the management of the note issue and of the Government balances will provide the Bank with an enormous source of revenue'. Begbie thought this too optimistic. He also expected some temporary curtailment in credit, with a loss of business to the State Bank, because the big shroffs and merchants who at present obtained credit from two or all three of the Presidency Banks would not be able to get as much in one sum from the State Bank.

To SIR JAMES BEGBIE, *10 November 1913*

Dear Sir James,

Many thanks for your notes on my memorandum, which I take in turn below:

(1) When I spoke of the 'rediscount' of sterling bills, I meant what you, more correctly, call their 'purchase'—that is to say, I assumed that the rate of exchange would be taken into account.

Also, it must necessarily be the case that their price will be governed by the London rate of discount for such bills, taken in conjunction with the rate of exchange, not by the local rate for rupee bills. I agree that the Bank could not expect to get sterling bills at local rates.

The position may be elucidated by some numerical examples.

London rate of discount for such bills	Rate of Exchange	Price in rupees of a 3 month sterling bill for £100
4	1s 4d	Rs $99 \times 15 = 1485$
$4\frac{1}{2}$	1s $4\frac{1}{16}d$	$98\frac{7}{8} \times \dfrac{240}{16\frac{1}{16}} = 1477$
$4\frac{1}{2}$	1s 4d	$98\frac{7}{8} \times 15 = 1483$
$4\frac{1}{2}$	1s $3\frac{15}{16}d$	$98\frac{7}{8} \times \dfrac{240}{15\frac{15}{16}} = 1489$

I expect I have done the arithmetic wrong, but these examples show the principle.

The inducements to be offered to the exchange banks to bring sterling bills to the State Bank for rediscount simply consist in quoting them a rate slightly more favourable, regarded as an exchange operation, than the other alternatives open to them.

For example, an exchange bank having bought a sterling bill in India can cover itself in two ways—by rediscounting this bill at the State Bank; or by rediscounting some other bill in London and buying telegraphic transfers with the proceeds from the London office of the State Bank. If the London rate of rediscount for bills of this type and maturity is $4\frac{1}{2}$ per cent and the London office is quoting 1s $4\frac{1}{16}d$ for telegraphic transfers, then any price below Rs 1477 (see above table) offered by the State Bank in India for a three months' sterling bill for £100 is an 'inducement' to the exchange bank to rediscount in India rather than buy telegraphic transfers in London. Of course, this is simply one possible example. The State Bank by adjusting its rate for bills and T.T.'s in London and its rate for the purchase of sterling bills in India could lead the exchange banks to take the alternative most convenient to itself.

(2) Perhaps, what I have said under (1) meets this point.

(3) I quite agree. The officials of the State Bank ought to exercise a wise discretion as to the extent to which and the persons to whom they make rediscount easy.

(4) I daresay I exaggerate. Anyhow the exact terms must be a matter of negotiation. Also so long as bills are not available as much as is desirable, the Bank is not precluded from using its funds in other ways. Yes, I was contemplating a transfer of some part of the Bank's present bills to the Note Department, and thus the release of funds for other purposes. Would the credit allowed to the big shroffs you refer to be reduced, unless they are now getting in the aggregate more than they have any business to get?

But I accept your criticism that I may have exaggerated the *immediate* profit. If a longer view be taken, I am inclined to think that there is a great deal in the scheme financially. India has such great potentialities in this matter.

I am very glad indeed to find that the criticisms you find occasion to make are not more fundamental. It was as to the acceptability of the general constitution of the Bank that I felt most nervous.

Sincerely yours,

J. M. KEYNES

Abrahams's reaction to Keynes's memorandum was mixed. 'As an intellectual achievement I greatly admire it:' he wrote (23 October 1913), 'and I am sure that it will do great good, whether its most important features are accepted or not.' When, however, he came to study it in more detail, he remarked (12 November 1913) on the absence of provision for India to use the profits of an economical currency—profits obtained on coinage, and by the release of purchasing power through expansion of the fiduciary issue that could be invested in Indian Government securities—for industrial investment (for example, the construction of railways). Keynes, he wrote, had disregarded or eliminated the possibility of gains for India of this kind.

Alas! Alas!! Alas!!! How much all this falls below the following admirable teaching: 'I believe that it contains one essential element—the use of a cheap local currency artificially maintained at par with the international currency or standard of value (whatever that may ultimately turn out to be) —in the ideal currency of the future.' (J. M. Keynes, *Indian Currency and Finance*, page 36[*JMK*, vol. I, p. 25].) What is the good of an economical currency if the fruits of economy are to be put in a sarcophagus? The economic error of India tends to be to hoard wealth instead of using it. It would be a calamity if the Government falls a victim to this error in its own action.

While Keynes did not provide specifically for industrial expansion in his memorandum, his scheme for proportionally increasing the fiduciary part of the note issue and furthering Government lending was designed to achieve an elastic money supply with the same kind of final end in view. It must have been that Abrahams was really taking issue with his treatment of the gold standard reserve. In evidence Abrahams, who regarded the reserve's true function as support of the exchange, had advocated limiting its growth (from interest on investments and profits on coinage) to £25,000,000, allowing only small accretions thereafter to cover the growth of trade. Keynes, on the other hand, wished to make additional use of the gold standard reserve as 'an ultimate safeguard and guarantee of the convertibility of the note issue' and called for it to be governed by 'ultra-conservative methods', holding a larger amount of gold than before.

In deference to Abrahams, it would appear, Keynes dropped an offending paragraph in the section on 'Other Functions of the Bank' in an early version of the memorandum, which looked forward to the conversion of the silver branch of the gold standard reserve into gold, and substituted for a sentence in the same vein under 'General Advantages of a State Bank' a quite different one calling attention to the greater opportunities for popularising the use of notes. Although he did not change the proposal to have a large sum in gold coin in the gold standard reserve, he later introduced an amendment to the gold standard reserve section of the Commission's report—not, however, incorporated as he had framed it—warning against the possibility that the Government might be tempted to accumulate needlessly high sterling reserves (p. 236).

When Abrahams appeared again before the Commission on 13 November he was questioned on his opinions about a state bank by several members, including Keynes. In spite of Abrahams's scrupulously held neutrality Keynes, with his help, was able to bring out his agreement on specific important points and to extract what amounted to a general testimonial. The extract which follows is from *Minutes of Evidence taken before the Royal Commission on Indian Finance and Currency*, vol. II (Cd. 7237).

FROM THE MINUTES OF EVIDENCE, 13 NOVEMBER 1913

(MR KEYNES) In 1900 the proposals that were brought forward were for what one could justly call, I think, a central bank as distinguished from a state bank?[1] (MR ABRAHAMS) *Yes.*

Are you in favour of a state bank or a central bank? *A state bank. In fact, I think that the general outcome of my memorandum was that if there is to be a central bank at all it must be a state bank.*

Do you attach importance to this state bank, though under the ultimate control of Government, being independent of Government from the point of view of day-to-day transactions? *Yes. I entirely agree with what you put (and if I may say so, put very admirably) in the memorandum[2] which I have read. I want to clear up a possible misunderstanding. In your memorandum you have proposed that the central board should consist of a Governor, who would be appointed by the King, a Deputy-Governor, to be appointed by the Viceroy, and the Government's representative; you also mention in the Appendix to the memorandum the practice of certain continental state banks, and you leave it to be understood or misunderstood that they are the models which your scheme follows. I believe actually that you do not wish an Indian State Bank to be an instrument of Government in the same way that the continental state banks are the instruments of their respective Governments, and that this appointment by higher authority of the Governor, Deputy-Governor, and Government representative, is not intended to subordinate them to the Government, but to make, at any rate, the Governor and the Deputy-Governor independent to a very great extent both of the shareholders and of the Government. It is on that understanding that I give my general agreement to your memorandum, and I mention it merely because the other view might easily be taken by anyone who read your memorandum rather hastily.*

I may say that what you have said is the right interpretation of what I meant. Is there anything of a general character that you care to say about the relation of the executive officers of the Bank to the shareholders? *My general view would be that the shareholders must have a considerable amount of influence on the behaviour of the executive officers of the Presidency Banks at the Presidency head offices as distinguished from the Central Board; but the influence ought not to be of such a nature that it entirely controls the action of the Presidency head offices. One wants practically the real government to be to some extent by shareholders and to some extent by the Government representatives.*

If the supreme power of the Bank is in the hands of a Central Board which is distinct from the Presidency head offices, is it possible, do you

[1] See Appendix xv (p. 355) in Cd. 7071.   [2] Printed as an Appendix to the Final Report.

think, to obtain that degree of decentralisation which is required for the dispatch of business in different parts of the country? *Yes. That is one of the problems which it was the object of your memorandum to solve, and I think you have solved it—I ought not, perhaps, to express too enthusiastic an agreement with you—extremely well. I was absolutely satisfied with your solution.*

What is your feeling as to the position of the Secretary of State in the event of the establishment of a bank of this kind, particularly in his relations to Parliament? *There again I can do little more than express my agreement with what you have put. You have explained that there are many subjects on which the Secretary of State would be able to say: This is a matter for the Bank and not for me. Of course that would not apply to the biggest subjects, I mean large questions of policy, but it would apply to everyday questions. I think that what you say about that is obviously correct; at any rate, to my mind it is absolutely convincing.*

Do you think that the Secretary of State would be in a more favourable position than he is now in the event of criticism of financial details, or not? *I think he would be in a more favourable position. He might have more questions put to him, but he will have better answers to them.*

I suggested that if there was an establishment in India in a position to buy sterling bills on London, some part of the Secretary of State's floating resources in London might be held in the form of sterling bills having an early maturity; what is your general opinion with regard to that suggestion? *I have no objection to that, provided it is accompanied with what I understood you to contemplate, a limitation of the bills to those which bear the names of firms or institutions of very great repute.*

Bank bills? *I think they would be bills either drawn, or accepted, or endorsed by the exchange banks. If it became a question of holding bills, the names on which were names of private firms, about whom it might be difficult to get information, then it would be undesirable that the State Bank should hold such bills; but you do not contemplate that.*

If that were done, do you think it would do anything towards meeting the criticism against holding a great deal of Indian money in London and using it for the general support of the London money market, and only indirectly for the support of Indian trade? *I think it would have some effect. I do not attach quite so much importance to it as you do in your memorandum, for two reasons. I do not suppose that the exchange banks would bring all their bills, perhaps not even the greater number of them, to the India Office, or to the State Bank in India, to be rediscounted; and I do not suppose that the State Bank would wish, on its side, to be regarded as the one regular resource for the rediscounting of bills, which would set up the idea that it undertook a greater obligation towards the exchange banks than it really wished to do. Perhaps I might mention this consideration, which no doubt you have not overlooked—that the chief difference between the present method of the Secretary of State making his remittances, and the new method which is proposed in your memorandum is that at present the Secretary of State gets the money before he pays out rupees; he gives no credit, but credit is given by the Bank to the Government. Under your method, the State Bank would be giving credit, and would be making payment before it received the equivalent. Although that is quite reasonable, one does not want to do it to an unlimited extent.*

If it is an alternative to lending money at short notice in London, what it amounts to is substituting the holders and backers of the bills for the brokers who now get the money, is it not? *The firm that now borrows money pledges not only its own general resources, but specific resources as well. That would not be the case if the State Bank rediscounted the bills for the existing bank.*

But you would not maintain, would you, that there was any appreciable risk in taking bank bills of that sort? *No, I should not say there was much risk; but when many millions were involved, you do not want to take even small risks. I am not arguing against doing what you propose; I am only arguing that it might not be advantageous to do it on a very huge scale.*

I should like to ask your opinion with regard to some of the main criticisms against a State Bank which we have heard. The one which I think we have heard most frequently from witnesses is that India is too large and various in local customs to be worked by a single bank? *I am not much impressed by that. I ought to be, perhaps, because I know most critics with a very great knowledge of India, like Sir Shapurji Broacha, attach very great importance to it. But if one considers how widely spread are some of the great banks, for instance, the Chartered Bank of India, Australia, and China, or the Hong Kong and Shanghai Banking Corporation, it does not seem to me that there ought to be any insuperable difficulty in having one bank which does business in various parts of one country. The same criticism, if there was any force in it, would apply to the Bank of Bengal, which has advanced certainly as far east as Burma, and as far west, I believe, as the United Provinces, but I do not know what is its westernmost extremity.*

(MR GILLAN) *They go into the Punjab area. If the same bank can operate in Rangoon and Mandalay, and in Lahore, I should think it could not be impossible for the same bank to operate in Calcutta and Bombay.*

(MR KEYNES) The criticism, perhaps of next importance, or at any rate, which we have heard most frequently, is, I think, that the local jealousies of Calcutta and Bombay are too strong for them to agree to work together in a common institution of that kind? *I have seen in the papers many indications that the Bank of Bengal, the Bank of Bombay, and the Bank of Madras are all prepared to look favourably on the scheme. I think that is really the best answer I can give. It would be useless for me to try to estimate the local jealousies. I have never been in India as you know; perhaps, when I come back from India in a few months hence, I shall have an opinion on the subject.*

During the negotiations in 1900–1 a good deal of emphasis was laid on the position of the exchange banks in the event of the establishment of a State Bank; do you think there is anything which interferes in an unreasonable way with the interests which those banks have established in the sort of proposals we are contemplating? *Nothing at all. I have read the evidence given by Mr Toomey and Mr Fraser. They were evidently contemplating a State Bank which would take exchange business out of their hands.*[1] *They very much disliked the idea, and I think any of us being in their position would have disliked it. But I should imagine that when they read the memoranda which you and I have drawn up about the State Bank, which provide most tenderly for the interests of exchange banks in respect of exchange business, they will probably feel that their only objection has disappeared. Perhaps I am rather confident, but it seems to me that the only substantial objection that they put forward is absolutely met by those memoranda.*

I think you have already, in answer to Sir Shapurji, dealt with the argument that there is no popular clamour for the bank, and also in an earlier answer to me in regard to the position of the Secretary of State. There is one other argument, the historical argument, which is held to prove the experiment of semi-state banks was not fortunate; is there anything that you care to say in regard to that? *The common argument is that the failure of the Old Bank of Bombay shows that the less the Government have to do with a bank the better it is.* [Abrahams here gave an account of the Report of the Commission of Enquiry into the failure of the Old Bank of Bombay, which had been caused by speculation on the part of incompetent and dishonest officials.]. . .*So far from supporting the view that the Government ought to have nothing to do with banking, this history supports exactly the opposite view—that Government control, if wisely exercised, is very salutary in regard to the management of a great bank.*

(LORD FABER) Do you think that any rules you could lay down over a series of years would prevent the existence of rogues? *No. One of my reasons for wanting Government directors is that, if you do not have them, you have to rely merely on rules, and I entirely agree with you that you want something more than rules—you want personal contact, knowledge, and supervision; and I think it is only by some Government participation in the management of a bank that you can have that.*

[1] Cd. 7069, Q.A. 2621, etc.

Chapter 4

KEYNES AND THE
COMMISSION'S REPORT

The Commission heard the second round of witnesses from 23 October to 14 November. Chamberlain and Blackett had composed a draft Report that Chamberlain hoped would satisfy the commissioners without substantial change. The commissioners were not so amenable; some felt that the Chairman was going too fast. Sir James Begbie was restive about gold. Gillan was particularly worried about the treatment of the Government balances; he wrote to Keynes (6 December 1913), mentioning that he had outlined a statement on the subject, but although he was convinced that there was a good deal seriously wrong in the Chairman's draft, he felt it a delicate matter to criticise it wholesale.

Keynes was less diffident about approaching the Chairman. Indeed he seems to have written to Chamberlain, Blackett and Cable all at once, judging from the three replies that he received all dated 8 December. Blackett wrote confirming Chamberlain's desire to finish up the next week's meetings with little more needed than a final revise: 'You and Gillan however seem to be likely to want more changes than this...' Cable said: 'You are voicing my sentiments', and spoke of 'watering-down and white-washing adjectives' in the Report. Cable was ready for a sub-committee to draft a stronger document. The situation was awkward, as he put it, 'because (confound him) the Chairman has fathered the Report'. But whatever Keynes wrote to Chamberlain must have overcome the difficulty of communication, because the reply was gracious and accommodating.

Dear Keynes,

Many thanks for your letter. If you will let me have any small alterations of detail or language which you think would be an improvement, I will endeavour to incorporate them as far as possible in my draft. I have already done this with suggestions received from three of our colleagues. As regards criticisms of arrangement or argument where you agree with the conclusions, very much depends upon the extent of the alteration which you want made. In some cases it will probably be desirable for you to move formal amendments. In others, it may perhaps be sufficient to raise the question either by letter to me or in discussion when we meet. You will realise the difficulty which every Chairman lies under of finding a language and an arrangement which meets the literary and argumentative sense of every individual colleague.

As regards your third class, namely questions on which you are in substantial disagreement with the Report, I think they must be brought up before the whole Commission, as, after circulating a draft, I do not feel authorised to make really substantial alterations in it without the approval of my colleagues. I think perhaps the best course would be that you should ask Blackett to print and circulate as an alternative your draft section dealing with gold currency. If the Commission prefers your draft to mine, we will simply strike out mine and take yours as the basis of discussion. If, on the other hand, they prefer my draft for a basis, we can probably improve my draft by incorporating a part of yours.

I am inclined to say much the same about the note issue and the lending from balances. On both these points I thought I was expressing only conclusions on which we were all agreed, but I may be mistaken. It will be one of the advantages of having a draft report before us that we shall know exactly where we stand in these matters. Personally, I am unwilling to advise the Government to lend from balances under present circumstances and in the absence of a State Bank. I regard this lending as something of an experiment and I should like to proceed very cautiously in the first instance.

There is one point in your letter on which I have not yet touched, namely, the purchase of silver. When drafting the Report, I became aware that we had arrived at no conclusion on this matter. My own view is embodied in the draft, but if the majority of the Commission take a different view, I should submit to having that paragraph struck out. It is not a question of very great importance.

I have received from Sir James Begbie what I think is quite the ablest statement of the case for the circulation of gold that has been presented to us. Unfortunately it only reached my hands on the same day that the draft Report was in the hands of my colleagues. It does not alter my opinion, but it might have led me to somewhat alter the line of my argument. As you are at work on the subject, I think it will be both interesting and useful for you to see it, but please treat it as confidential and return it to me at your earliest convenience.   Yours very truly,

8 December 1913   AUSTEN CHAMBERLAIN

Keynes's reaction to this was communicated to Cable in a letter that has unfortunately not survived, but something of its flavour is conveyed by Cable's comment: 'Your description of chairman's brain makes me shriek with laughter.'

But Chamberlain accepted Keynes's redrafting of the gold currency section at once. 'The Chairman is remarkably free of petty jealousies', Blackett had observed in an earlier letter. During these weeks Chamberlain was engaged in a desperate private attempt to arrange a compromise on the Irish question between the Government and his own party—which might account for what Gillan described as a 'mixture of scurry and delay' in handling the Report.

Chamberlain's letter of 8 December indicates to a certain extent the changes in the Report that Keynes wanted, but more can be learned from Keynes's copy of the printed draft, marked with alterations in wording and queries of fact, and with the latter half scissored out of it and replaced by a handful of pages consisting of redrafted paragraphs—Chamberlain's comments in the margins showing that this document must have passed between them. What concerned Keynes most was the treatment of the internal currency, the gold standard reserve and the paper currency reserve.

The Commission met for three days before the Christmas vacation to discuss the draft Report. Keynes wrote to his mother (20 December 1913) of the strain of these meetings:

> The Commission is very nearly finished now, and most of the Report is in its final form. The last three days have been about the most exacting to character and intellect that I have ever been through and I feel rather a wreck—wishing very much that I was off to the South of France for an immediate holiday. We sat for seven hours a day, and one had to be drafting amendments at top speed and perpetually deciding within thirty seconds whether other people's amendments were verbal and innocent or substantial and to be rejected. I must say that Austen came out of the ordeal very well, and I believe he may yet be Prime Minister—I don't suppose on the purely intellectual score that he is any stupider than Campbell-Bannerman...

The Commission adjourned for the vacation and Keynes went to the south of France. When the members met again on 12 and 13 January of the new year, prepared at the request of the Chairman to 'sit late' if necessary, he was still in Mentone suffering from what was first diagnosed as quinsy but proved to be diphtheria. His absence played havoc with the proceedings, so far as the proposals for the paper currency were concerned.

Gold, however, was the first matter for discussion. Several of Keynes's colleagues provided him with accounts of what went on but as none of them mentioned the reception of his draft on 'Gold in Internal Circulation' which

Chamberlain had substituted for his own, it must have been accepted with little discussion. In writing it Keynes retained much of Chamberlain's original version, making only verbal changes in the first six and the last three paragraphs. But in the central part both argument and expression are entirely Keynes's. Here he expanded and developed the reasoning against a gold circulation as a support for the exchange and introduced an additional argument against the contention, upheld by Sir James Begbie, that the coinage of new rupees was harmful. 'It puts quite a different complexion on the part you have re-written', Gillan had remarked (15 December 1913).

The changes between Keynes's draft as it was distributed to the Commission and the final Report are so slight and so purely literary, that it can be assumed that these were Keynes's own improvements and that the draft was accepted in its entirety. The version given below is from the published Report, with the paragraphs where Keynes's contribution was editorial only in small type.

GOLD IN INTERNAL CIRCULATION

53. From time immemorial India has continually absorbed the precious metals. But in quite recent years gold has been imported into India in the form of bullion or of sovereigns in greatly increased quantities. Apart from imports of gold bullion, the absorption of sovereigns by the public for all purposes (hoards, circulation, and the melting pot) during the twelve years ending the 31st March 1913, that is, the excess of the net amount imported over the amount retained in the hands of the Government, somewhat exceeded £60,000,000, an amount little less in value than the new coinage of rupees during the same period. Between the 1st April 1909 and the 31st March 1913 the absorption of sovereigns by the public was close on £30,000,000 (see Appendix I, page 21).

54. To what extent and how widely the sovereign has established itself as an actual medium of circulation, it is difficult to determine with any great degree of certainty. On the one hand, it is quite certain that a large portion of these 60,000,000 sovereigns is not in active circulation, and that in many parts of the country the public have shown a preference in currency uses for rupees (or notes) But there is undoubted evidence that in the last four years there has been a distinct increase in the use of the sovereign for purposes of currency in certain provinces and districts, such as parts of the Bombay Presidency and of the United Provinces, the Punjab, and Cochin in the Madras Presidency. Speaking generally, no district which wanted gold seems to have experienced in the last four years any difficulty in obtaining it.

55. In these circumstances it cannot be maintained that the public have been prevented from obtaining gold by the course pursued by the Government. On the contrary, the official policy has been to give the public whatever form of currency they wanted, and the only official preference for one form of currency over another which we can trace is, as already recorded, in favour of gold. Those, therefore, who advocate a gold currency for India, meaning by this the use of gold coins on an extensive scale for internal circulation, must take the responsibility of urging the Government of India to force upon the public more of a particular form of currency than they at present want. It may be added, at this point, that the majority of the witnesses heard by us were distinctly unfavourable to the coinage of a 10-rupee gold piece. There is little reason to believe that it would be any more popular as a medium of internal circulation than is the sovereign, while there are strong prima facie objections to the introduction of a new gold coin slightly more expensive and less convenient than the sovereign, which has been gaining an ever-increasing range of general acceptability for the purpose of meeting payments outside India. On the other hand, in so far as a 10-rupee piece was successful, it would be likely to prove a more dangerous rival than the sovereign to the smaller denominations of notes.

56. Is it then desirable that the Government of India should urge or encourage the circulation of the sovereign? The chief arguments which have been adduced in favour of such action appear to be as follows:

(i) That gold is a more convenient and portable medium of circulation than the rupee.

(ii) That a gold currency is a necessary step towards what may be regarded as the ideal currency, viz., paper backed by gold in reserve.

(iii) That some prestige attaches to the possession of a gold currency, whereas a silver circulation is the mark of less progressive peoples.

(iv) That a large amount of gold in circulation is a strong, and, in the view of some people, the only adequate support for exchange.

(v) That the constant mintage of fresh supplies of rupees is objectionable, and would be obviated by an increasing circulation of sovereigns.

(vi) That until India has a gold currency in active circulation, India will continue to possess an artificial and managed currency.

(vii) That India should be encouraged to absorb gold in order to protect the world in general from a further rise of prices due to the greatly increased production of gold.

57. The first argument is valid only in so far as concerns large payments which for any reason cannot be discharged in notes; but India must continue

for many years to use rupees for payment of the small amounts which form the bulk of internal transactions.

58. On the second argument we would say that history gives no support to the view that a paper currency can only be reached after a gold currency has been in circulation. A paper currency, if readily encashable, is the most economical medium of circulation, and at the same time provides a readily available reserve of gold for foreign remittances.

[Keynes's contribution begins here]

59. The argument that some prestige attaches to the possession of a gold currency is chiefly due, we think, to a confusion between a gold standard, which has undoubtedly become in the last forty years the mark of a progressive people, and a gold currency, in the sense of a preponderating use of gold for the purpose of effecting internal exchanges. So far as the internal circulation is concerned, a widespread use of cheques is generally agreed to be the most progressive system. After this comes the use of notes, which compose by far the greater part of the currency of most European countries. The preponderating use of gold coin is not characteristic of a single one of the Great Powers of the world, and it may be said that the only country which really conforms to this ideal is Egypt, where the continual inflow and outflow of sovereigns is an economic loss to Egypt herself and a cause of recurrent inconvenience to the money markets of the world.

60. The fourth argument, that the encouragement of a gold circulation is calculated in the long run to strengthen exchange, is probably that which carries most weight, and has been supported before us, in one form or another, by several witnesses who were in a position to speak with some authority. It requires, therefore, careful consideration.

61. In the first place, some witnesses seemed to imply that, if gold were to be used in India to the same extent that it is, say, in the United Kingdom or in Germany, the exchange problem would have been largely simplified. We think that this view is mistaken. The ability of these countries to meet at all times their immediate foreign indebtedness depends on the central reserves

of the banks of these countries, on the influence exerted by these banks on the other constituents of the money market, and on their bank-rate policy. It is not possible to point to any occasion in contemporary history on which sovereigns in the pockets of the people have proved a resource on which to count for easing the situation when a monetary crisis threatens the Bank of England's gold reserve. So little are the authorities of the Reichsbank impressed by the value of gold in active circulation for the purpose of settling international indebtedness, that they have been lately engaged in an active policy of replacing some part of this gold by notes of smaller denominations than were formerly current, whilst the gold itself has been used to strengthen the central reserve. It is useless to suppose that the advantages of the existing monetary system of the United Kingdom can be obtained for India by imitating what is, perhaps, the least vital part of this system, namely, the use of sovereigns for that small class of payments which are made in actual cash, while ignoring the nature of the complex banking and financial system upon which the stability of exchange really rests.

62. In the second place, it is important that advocates of a gold currency should be clear as to the scale on which they think it would be feasible and wise to introduce such a currency in the near future. If it is their desire and their intention that gold should be used in active circulation to the same extent that it is used, for example, in Egypt, then no doubt gold from circulation would be available for export in considerable quantities at times of depressed trade. For, in that country a large part, measured in value, of the total transactions, instead of a very small percentage, as is the case both in the United Kingdom and in India, is carried out with gold, so that a contraction in the amount of business is likely to release a nearly proportionate amount of gold for export. In order to attain, however, to this state of affairs in India, or even to approximate to it, it would be necessary to reduce the note issue to a comparatively insignificant position, and to withdraw from circulation, at large expense, no incon-

siderable part of the existing circulation of rupees. If, however, the advocates of a gold currency contemplate only such an addition of gold to the currency as can be made through the gradual increase of the aggregate circulation, without detriment to the existing circulation of notes or withdrawal of rupees now circulating, gold must continue to occupy for a good many years to come no more than a subsidiary position in the currency system. We do not believe that exchange would materially benefit from the circulation of gold on this scale. There would still be so many rupees in circulation that a considerable quantity could be spared at times of depressed trade, and it would be rupees which, as at present, would flow back into the hands of the Government at such times. All experience goes to show that, so long as the public have the option of making payments in tokens or in gold, it is the surplus tokens and not the gold in circulation which will seek an outlet at a time of weak exchange; and this will continue until the supply of tokens has been so far contracted that they are no more than sufficient for the ordinary business in the transaction of which coins of a low denomination are alone convenient. Thus it is a mistake to believe that to have 10 or 20 per cent of the total active circulation in the form of gold means 10 or 20 per cent of the advantages, such as they are, of having nothing but gold in circulation. During the crisis of 1907–8, while £4,179,000 in gold was withdrawn by the public from the paper currency reserve, only £250,000 was exported on private account. We do not believe, therefore, that the circulation of gold on a moderate scale only would materially reduce the liabilities which Government ought to be prepared to meet.

63. In the third place, it is of great importance to consider from what source any gold which may find its way into circulation is likely to come. If the gold merely takes the place, not of notes or of rupees now circulating, but of new rupees which it would be necessary otherwise to mint, the effect is to diminish the strength of the gold standard reserve by the amount of the profit which would have been made from the new coinage. This

would bring to an end the natural growth of the gold standard reserve (except in so far as its present funds might be invested and earn interest), and it is very improbable that so moderate a public circulation of gold as could possibly be obtained in this way would be as valuable in supporting exchange as gold, even though of a less aggregate quantity, in the gold standard reserve. But it has to be remembered that India's demand for additional currency has been exceedingly irregular; and it would be rash to base currency policy on the assumption that this demand will be large, on the average, over the period of years immediately in front of us. For if, on account of a falling off in the demand for additional currency or for any other cause, such as a greater success in the popularisation of gold than most of its advocates now anticipate, gold in circulation were to take the place of notes or of rupees now circulating, the necessary and immediate consequence of this must be a rapid depletion of the gold now held by Government in the paper currency reserve. Now it must be conceded, and has in fact been acknowledged by most of the witnesses who have pressed for a gold currency, that, sovereign for sovereign, gold in circulation is less effective than gold in reserve for supporting exchange. The depletion, therefore, of the gold in the paper currency reserve, which now serves as a substantial aid to the gold standard reserve in the support of exchange, might gravely weaken the Government's position at a time of exchange difficulties; and the policy of popularising gold, so far from helping exchange, would have jeopardised it. Advocates of a gold currency are met, therefore, by the difficulty that the circulation of gold on a moderate scale only is of no substantial use, while, on the other hand, the circulation of gold on a large scale, at any time in the near future, must necessarily be at the expense of the existing reserves and, so far from increasing the gold in the country, must have the effect of making what gold there is less available for the support of exchange. Advocates of this policy have also to remember that every step in the direction of popularising gold makes it more likely that people will cling to the gold they have and seek to obtain what additional gold they can, on any occasion of crisis or general want of confidence.

64. The argument that the coinage of fresh rupees is objectionable and ought to be avoided is largely bound up with the argument just examined; for the possible danger to exchange of a very large circulation of tokens is the main ground of the objection. But this is a convenient place at which to point out that it is by no means certain that an increase of gold in circulation will be altogether at the expense of rupees. In many respects gold is a far more formidable rival to the note issue than to rupees, since for many purposes a coin of so high a value as the sovereign cannot possibly take the place of rupees, whilst experience elsewhere has shown that a public preference for gold, or alternatively for notes, is largely a matter of habit and custom. To habituate a people, therefore, to the use of sovereigns is almost certain in the long run to militate against the use of notes, even though at first the sovereign is able in some cases to obtain a vogue where, at present and immediately, this is not possible for notes. A people who have adapted their habits to the use of gold will not easily be won from them, so long as gold is easily available. Advocates of a gold currency have repeatedly told us in evidence that they by no means advocate gold in preference to notes, which they regard as a more desirable form of currency; but the policy they favour may have, nevertheless, the consequence they deprecate. There is, indeed, some evidence that the increased popularity of the sovereign in certain districts during the last two years has already hindered in some degree the growing use of notes. In his latest report (for 1912–13) the Head Commissioner of Paper Currency states (paragraph 59):

In paragraph 44 the conclusion has been drawn that gold has replaced rupees to a large extent in the Punjab, and to a smaller extent in Bombay and the United Provinces also. The question now arises whether the increased use of gold has affected the note circulation at all. In the Punjab it is certain that the circulation of 5- and 10-rupee notes has been affected. The gross circulation of the 5-rupee note after nearly doubling in the three years 1908–9 to 1911–12 increased by 0·5 per cent only in 1912–13. The gross circulation of the 10-rupee note in 1910–11 was more than double what it was three years before. In the last two years it has increased by 1 per cent only. These figures considered in conjunction with the large increase in the use of sovereigns in the last two years are irresistible.

In Bombay the gross circulation of the 10-rupee note after increasing by nearly 30 per cent in the two years 1908–9 to 1910–11 has increased by 0·6 per cent only in the last two years.

On the whole, it may now be definitely stated that, but for the use of gold as currency, the circulation of the smaller currency notes would have expanded much more rapidly in the Punjab, Bombay, and the United Provinces.

65. This conclusion is corroborated by some interesting figures placed before us by the National Bank of India and by the Presidency Banks as to the percentage of their receipts and disbursements at various centres in the form of notes, rupees, and gold respectively (see Appendix XVIII, pp. 541, 542, and Appendix XLIII, pp. 724–6). It is remarkable how uniformly in districts where the use of gold is considerable the use of notes is below the average.

[This concludes the section redrafted by Keynes]

66. There remains the argument that without gold in active circulation India's currency system must remain a 'managed' system, it being implied that a managed system is a bad system. The ideal with which this managed system is contrasted seems to be the system of the United Kingdom where fresh supplies of the only unlimited legal tender coins, the sovereign or the half sovereign, can be obtained at will by anyone who takes gold to the mint for coinage.

In our opinion this contrast is of no value. There does not appear to us to be any essential difference between the power to import sovereigns at will and the power to have gold coined into sovereigns in India. The only point of the criticism that India's currency system is managed in a sense that is not true of the currency of the United Kingdom lies in the fact that the rupee is a token passing at a value above its intrinsic value and at the same time is unlimited legal tender. It is true that it is not practicable even to consider the limitation of the amount for which the rupee is legal tender. In this sense therefore the system must remain a managed one. But we demur altogether to the idea that because it is to this extent a managed system it must be a bad system. It is not, in fact, possible for the Government of India to manipulate the currency for their own ends, and they cannot add to the active circulation of the currency except in response to public demands.

67. With the argument that India should be encouraged to absorb gold for the benefit of the world in general we do not propose to deal. The extent to which India should use gold must, in our opinion, be decided solely in accordance with India's own needs and wishes, and it appears to us to be as unjust to force gold coins into circulation in India on the ground that such action will benefit the gold-using countries of the rest of the world as it would be to attempt to refuse to India facilities for obtaining gold in order to prevent what adherents of the opposite school have called the drain of gold to India. In any case these arguments (which it will be noted are mutually destructive) are irrelevant to the inquiry which we were directed to make and to the terms of reference, which confine us to a report on what is 'conducive to the interests of India'. They raise vast controversies upon subjects which are beyond our scope, while giving no reason for the adoption of either policy in India's own interest.

68. We conclude therefore that it would not be to India's advantage to encourage an increased use of gold in the internal circulation.

It is a problem to know how far Keynes went in attempting to rewrite the 'Gold Currency in India' part of the Report. It has three subsections: 'Gold in Internal Circulation' (reproduced above), 'Proposed Gold Mint for India' and 'Conclusions'. Chamberlain's paragraphs on the proposed gold mint were redrafted by someone, and the tightening of the writing and the argument could be described as typical of Keynes, but there is no documentary proof. The 'Conclusions' were redrafted by Keynes and submitted to the Commission as an alternative. 'The Commission (which was in a conservative mood) preferred the original draft to your redraft', Blackett wrote (17 January 1914) describing the meeting.

Keynes's 'Conclusions' were much more explicit than the version adopted and would have made this part of the Report much stronger. His draft emphasised the point which he had introduced into the 'Gold in Internal

Circulation' discussion, that a gold currency was positively dangerous—not simply uneconomical, as stated by the Commission. It also included a paragraph, which has no counterpart in the Report, urging the Government of India to disallow any further efforts by officials towards the popularisation of gold (one of the witnesses examined had recently tried such an experiment). What follows is his draft of the 'Conclusions'.

GOLD CURRENCY: DRAFT 'CONCLUSIONS'

74. We have already stated that it is not to India's interest that further efforts should be made to encourage the circulation of gold as currency. We have there given our reasons for believing that such quantity of gold, as could flow into the circulation in the not distant future without involving the displacement of notes and the withdrawal of rupees now circulating, would afford but little support to exchange and might result in a weakening of the existing reserves. If we take a larger view and look to the more remote future we are in sympathy with the school of thought which regards gold in circulation as essentially wasteful, and which holds that India should be encouraged in all reasonable ways to develop economical habits in matters of currency. In the long run the encouragement of the inclination to handle metallic coin must result in the locking up of much wealth in a barren form. In the immediate future, therefore, a somewhat increased use of gold would not help exchange, while it would develop the habits of Indians along the lines which are not ultimately the most desirable. In dealing with the paper currency system of India we shall make some suggestions relevant in this connection.

75. But while educating the people in the use of more economical forms of currency, the Government should continue to act on the principle of giving them the form of currency for which they ask. Though holding that the coinage of new rupees should be limited as closely as possible to the probable requirements, we recognise that for many years to come there will be a vast number of transactions in India for which rupees alone are suit-

able. And there will be opportunities for the use of gold coins rather than rupees in circumstances for which notes are not adapted and rupees are inconveniently cumbrous. It is likely, moreover, that a long period will elapse before the growth of habits of banking can put an end to the existing demand for gold coins in hoards by taking their place as a means to make savings secure. The line between gold in hoards and in circulation is an indefinable one, and the hoarding habit is sanctioned in India by the experience of centuries and by religious and racial laws and customs, with which the Government of India have neither the inclination nor the power to interfere. The people of India have as much right to expend their resources without hindrance on the absorption of gold for such a purpose, as on any other object of luxury or distinction. Any attempt, therefore, to refuse gold would be likely to cause alarm and inconvenience, and unlikely to achieve its object.

76. There is, however, a clear line between meeting a definite demand for gold coins, which it would be unfair and impolitic to refuse, and encouraging a further demand for gold beyond what would exist otherwise. While giving gold freely to those who desire it, the Government of India should definitely discountenance experiments on the part of their officers in the popularisation of the sovereign, and should always have before their eyes the gradual education of the people in the use of economical forms of currency, as opportunity serves. So far from agreeing with the view which has been expressed to us, that the popularisation of gold is a necessary first step to the replacement of coin by notes, we regard this policy as likely to lead to serious and needless delay in the attainment of its ostensible object.

77. To sum up, our view is that India does not require greater facilities for the supply of gold coin than exist at present, that the most suitable media of internal circulation in India in the immediate future are rupees and notes, and that the Government should do all they can to encourage notes, while providing—and

this is the cardinal feature of the whole system—absolute security for the convertibility into sterling of so much of the internal currency as may at any moment be required for the settlement of India's external obligations.

Keynes had made several suggestions regarding the next section of the Report, on the gold standard reserve, in the comments that he had exchanged with Chamberlain. The most important of these concerned the question of the proper size for the reserve and particularly whether some limitation should be placed on it, as Abrahams had proposed. Keynes had written to Chamberlain:

From a letter to AUSTEN CHAMBERLAIN

Two important witnesses, Mr Abrahams and Lord Inchcape, urged us not to forget the possibility of wastefulness in the accumulation of needlessly high sterling reserves. I think we owe it to them to make our position clear on this point and not to lay our whole emphasis on the risk of the reserves being too low, especially in view of the enormously strong financial position of the Government of India at the present time. With this object in view, therefore, I suggest a revised form for §§83–5.

J.M.K.

His revision follows. It differs from the original draft in the importance given to the aggregate reserves—the gold in the paper currency reserve as well as in the gold standard reserve—as a support to the exchange. This made it possible to alter the emphasis of the original, which insisted on the deposit in the reserve of all the profits obtained from coining rupees and interest on loans, with no diversion as in the past for railway development, to a more progressive proposal looking forward to the future when an increased gold standard reserve would be strong enough to support the exchange alone, and the gold in the paper currency reserve could be turned to profitable investment.

DRAFT: THE GOLD STANDARD RESERVE

83. We do not accept, therefore, the figure of £18 million, which was the measure of the demand made by the crisis of 1907–8 upon the sterling reserves of the Indian Government, as an adequate guide to the amount which may be required in a similar

crisis in future. Experience of a second period of adverse exchange is necessary before it will be safe to prescribe with any degree of precision the proper magnitude of the aggregate sterling reserves. We can say no more than that, with India's foreign trade on its present scale, aggregate reserves of anything from £30 million to £40 million would not be, in our opinion, in any way extravagant.

84. When the question of the aggregate amount of the sterling reserves has been settled, it still remains to determine what part of the burden ought to fall on the gold standard reserve and what part on the gold in the paper currency reserve. It is the declared intention of the authorities at present to increase the gold standard reserve up to a total of £25 million and then to reconsider the necessity of continuing to appropriate to it the whole of the income from its present sources of supply. Of the paper currency reserve the gold ear-marked in London (at present £6,100,000) is commonly regarded as a far more reliable support to exchange than the gold held in India, and as the part of which account ought primarily to be taken. We incline to the view that reliance ought to be placed on gold in the paper currency reserve for the support of exchange, only in so far and so long as the gold standard reserve is not yet adequate to support the burden itself. There is no great likelihood of this in the immediate future and we do not think, therefore, that it would be useful for us to attempt to lay down at present any hypothetical limit beyond which the gold standard reserve should not be accumulated.

Our unwillingness to set a limit to the accumulation of the gold standard reserve, so far as this is due to profits on the coinage of rupees, is increased by the fact that otherwise Government may appear to lay themselves open to the charge that they can (if foreign exchanges be left out of consideration) provide themselves with as much money as they like for internal expenditure by the simple process of coining rupees without limit. We do not suggest that it is even conceivable that the Government of India would actually take this suicidal course. But at the same time it appears to us undesirable that any Government should be open to attack in this way if it is possible to avoid it.

85. While we do not see our way to setting any present limit to the accumulation of the gold standard reserve, we think, nevertheless, looking beyond the immediate future, that the Government of India ought to be alive to the possibility of the aggregate sterling reserves eventually reaching an unnecessarily high figure. In the case of a country with such large and unsatisfied claims, as India has, for further capital development, it would be a great misfortune if more wealth were accumulated in a barren form than is absolutely necessary. We hold, first, that it is worth India's while to make absolutely sure of the maintenance of exchange; and, second, that, when this point has been reached with the aid of the gold standard reserve and the earmarked gold in the paper currency reserve taken together, the preferable course will probably be, not to divert funds from the gold standard reserve, but rather to throw a large share of the burden on this reserve. It should then be a matter for consideration whether the time may not have come, when, account being taken of the magnitude of the gold standard reserve, it is safe to invest, and so to enjoy the profits of, a larger proportion of the paper currency reserve than formerly.

Blackett reported: 'As I rather suspected, as soon as the Commission studied your redraft here, they clamoured against it.' The final result was that they accepted Keynes's rewording, which was more easy to follow than the original, but not his position. They dropped the references to the aggregate sterling reserves in the first and second paragraphs and reinstated their original dictum that £25 million in the gold standard reserve was not enough, even with the ear-marked gold of the paper currency reserve taken into consideration. After Keynes's third paragraph they reinserted their disapproval, ignored by Keynes and revived by Chamberlain, of the suggestion of one witness—it was Abrahams—that the gold standard reserve represented great sacrifices from the revenues of India by way of forgone investments. Keynes's final paragraph 'was deleted altogether', wrote Blackett, 'but on my urgent request that something should be done to meet you, the first sentence of §89 [Keynes's final paragraph] was placed at the beginning of

§88 [the original conclusion for this section, §89 in the published Report]'. Thus, while it was acknowledged in a subordinate clause that the aggregate sterling reserves might possibly grow in the future to an unnecessary size, the course recommended was to continue accumulating gold for the present, with no diversion for development. (In the published Report paragraphs 85–7 correspond to Keynes's first and second paragraphs above.)

Keynes was governed by his desire to make possible a much greater use of the paper currency reserve, and it was in the treatment of the paper currency reserve that he left his mark on the Report. *Indian Currency and Finance* had criticised an otherwise admirable system for its lack of flexibility in providing funds for lending. India suffered a periodic demand for money, in the cycle of busy season following slack season. The means to satisfy the demand existed—the abnormally high balances standing idle in the Government Treasuries—but these could only be released by selling Council bills in London and there was no machinery for making the funds available in India. The situation was aggravated by the annual movement of money, in the form of taxes and revenues, out of the public circulation into the Reserve Treasuries just at the time when it was most wanted.

The need was for temporary loans to tide business over from season to season. The only source other than the Reserve Treasuries was the paper currency reserve. This was modelled on the British system with a fixed fiduciary issue—so low, in spite of past increases, in relation to what it could safely lend and to what was needed, that the maximum available for lending had become in effect a minimum of permanent investment. Without a change of law, there was no money free for short-term loans.

Keynes had already outlined his ideal solution in his State Bank memorandum, but with no State Bank to manage the paper currency the commissioners had to seek another remedy. The proposal made in Chamberlain's draft Report was to fix the fiduciary issue at one-third of the gross circulation of notes—both the notes out with the public and the banks and those in the Reserve Treasuries. Thus investments would increase as the total note issue increased. This plan, however, made little provision for short-run changes in the gross note circulation—the large temporary demands for money that regularly occurred. A solution of the problem was attempted by allowing a four-month period of grace before securities in excess of the permitted maximum would have to be sold. But, in spite of good intentions, the proposal betrayed a nervousness towards departure from the traditional dogma that every note must be backed by gold or silver.

Moreover, by limiting lending to one-third of the gross circulation, the plan freed only one-third of the balances in the Reserve Treasuries for investment. Gillan, when writing to Keynes of his dissatisfaction with the draft Report, had expressed a fear that 'the inclination on the financial side now is to drop loans in India from Treasury and confine our recommendations to the paper currency reserve'. He mentioned that he had blocked out roughly what he thought ought to be said on the subject.

Gillan's draft appears to survive as an unsigned, undated carbon typescript in Keynes's files. It is possible (though unlikely, if only on stylistic grounds) that the paper is Keynes's work at a half-way stage; but Gillan was much concerned to promote lending from the balances while Keynes looked more to the paper currency reserve for assistance. It seems much more likely that Gillan's comment became the germ of an idea which Keynes developed. The typescript is as follows:

The suggestion which we [the Commission] have made in regard to the fiduciary portion of the paper currency reserve is that loans should be made from that reserve in India up to a maximum of one-third of the gross circulation. In so far as the balance kept in the Reserve Treasuries consists of notes, this proposal will enable the Government to make available by means of loans from the paper currency reserve a maximum of one-third of the amounts at present immobilised in the Reserve Treasuries, and will mitigate to this extent the effect of the Reserve Treasury system in causing stringency in the money market. It would obviously be possible to make the remaining two-thirds available for the market by so modifying our scheme as to allow the permanent or temporary investment of the paper currency reserve up to a maximum of (a) one-third of the amount of the gross circulation less the notes in the Reserve Treasuries *plus* (b) the whole of the amount of the notes in the Reserve Treasuries. But it appears to us that such a scheme is cumbrous and that so long as the paper currency reserve and the Government of India's balance are kept distinct it is preferable, even as a matter of book-keeping, to regulate the fiduciary portion of the note issue according to the gross circulation, and to treat separately the question of making the surplus balance temporarily available on the Indian money market. If this view be taken, our proposals in regard to the paper currency reserve will not provide a complete alternative to loans from balances, and so long as the Reserve Treasury system is maintained, there will always remain the possibility of the locking up of funds in the Reserve Treasuries causing stringency on the market.

We are therefore of opinion that the Government should go so far in the direction of releasing funds from the accumulations in the Reserve Treasuries as to make a regular practice of granting loans to the Presidency Banks, as a measure supplementary to the grant of loans from the paper currency reserve, on the same conditions as we have recommended for loans from that reserve. The exact conditions for the loans can best be settled by the Government of India in consultation with the banks on the spot and may require to be reconsidered at fairly frequent intervals. Incidentally we may observe that, besides being an act of justice on the part of Government to that part of the business community which suffers under the present system (and through them to the Indian public generally), the loans will provide a new source of revenue to the Indian Exchequer in the shape of interest on funds which at present produce no return.

We do not suggest that the Government of India should allow its balances to accumulate for the purpose of making such loans, or that any reduction should be made in the amounts now made available by the Government in India for meeting the Secretary of State's sales of Council drafts in order to increase the sum available for lending in India. It is not, in our opinion, desirable that the practice of making loans from balances in India should be allowed to interfere with existing arrangements in other directions.

The important point here was that the notes in the Reserve Treasuries were in fact the Government's own debts to itself, or debts owed by one branch of the Government to another. Since the cashing of these notes was in the hands of the Government they did not constitute a risk to the paper currency reserve, as did notes in public circulation or with the banks. This was the real reason why Gillan was able to suggest lending out the balances independently of loans from the paper currency reserve. While he accepted the Commission's plan to apportion the fiduciary issue in relation to the gross circulation, his 'cumbrous' formula for investment up to a maximum of '(a) one-third of the amount of the gross circulation less the notes in the Reserve Treasuries *plus* (b) the whole of the amount of the notes in the Reserve Treasuries' amounted to saying 'one-third of the amount of the *net* circulation, plus the whole of the amount of the notes in the Reserve Treasuries'. It was only the notes in the net circulation—at large with the public and the banks—that the paper currency reserve would be called upon to cash and against which it must provide a reserve.

Keynes's criticism of the draft proposal went farther and deeper than Gillan's and concentrated on the paper currency reserve, but he incorporated Gillan's idea of the theoretical usefulness of *all* the government balances. In the note that he wrote to Chamberlain disagreeing with this part of the draft Report he pointed out the essential inflexibility of the scheme in operation and suggested an ingenious alternative. Instead of stipulating a maximum fiduciary issue of one-third of the gross circulation as the basic requirement, he would impose a cash reserve requirement of two-thirds of the net circulation, thereby releasing the amount in the Reserve Treasuries for lending. In transforming the allowance of a fiduciary issue of one-third of the net circulation suggested by Gillan into a cash reserve requirement of two-thirds of the net circulation, he emphasised the need for enough cash to back the net circulation as the crucial factor in determining what the Government could safely lend.

This is not made explicit, however, and the main weight of Keynes's criticism rests on the need to give the authorities a greater margin for discretion in lending. To this end Keynes recommended a rule setting the maximum fiduciary issue at one-third of the gross circulation, leaving any reduction from this amount to the judgment of the Government. In the same spirit the second part of the note urges that the Government be left free to ascertain the most appropriate rate to be charged for loans.

CRITICISM OF DRAFT RESERVES PROPOSAL

I am in sympathy with the objects arrived at in these two paragraphs [111 and 112 of the draft report], but am not quite satisfied with the details of the proposed scheme.

S. 111. The fault of the proposal here is that there is little or no margin between the working figure for the invested portion of the paper currency reserve and the maximum figure allowed by law. The legal figure, that is to say, has been fixed at about that proportion up to, or nearly up to, which would be thought reasonable to work in normal times. This seems to me to be a vicious plan and to be a likely occasion of inconvenience: for a comparatively small divergence from the normal would make it legally incumbent on Government to draw in its advances suddenly and even to sell its securities, although in the opinion of Government the existing situation were of the most temporary character and not in the least such as to justify any strong measures. Indeed the rule might act in the most ridiculous way imaginable: suppose, for example, the fiduciary portion was near the legal ratio of one-third, and the Government were called on to make disbursements involving a reduction in the amount held in the Reserve Treasuries, then for every lakh they had to disburse they would have to call three lakhs from the market. The Government might be legally bound to take action, which would provoke grave stringency, in calling from the market money in which they were of no need.

Or take the situation in October of this year. The gross issue of notes fell to 6,050 lakhs. If the permanent investments had been at 2,000 lakhs (as proposed), not only would all temporary loans have come to an end, but the Government might even have had to consider selling securities at a most unfavourable moment. Yet there was nothing in the actual situation to justify in the least either of these measures.

The period of grace of four months, which is proposed, goes a little way towards modifying these objections. But the Government would have to act on the safe side and to take action some time before the period of grace had elapsed. It gives a little 'play', but not, I think, nearly enough. The proposal involves the appearance and the disadvantages of a rule-of-thumb system, without its reality or simplicity of working. It is in fact useless to hope that elasticity can be introduced into the note issue without a sacrifice of rule-of-thumb.

There seem to be two lines of solution, in the absence of management by a bank:

(1) A rule that the fiduciary portion must not be *increased*, so long as it exceeds one-third of the gross circulation, while leaving it entirely to the discretion of Government as to whether or at what date it need be *reduced*.

(2) A rule fixing the legal proportion considerably above the normal working proportion.

A number of rules could be propounded which would satisfy condition (2). One which occurs to me is that the cash in the paper currency reserve should not fall below two-thirds of the *net* circulation. This would have the effect of making available for fiduciary purposes, and for loans and investment through the machinery of the paper currency reserve, one-third of the net circulation together with the whole of the sums held by Government in their Reserve Treasuries. Such a rule would err, if anything, in the direction of making the legal figure still too near the normal working figure.

I suggest that provision (1) above might be adopted *as well as* some provision under (2).

S. 112. I deprecate a rule fixing the rate charged for loans at 1 per cent below bank-rate. I should prefer to leave the rate entirely to the discretion of Government, to be settled by bargaining with the Presidency Banks according to circumstances.

Certainly a rate 1 per cent below bank rate would often have the effect of preventing any business being done. The banks could not lend from the proceeds of loans placed with them for short periods absolutely up to the hilt. Suppose for example that the bank rate were 6 per cent and the Presidency felt free to lend 5 lakhs out of every 6 placed with them by Government; in this case they would be lending 5 lakhs at 6 per cent and paying 5 per cent on 6 lakhs, which would leave them no margin of profit. The proposed terms are only reasonable on the assumption that the bank can lend up to the hilt, or that, as in England, to place additional cash with the bank increases its power to lend to a more than corresponding amount. Such an assumption would not always be justified in India.

The Government of India ought to be allowed to feel their way in this matter of loans and to experiment as to the proper rate chargeable for them; and, at any rate in the first instance, it will be unwise to tie them down to one particular method.

J.M.K.

Chamberlain reacted to this in an orthodox fashion. In the margin of Keynes's first page he wrote:

This is a very difficult subject but I should be very much afraid of your solution which it seems to me is equivalent to saying to the Government 'You may do what you like with this Reserve'.

At any rate, after trying, I cannot draft anything on your lines to my liking. You may perhaps be more successful.
A.C.

Keynes and Gillan then submitted a revision of Chamberlain's draft for the Commission's consideration. The scheme they proposed followed the outline suggested by Keynes in his note to Chamberlain—a reserve with a cash requirement of two-thirds of the net circulation and a fiduciary issue consisting of at least 20 crores of permanent investment. With two-thirds more of the Government balances free for lending than would be available under the Commission's proposal, it would be possible to make temporary loans in addition to this permanent investment, from either the balances or the paper currency reserve, as the Government saw fit.

The paper explained in some detail the reasoning that led to this formulation; central banking was a little-explored field at the time and these were novel ideas. As later events showed, this draft was essentially Keynes's work.

PAPER CURRENCY: REVISED DRAFT

113. The change which we propose in the principle governing the invested portion of the reserve is more fundamental, and is directed partly towards an immediate increase in the permanent investments and, as the circulation of notes grows, their further increase in the future without special legislation; partly towards some amelioration of the fault in the existing system, to which we have already referred, by the introduction of temporary investments. We will deal first with the total amount of the invested or fiduciary portion, and then with its division between permanent and temporary securities.

114. In the past the invested or fiduciary portion of the note issue has been fixed in absolute amount. There has been no discretionary power to vary it in accordance with the permanent growth of the circulation or with the fluctuating demand for currency at different seasons of the year. Experience in the management of note issues elsewhere points, first, to the desirability of fixing the legal maximum of the fiduciary portion by reference to a proportion rather than to a fixed amount, and, second, to the importance of fixing the proportion, which cannot be exceeded legally, well above the proportion normally worked to. The significance of the second of these considerations may be brought out thus—if the legal maximum to the fiduciary

portion were fixed at one-third, and if the investments stood at 20 crores and the circulation at 62 crores, 3 crores could not be cashed immediately on presentation without a suspension of the Note Act (since 20 crores exceeds one-third of 59 crores). Thus a relatively slight departure from normal conditions might force the Government to liquidate securities, at a time when, apart from the letter of the law, the balance of advantage might be opposed to this course. To compel the Government to take such stringent measures on an occasion of moderate departure from normal conditions would be calculated to aggravate, rather than to relieve a troublesome situation.

115. Four ways of avoiding this difficulty suggest themselves: (1) to fix the legal maximum well above the normal working maximum, in order to allow a very wide discretion in times of emergency or abnormal conditions; (2) to fix the legal maximum well above the normal maximum, but to exact a fine when the working figure, although still below the maximum, exceeds a certain other proportion or absolute amount, so as to allow a wide discretion while discouraging a too free exercise of it; (3) to combine the principle of a proportionate fiduciary issue with the principle of an absolute maximum, so as to set a limit to the volume of securities which it may be necessary to liquidate urgently; (4) to allow the invested portion, when once it has legally reached a given total, to remain at that total for a certain period of time without regard to its proportion, so as to permit the more gradual liquidation of the securities.

116. To give the Government so free a hand as would be involved in the adoption of the first method by itself, while probably the safest and most convenient method in practice, so long as reliance can be placed on Government's using their discretion prudently, might possibly have a weakening effect on popular confidence in the note issue, and would be a somewhat violent departure from the rigour of the existing system for immediate use, and before experience has been gained of the capacity of Government officials to work an elastic system wisely.

The second method has been used with much success in countries where the note issue is managed by a central bank, but is out of the question in the case of Government management, since there is no one but themselves to whom the Government could pay the fine. The remaining two methods, while somewhat makeshift in character and unsupported by experience, may contain ideas of some practical usefulness. Indeed, the elastic systems of note issue in other countries of the world are so inseparably connected with the existence of a state or central bank, that any attempt to set up an elastic system under purely Government management must be largely experimental; but on the whole we recommend for India a moderate use of the first method, in combination with the third; though we do not desire to rule the fourth method out of consideration altogether.

117. When we come to fix the proper proportion of the cash reserves to the circulation, the practice of other countries affords but a misleading analogy. In the case of the state banks of Europe the reserve of cash held against the note issue serves the purpose not only of a reserve against the possible encashment of notes, but is also the ultimate banking reserve of the country and the support of the exchanges in the event of an adverse balance of international indebtedness. It serves, that is to say, the joint purposes of the Indian paper currency reserve, the gold standard reserve, and the cash reserves of the Presidency Banks; so that what in India is three funds, with them is one. Thus the circulation of most note-using countries corresponds, not to the gross circulation in India, but to the active circulation, from which the notes held by the Government or by the Presidency Banks are excluded; and the proportion of cash in the paper currency reserve to the active circulation corresponds to the proportion of cash to total circulation in most European banks. In the case of India, it would not be convenient to take the active circulation as the starting point for the calculation of the legal reserve, because the amount of notes held by the Presidency Banks is not a direct concern of the Government. Nor would it

be convenient to treat notes in Government Treasuries up and down the country as unissued for the purpose of calculating the reserve, since their amount is constantly fluctuating and is not within the daily cognisance of the central authorities. Both financial propriety and convenience, however, point to what is known in India as the *net* circulation, namely, the gross circulation less the notes held in the Reserve Treasuries, as the most suitable basis for the calculation of the legal reserve. It is a further advantage of this method of calculation that, whether the Government choose, as a matter of form, to make temporary loans from the cash balances or from the paper currency reserve, it makes no difference to the legal position; whereas, if the gross circulation is taken as the basis on which to calculate the legal reserve, it may make a great difference from which source a loan happens to have been made on a particular occasion.

118. We are now in a position to proceed to the details of our recommendation. We propose that the cash portion (rupees and sovereigns) of the paper currency reserve should not fall below two-thirds of the net circulation, subject to the proviso that the investments need not be reduced below 20 crores, the permanent nucleus of investment being placed at this figure instead of at 14 crores as at present.

119. If the recommendations which we make in regard to the use of balances in India are accepted, the Government will have a discretion to make temporary loans from their cash balances. When Government have funds in their own balances which they desire to lend we see an advantage in making the loan from the Treasury inasmuch as Government are then seen to be dealing with their own funds. At the same time there is a very close connection between Treasury loans and paper currency investments, and it remains true that, in a crisis, Government must be prepared to employ all the resources available to them in whatever fund they may be deposited. We suggest, therefore, that in dealing with the Reserve Treasuries Government may employ alternative methods. Either, that is to say, they may make a loan

as from the Treasury, reducing consequently both their balances and the gross circulation, and possibly a further loan from the paper currency reserve at its reduced level, or they may leave their surplus balance in the paper currency department, and make the loan from the aggregate funds thus accumulated there. In favour of the second alternative it may be observed that there are clearly advantages in dealing with funds as a whole instead of in compartments. When money is available it may not always be necessary to distinguish the advances made as being so much from the Treasury and so much from the paper currency; and further, a larger loan may, at times, be possible from the aggregate fund, than it would be desirable to advance from either of its constituents.

120. The final choice, however, between the alternative method of granting loans which we have indicated must rest on actual experience of the working of the system, and we cannot do more than outline the general considerations which seem to us to bear on the question.

121. We must add that a Government without responsibility for or control over the bank rate or credit facilities generally ought, in our opinion, to work an elastic system of note issue with the utmost caution, and that the Indian business world should not entertain too high hopes as to the amount of relief from seasonal stringency which they may expect to obtain under the system which we have proposed. As we have pointed out above, it is necessary in order to avoid the difficulties which otherwise would follow a reduction in the note circulation to provide an adequate working margin against a considerable departure from normal conditions. This the Government can do, under the system which we put forward, only by keeping their investments well within the permissible limit, and in the paper currency apart from the Government holding there will be little room for this until the circulation has increased considerably. The margin, however, is increased by the extent to which the Reserve Treasury balance is retained in the paper currency

reserve. Thus, to take hypothetical figures, if the gross circulation stood at 65 crores and the net circulation at 55 crores, the Government might invest a little over 18 crores as against the net circulation and the whole of their Reserve Treasury balance of 10 crores. They might, however, think it safe to invest no more than 22 crores, and in that case the cash in the reserve being 43 crores, 20 crores of notes could be redeemed before it would be legally obligatory to liquidate any part of the 22 crores of investments. In the case assumed the cash belonging to the Government holding is really hypothecated for the purposes of the paper currency reserve, but it is not necessarily objectionable to use it in this manner, otherwise the Government in making their investments must be content to follow at some distance the development of the net circulation.

122. The division of the invested portion between permanent and temporary securities ought not, we think, to be the subject of any statutory provision. At present the permanent investments should not exceed the 20 crores below which we propose that the total investments need never fall. We propose that the 6 crores of additional investments, which would be required to bring the present investments up to this figure, should be obtained by a transfer (at market value) of securities to this amount from the gold standard reserve in exchange for 6 crores of the gold now in the paper currency reserve in India.

123. Such part of the balance still remaining available for investment, as it is thought advisable to deal with, should be temporarily invested either in London or in India. In India such temporary investment should take the form of loans to the Presidency Banks against the deposit of securities of the Government of India or port trust stocks or similar securities. We do not think that it would be advisable, on the basis of such experience as is now available, to prescribe exactly on what terms in relation to bank rate these loans should be made. The rate on each occasion should be a matter of negotiation between the Government and the Presidency Banks. Nor do we think that

any absolute rules should be laid down as to the length of time for which such loans should be made, though they ought not on ordinary occasions to exceed a period of three months at the most. In London the Secretary of State should have power to make temporary investments or to lend sums in the London money market on account of the paper currency reserve, in the same manner in which he makes loans from his cash balances. But this power ought, in our opinion, to be exercised only for exceptional reasons or when the Presidency Banks have been unable to offer satisfactory terms. We have considered the possibility of holding a limited amount of commercial paper against loans either in London or India, but we are of opinion that Government officials, who are necessarily without banking experience, are not in a position to undertake this class of business.

124. We hope for the following advantages from our recommendations: (1) While the permanent addition to the invested portion of the reserve will be no more than is justified by past practice and experience without in any way endangering the complete convertibility of the notes, the revenues of India will secure the profit earned by investing the amount now held idle in the form of gold in India. (2) There will be occasions, especially in the busy season, when it will be safe to lend temporarily sums which it would be unwise to invest permanently. The power to make such loans will, therefore, enable the Government to earn interest on sums which would otherwise lie idle needlessly, and will provide at the same time a much needed facility for a temporary expansion of the currency in the busy season, by virtue of which the market may obtain some relief, though not at first, perhaps, a very great amount, from its recurrent stringency. (3) The power to make temporary investments in London on account of the paper currency reserve will be a convenience to the Secretary of State in permitting him to sell Council drafts against the paper currency reserve, in anticipation of silver purchases or for any other cause, without the loss of

interest and other disadvantages which might sometimes come about if he were compelled, without discretionary power, to utilise the entire proceeds of such sales in ear-marking gold. (4) As the circulation of notes in India increases, it will be within the power of the authorities to increase as and when desirable either the permanent or the temporary investments of the reserve or both without a special act.

The document seems to have been produced hurriedly—Keynes never saw a proof—and some of the argument is very compressed. In paragraph 119, for example, Keynes assumed without explanation that notes loaned from the Reserve Treasuries would be immediately cashed from the paper currency reserve (hence the reduction in the gross circulation). This paragraph and paragraph 121 implicitly confined attention to notes held in the Reserve Treasuries (the difference between the gross and the net circulation), which notes either could be lent out directly from the Treasury balances, or could serve to free cash for lending from the paper currency reserves.

It is no wonder that Chamberlain had difficulty in following these paragraphs. 'Is it a fact', he queried through Blackett, 5 January 1914 (in a letter which Keynes did not receive until his belated return to London), 'that as appears to be here suggested, the balances in the Reserve Treasuries must equal the difference between the net and the gross circulation of notes? May not that balance be partly notes and partly rupees and partly gold? In other words, in the case stated in the section is the 10 crores of notes in the Reserve Treasuries all that is in them? Will there not be rupees and gold in addition?'

A related source of confusion was the shift from a conventional to an unconventional mode of thought. When Keynes described the permanent investment provisions for the paper currency reserve as an 'absolute maximum' what he really meant was a minimum that it would be legal to hold. He did indeed make it quite clear that he wanted to insure the holding of a certain amount of permanent investment which the reserve could not be forced to cash—a privilege, rather than a restriction—but the traditional language for these matters was repressive, not permissive, and in slipping into it, Keynes helped to befog the issue.

When the Commission reassembled in January—without Keynes—they, in the words of Blackett's 17 January letter, 'unanimously expressed themselves unable to understand clearly what you and Gillan were after, and led by Kilbracken wanted to stick to the old scheme'. They were, as Gillan described them, dominated by impatience to be done with their job and faced with a tricky subject which they had failed to master in a written exposition. Gillan put up a fight but was not able to meet a criticism that he had not expected; 'the rock on which I foundered was "complexity"' (letter of 27 January).

Cable wrote: 'If your memo had given just *one simple method* to secure elasticity it might have gone through—but you *over-elaborated*, I think' (24 January). The extent of the confusion may be appreciated by the fact that Blackett, the secretary, in telling Keynes how the Commission had gone on to modify the original scheme, got some of the details wrong.

As Gillan said, Keynes's absence from the Commission was 'little short of a calamity'. There certainly was a guilty hastening to pen and paper afterwards on the part of his correspondents. The first to write was the Chairman, promptly on the day of the second meeting, 13 January. Chamberlain started his letter, marked 'Private', with 'Dear Mr Keynes'—certainly a slip, since it had been 'Dear Keynes' since August and it must have been 'Dear Chamberlain' for some time as well, as a note from him to Keynes, 29 October 1913, begins: 'Need we "Mr" one another any longer?'

Dear Mr Keynes,

I was very sorry to receive your letter yesterday with news of your illness and doubly and selfishly sorry that it had come at such a moment. We greatly missed your assistance at our meetings yesterday and today.

Owing to your absence you had not received some of the papers circulated to the Commission. Among these was a draft on Balances and Councils which adopted Gillan's arrangement, modified or omitted some of his propositions and embodied a good deal of the original draft as well. This was taken by the Commission as the basis of their discussion and was adopted by them with amendments some of which were taken from your communication to me. I do not think that there is anything in it to which you will take serious exception.

On the other hand there were some paragraphs on paper currency to which you and Gillan had taken exception and to which you had circulated an alternative.

I made some criticisms on this alternative which went to your London address and unfortunately had not reached you when you wrote.

I do not think that Gillan was very successful in meeting them and I had to confess after some discussion that I did not understand your alternative draft. Cable said he understood it but could not explain it, and all the Commissioners except Gillan preferred to take the original draft with some amendments. This is therefore what we have done, and I hope that it will not cause you to record any dissent.

The result of our proposals is certainly not to give any large discretion to the Government in dealing with the note issue; but, as you have perceived, the fact is that such wide discretion would only be safely given to a bank. We have taken the *net* issue as the measure of the fiduciary portion instead of the gross, but we allow a minimum investment of 20 crores. This leaves our gold standard reserve proposals intact.

Considering the great difficulty and intricacy of the matters with which we had to deal and the divergency of opinion even on the Commission, it will be a great triumph for us all if we can get a report whose unanimity is marred by only one dissent—Sir J. Begbie's. He has behaved with great fairness but he wants a gold standard pure and simple. This is the biggest thing in the Report and I earnestly beg you to give your most favourable consideration to what we have been obliged to do in your absence and if, as I believe, you agree in the main on the big issue of which your book has made you the champion, not to mar our agreement by recording dissent (if you feel it) on a minor point of note issue management.

Please let me know when you will be in London, so that I may give you any further explanations you desire, and believe me.

With best wishes for your recovery
Yours sincerely

AUSTEN CHAMBERLAIN

The Commission had indeed been affected by Keynes's arguments, but strangely. They seem to have grasped at the idea of using the net circulation but misunderstood the difference between a minimum cash requirement and a maximum fiduciary requirement, and they balked at granting so much discretion to the Government. What they had done was to fix a fiduciary requirement in proportion to the net circulation (one-third), allowing discretion in lending from the balances, and to provide for an increase of the permanent investments to 20 crores (by transferring rupees from the gold standard reserve—Chamberlain's reference to leaving 'our gold standard reserve proposals intact'). In effect, however, their well-intentioned attempt at flexibility was cancelled entirely by the 20-crore specification which choked off any temporary loans from the paper currency reserve until the net circulation reached a very high figure.

There is no copy of any answer by Keynes to this letter but on 21 January Chamberlain wrote again. Blackett had told Keynes in his letter of 17 January that the Chairman was 'very anxious to have as few further changes as possible, as your colleagues are many of them drifting in your direction and don't mean to come back at any price'.

Dear Keynes,

I am very glad to hear that your convalescence proceeds satisfactorily, but even this good news does not console me for your absence from our last meeting.

The Commission did, I am afraid, take the course which you deprecate. They kept as closely to their original proposal as they could, whilst substituting the net for the gross circulation as the test to be applied for determining the extent of the fiduciary issue in future.

I quite recognise that this does not give the kind of elasticity which you desire to the currency, but apart from other difficulties connected with your proposal, which we were unable to overcome in your absence, I would say for myself that I gravely doubt whether it would be wise or right to entrust to unskilled Indian officials without special training, the kind of responsibilities that would be involved in working any of the proposals that you sketched.

I think that this is essentially one of the points on which practical bankers' experience would be needed, and I doubt if your proposal could be carried out except in connection with the establishment of a State Bank.

I hope that this difference will not prevent you from signing our report, or compel you to add any addendum to it. It may certainly serve as an argument in your further writings for the conclusion to which I know you have come, that there can never be a perfectly satisfactory system until such a bank is established, and I hope that this thought may console you for any disappointment which you feel about the conclusion to which we came.

I am kept a good deal on the jog by political meetings, but I shall hope to see you when you are passing through London.

Yours very truly

AUSTEN CHAMBERLAIN

Keynes, still at Mentone, stuck to his position.

To AUSTEN CHAMBERLAIN, *23 January 1914*

Dear Chamberlain,

After much consideration, I feel clear that I cannot agree to the paper currency proposals, although I have not yet seen the actual text of them, and, while of course signing the Report, I must append a note to my signature in respect of them.

Your suggestion, that the worse the paper currency scheme we propose the more likely is a State Bank proposal to be acceptable, appeals to me so long as the paper currency scheme in question is set forth by others. But I feel it too jesuitical to go so far as to recommend the scheme *myself* on these grounds. Moreover I should not feel quite free at a later date to point out, as you suggest I may want to, the extreme weakness of the scheme now proposed, if I had myself recommended it without reservation.

I object to the scheme now recommended because it leaves the paper currency entirely deprived of elasticity and must have the effect, at any rate for some time to come, of precluding *altogether* temporary loans from the paper currency reserve. You yourself have swung on this matter from one extreme to the other. In the original draft temporary loans were to be allowed from the P.C.R. *only*. Now *no* such loans (in effect) are to be allowed from this source, although I had believed the Commission to be moving in favour of permitting them. With the argument that officials without banking experience cannot well be entrusted with loans on a *large* scale, I am, as you know, in sympathy. But your use of it in this connexion does not impress me because it applies in an exactly equal degree against the loans from the cash balances to which you have agreed. There is no difference whatever in the machinery of loans from the two sources.

I am also of opinion that, if no margin of discretion is to be allowed, the *net* circulation is not the convenient basis. My objections on this score, which are of a practical character, have, however, no present force; and I need not, therefore, detail them. They only have force in the improbable event of temporary loans ever being made under the proposed rules. I may add incidentally that, as the S[ecretary] of S[tate] will not be able to make temporary loans in London against the P.C.R., he will not be able to make temporary remittances from this source without ear-marking gold—so that one of the old pretexts for the silver branch of the G.S.R. will remain untouched. I know Abrahams attached some practical importance to the power of temporary loans in London against the P.C.R.

My objection to a very rigid and conservative treatment of the P.C.R. is increased by the changes I understand you to have made in the passages dealing with the future of the gold standard reserve. The whole bias of the report now lies in the direction of the policy of 'shut your eyes and blindly accumulate gold'. I am altogether in favour of safety, but this blind policy, easy though it is to formulate and to defend with maxims, is not the wise one; and I agree with Abrahams and [Lord] Inchcape [a witness] in deprecating it.

Lastly I feel averse to what I regard as the spurious character of the present proposals. They toy with the idea of temporary loans, even suggest to the ordinary public that they encourage them, and do this only to deceive. To a frank statement—'This is not a satisfactory system of note issue but we do not believe that any really satisfactory system is possible without a State Bank and do not care in the meantime to attempt experiments'— I could subscribe. But from all frankness on these matters the Bank compromise has cut us off. I do not like a facile make-believe at reform, which when analysed comes to nothing.

I am very sorry to have come to this conclusion when agreement had been carried so far; and I greatly regret that my absence from the final proceedings of the Commission has deprived me of an opportunity to attempt the conversion of my colleagues. As I was not present at the meeting, I do not know whether any other members share my view. In any case a point comes when it is neither politic nor right to attempt to gloss over a difference of opinion.

For letters posted after midday on January 26, King's College, Cambridge, will be my safest address. At any rate a duplicate of any letter had better go there.   Sincerely yours,

J. M. KEYNES

Keynes wrote again when he had received the revised Report. He retained a copy only of the part of the letter that dealt with the paper currency section.

To AUSTEN CHAMBERLAIN, *27 January 1914*

Dear Chamberlain,

The revised draft of the Report has now reached me, and I am able to see the paper currency proposals in their context. I can't help but think that one more meeting of the Commission, if that is not impossible and altogether inconvenient, might clear things up a great deal. Apart from my unwillingness to write a note of dissent if it can be avoided, I feel very unhappy about the Commission's proposals going forward in their present form. You have retained a preamble and a summary of consequences which were written for quite a different scheme, and have not changed them with the change of scheme. §114 in particular seems to me scarcely honest now. For, except in an indefinite future, none of these advantages can possibly accrue from what is now proposed.

I have also studied the draft put forward by Gillan and myself, and don't altogether wonder at the way you treated it. I never saw a proof. It is certainly over-elaborated and much too long and not particularly clear. But I believe I could draft something which would not cut the existing draft about too much, and I should much like an opportunity of *explaining* at any rate to my colleagues why I feel so definitely hostile to the present scheme. I can't believe that the Commission had really thought out its consequences.

I have read through the revised draft dealing with balances; and only have some minor suggestions to make—I think you let off [Sir Guy] Fleetwood Wilson [a witness] a little too lightly. This draft as a whole seems to me exceedingly good in its present form.

J.M.K. [The copy ends here]

The letters Keynes received from Cable, Gillan and Blackett show that he was exploring all possible means to repair the damage, but they did not offer much encouragement and tried to reconcile him to the situation. Gillan hoped, as he wrote on 27 January, that 'The authorities, since they will now have to work with the ideas of lending on practical terms and of elasticity in currency will consider means of combining the operations, so that what we have done may well have prepared the ground for a further advance...'.

But Cable and Blackett, though willing to take Keynes on faith, did not grasp the significance of his protest, nor the difference between the Commission's loans from the paper currency reserve plus loans from balances and Keynes's loans from an aggregate fund.

'If you and I go through [the] report we may get some alterations in', wrote Cable (24 January).

> Rather than a minute of dissent, you might append a footnote on the page itself signed by you—(same effect but less marked).
>
> You must explain to me why the Commission proposal is a sham.
>
> You and I can see Blackett together also.
>
> The *rest* of the Commission (except Gillan) are so tired they will agree to anything—Gillan is pigheaded—Austen *rather* contemplates one more sitting.

As to the likelihood of another meeting, Blackett wrote (29 January) that

> ...the final meetings of the Commission as a body have been held and we shall never get more than two or three to meet again however hard we try. But there was a definite understanding among them that you might want to have a further say on some points, though it was felt that the alterations to be proposed by you would have to be of small moment if they were to be accepted. It comes to this, that anything you say on small points will have a good chance of acceptance but that the Commission will not meet you on the gold standard and paper currency sections, without very great pressure, and then doubtfully...

But Keynes had his way. Back in England, he convinced Cable and produced a final memorandum, dated 3 February, very carefully elaborated, which convinced Chamberlain.

It was a hazardous argument, under the circumstances, to entrust to paper. Keynes's colleagues had been perplexed by his rejection of their scheme because both his plan and theirs allowed the Government to lend exactly the same amount, and—so they thought—both achieved the same results. They had seized on his device for increasing the amount that could be lent by fixing the cash and notes in the paper currency reserve in proportion to the net circulation but had not appreciated its full significance: not only did it make the total amount of the balances available for lending, but also the part of the paper currency reserve held against the notes in the balances. The Government's capacity to make temporary loans depended on the total amount in these two funds—and the discretion to lend from one or both, to the best advantage—as Keynes had pointed out, but the Commission had either not grasped or preferred not to entertain the idea. From their original proposal to lend only from the paper currency reserve, they had shifted to lending only from the balances, but this was the unintended effect of their stipulating a 20-crore minimum of permanent investment in the paper currency reserve. They had permitted discretion in lending from the balances, but not from the paper currency reserve, showing that they regarded these two funds as distinct.

MEMORANDUM BY MR J. M. KEYNES ON THE COMMISSION'S PAPER CURRENCY PROPOSALS

I greatly regret that my absence from the final meetings of the Commission prevented my laying before them my views on paper currency.

I hope the Commission fully realise the consequences of the system which they have now decided to recommend. These consequences seem to me to differ very considerably from what I understood to be their wishes before the Christmas vacation, and I find myself unable to concur in their new recommendation. I have had an opportunity of discussing the question with Sir Ernest Cable who agrees with me. I present my reasons for dissent herewith.

1. The Commission have retained without alteration a preamble (enlarging on the benefits and the need of elasticity) and a summary of advantages to be obtained from their proposals (paragraph 114), which were written for quite a different scheme. With reference to this previous scheme these passages were relevant and truthful; but with reference to the new scheme they are, in my opinion, neither the one nor the other. If the Commission believe that the disadvantages referred to in paragraph 105 [inelasticity of the currency due to restrictions on the note issue] can be cured, or the benefits (2) [temporary loans] and (3) [loans in London from paper currency reserve] of paragraph 114 can be obtained, at any rate for some years to come, from the scheme they are now recommending, they are unquestion-

ably deceived. If, as I presume, they only acquiesced in this scheme in the belief that advantages (2) and (3) would really accrue from it, they ought to reconsider the matter. The recommendations as they now stand are of a spurious character. They toy with the idea of temporary loans, even suggest to the ordinary reader that they encourage them, and do this only to deceive. This make-believe element in them is open, I think, to criticism of an exceedingly damaging kind.

II. (i) Advantages (2) and (3) of paragraph 114 are unreal, because, while the scheme purports to encourage temporary loans from the paper currency reserve, no such loans can possibly be made, at any rate for some years to come. The average net circulation is at present not quite 55 crores. It must rise to 60 crores before any temporary loan is legally possible; and it must rise considerably above this before a loan can be wisely made without a risk of breaking the law. For though at 63 crores 1 crore can be legally lent, the least reduction in the net circulation would render the position illegal. I do not suppose that with these rules the Government would care to lend 1 crore from the P.C.R. until the net issue had reached 66 crores. Thus the net circulation must increase 20 per cent above its present level before even so trifling a sum as 1 crore can be temporarily lent. By the time the net circulation had increased so much as this, the Government might reasonably take the view that some increase in the permanent investments could be safely made. All talk of introducing elasticity into the paper currency by means of the present proposals is therefore vain.

(ii) The conveniences, pointed out in paragraph 114, of occasional temporary loans from the P.C.R. in London cannot possibly, for the same reason, be realised in practice.

(iii) We have the somewhat anomalous position, under the Commission's scheme, that if notes are transferred from the Reserve Treasuries to the other Government Treasuries, to the Presidency Banks, or to the active circulation, the amount which may be lent from the paper currency reserve is increased, although the Government's real strength and real capacity for lending is diminished. The Government cannot lend (from the paper currency reserve—I am not dealing here with the balances) against notes held by itself, until it spends them, or at any rate has despatched them to some up-country treasury. The absurdity may even be greater than this—a temporary loan from the balances (since it transfers notes from the Reserve Treasuries to the Presidency Banks and the general public) has the effect of *increasing*, instead of diminishing as it ought, the amount which can be lent from the paper currency.

III. The inhibition of lending, which leads to the disadvantages (i) and (ii) above, and the anomalies outlined in (iii), are due, not so much to any excessive caution in the scheme, as to the division of the net issue of notes and the Reserve Treasury notes into two watertight funds. The Government's real capacity to make temporary loans depends on the sums in their paper currency reserve and in their balances regarded jointly. The rules, suggested by the Commission, do all they can to prevent the Government from regarding the question in this light. This will be best elucidated by a comparison between the Commission's plan and that suggested in the draft put forward by Mr Gillan and myself.[1]

IV. In the scheme proposed by Mr Gillan and myself the Government were to be permitted to lend (temporarily or permanently) (i) one-third of the net issue and (ii) the sums in the Reserve Treasuries. The sums in the Reserve Treasuries they were free to invest either as paper currency money or as balances, as might be most convenient. Further the total invested from the paper currency, whether from the net issue or from the Reserve Treasuries, need not fall below 20 crores.

In the scheme now proposed by the Commission, the arrangement is precisely as above, except that the Government is in effect prohibited from lending sums in the Reserve Treasuries as paper currency money. These funds may only be lent as balances.

[1] This draft was over-elaborated. I am told that the Commission found it obscure.

The amount which can be *legally* lent by the Government is precisely the same in the two schemes. The only difference is that the former allows the Government more latitude in the machinery it may employ. The difference seems small. But I attach importance to it for the following reason.

It may often be prudent to lend more from two funds taken together than can be lent from the two regarded separately. Thus, if the net issue is at 54 crores and the gross issue at 66 crores (so that there are 12 crores in the Reserve Treasuries), it might in certain circumstances of the market be prudent to lend (say) 4 crores temporarily, in addition to 20 crores of permanent investment. Under the rules I have suggested these 4 crores could be lent partly from the paper currency, partly from the balances. Perhaps in this case $2\frac{1}{2}$ crores would be lent from the P.C.R. and $1\frac{1}{2}$ crores from the balances. This would, in fact, be perfectly safe, and there would be nothing in it to excite remark. Of the 4 crores lent at least 1 crore might be taken in the form of notes. Thus

	Net issue	Gross issue	Cash	% of cash to net issue
Before lending 4 crores	54	66	46	80·5
After lending 4 crores	55	$65\frac{1}{2}$	43	78

Under the rules proposed by the Commission, however, nothing whatever could be lent from the P.C.R.; and although it would be *legal* for the Government to lend the 4 crores from the balances, it might justly excite remark if they were to lend no less than one-third of their Reserve Treasury resources. I have taken very moderate figures, and could make a much stronger case by taking hypothetical figures which may easily be real in the next year or two. The Commission's rules tend to prevent the Government when making loans from the P.C.R., from taking account of what is held in the Reserve Treasuries; and *vice versa*.

In fact, the proposed scheme extends and perpetuates the multiple reserve system which is anyhow a great defect in the

Indian system. We have had the gold standard reserve, the paper currency, and the Presidency Bank reserves quite distinct. Now in future we are to have the notes in the net circulation distinct and separately regarded from the notes in the Reserve Treasuries.

v. I would add:

(i) When we allow for the fact that in other countries the note reserve serves the joint purpose of paper currency reserve, gold standard reserve, Government balances, and Presidency Bank reserves, even if the Government lent temporarily up to the last rupee legally permitted by either scheme, the Indian system would still be *far more* cautious and conservative than that of any other country.

(ii) The more conservative the treatment of the gold standard reserve, the less the need for hampering the Government in the treatment of the paper currency reserve. For it is not always realised that a drain on the gold standard reserve alters, not its volume, but only its form. However great the exchange crisis, there is just as much legal tender money in the gold standard reserve (the sovereigns having been turned into rupees) available for transference to the paper currency reserve, in exchange for the sterling securities there, as there was before. After the G.S.R. has been used to its last sovereign for supporting exchange, its vast holdings of rupees are, therefore, still available for the P.C.R. Such a transfer (of rupees for securities) would be politic and financially sound on every ground; and if the rupees were only issued from the P.C.R. in exchange for notes previously circulating, the total reduction of currency would be no less than before. This is a fundamental and vital factor in the situation, (and possibly an argument for the amalgamation of the P.C.R. and G.S.R.), which has not been clearly brought, so far as I can remember, before the notice of the Commission.

vi. The amendment in the existing draft Report, which would be required, in order to bring about the modification I desire, is a simple one.

In § 112, read 'so long as the gross circulation is above 60 crores'

in place of 'when the net circulation rises above 60 crores'
and after the words 'for the time being'
insert 'fixed at the amount of notes held in the Reserve
Treasuries plus one-third'.

This gives the Government the liberty to lend their Reserve
Treasury money either through the paper currency reserve or
direct from the balances, according to their discretion. It does
not increase the total sum which they may legally lend from the
two sources together.

3 February 1914   J.M.K.

It is not clear from Keynes's papers exactly by whom or in what circumstances this memorandum was ever discussed. Gillan wrote, 9 February, to
congratulate him on his 'success with the Chairman. Your memorandum
was such a smashing document that I am not surprised at his giving in...'
A short list in Blackett's handwriting of 'Amendments recommended by
Chairman' suggests that the memorandum may have been distributed to the
other members of the Commission for their assent.

The brilliance of Keynes's understanding and political sense is revealed
in the seeming simplicity of the two small changes of wording for which he
asked. They gave him all he wanted: '*so long as* the gross circulation is above
60 crores' overcame the limitation set by the 20 crores of permanent investment and enabled temporary loans to start immediately; '*the amount of the
notes held in the Reserve Treasuries plus* one-third of the net circulation' gave
discretion in lending from the combined paper currency reserve and balances.
The two paragraphs of the Report on which all this discussion had focused
finally appeared thus:

112. Our next recommendation is that the fiduciary portion of the paper
currency reserve should be increased at once to 20 crores. But instead of
merely fixing this figure as a maximum, we propose that the maximum of
the fiduciary portion should be fixed at the amount of the notes held by the
Government in the Reserve Treasuries *plus* one-third of the net[1] circulation
for the time being. Under this proposal the invested portion of the reserve
will be at once increased by six crores. We recommend that this result should
be effected by a transfer (at market value) of sterling securities to that amount
from the gold standard reserve in exchange for six crores of the gold now
in the paper currency reserve in India.

[1] By net circulation we mean the gross circulation less the amount of notes held in the
Reserve Treasuries, cf. para. 102.

113. So long as the gross circulation exceeds 60 crores, it will be within the power of the authorities to increase the investments of the reserve and we propose that the Government should have power not only to make such further permanent investments as they think fit but also to make temporary investments or to grant loans either in India or in London. In India such loans should be made to the Presidency Banks on the same terms as we propose hereafter in the case of loans from balances, while in London the Secretary of State should have power to lend out in the London market sums received in payment for Council drafts sold against the currency reserve in the busy season so long as the total of the cash portion of the reserve does not fall below two-thirds of the net circulation.

Keynes also managed to slip in an addendum in favour of regarding the paper currency reserve and the gold standard reserve as a joint fund. Paragraph 110 of the Report had been drafted as follows:

We are of opinion that considerable improvements can be made in the location and disposition of the paper currency reserve.

In the course of our inquiry the suggestion has frequently come up for consideration that the gold standard and paper currency reserves should be amalgamated. The overlapping which occurs between the functions of the two reserves makes this suggestion attractive, and it is possible that an amalgamation may be found desirable in the future. But for the present we think that the balance of advantage lies in the maintenance of two separate reserves.

Keynes's words, adopted by Chamberlain at this final stage, follow immediately in the published Report:

A very conservative treatment of the gold standard reserve may, however, in certain circumstances strengthen the position of the paper currency reserve. A drain on the gold standard reserve for the support of exchange alters, not its volume, but only its form; and when rupees have accumulated in this reserve, as a result of providing gold for payments abroad, these rupees are available, if necessary, for transfer to the paper currency reserve in exchange for sterling securities. Such a transfer would be financially sound from the point of view of both reserves; and, provided that the rupees were only issued from the paper currency reserve in exchange for notes previously circulating, the total reduction of currency would be no less than before. In the consideration of the paper currency reserve, therefore, the increase of strength which would accrue to the gold standard reserve, if our proposals under that head are adopted, ought not to be entirely overlooked.

Finally, on Chamberlain's recommendation, paragraph 158 of the 'Indian Balances' section was amended to read:

It would accordingly make no practical difference to the Indian money market whether loans were made from the balances or from the paper currency reserve, if the amounts lent were the same; and provided that due precautions are taken we think that both sources may be used for the purpose of loans. We therefore recommend that the Government should declare their willingness to grant loans from balances in India when it is in their power and interest to do so...

There were, of course, other instances, less important, of Keynes's influence on the final Report. A minor example was his suggestion that the India Office, if called upon to dispose of Consols from the gold standard reserve at a loss, be allowed to pledge them against an advance as an alternative.

Keynes's ideas on the financial organisation of the India Office, stemming from personal experience, were substantially incorporated in Chamberlain's draft. A memorandum by Keynes, dated 11 November 1913, pointed out that with the increase of India Office financial business the Financial Secretary had become overburdened, mentioning Abrahams's occupation of this post. The important decisions which were the responsibility of this officer required freedom from the pressure of routine work. He suggested that there should be two Secretaries for the Financial Department, one concerned with the more routine business of Treasury control and one with some specialised experience for dealing with technical financial matters. He also criticised a proposal of the Secretary of State to replace the Finance Committee (five members of the India Council attached to the Financial Department as advisers) by a single member of Council, because it would sacrifice the various different kinds of business experience offered by the individual members of the committee. (Keynes could not forbear to add that with a State bank having a London office and a London board, the need for a Finance Committee would largely disappear.) These two ideas became part of the Report.

In commenting on Chamberlain's draft Keynes remarked:

...our reference to what is, I understand, one of the principal objects of Lord Crewe's scheme, namely the expediting of business, seems a little lukewarm. Might we not say that there is plenty of room, in our opinion, for improvement in this direction, and that a change of system, directed to this end and not incompatible with the conditions laid down above, would command our full concurrence?

At Chamberlain's request Keynes drafted a paragraph to this effect (paragraph 214 of the Report).

A final point of interest is Keynes's opposition to a proposal in Chamberlain's draft favouring regular purchases of silver for rupee coinage in order to satisfy recent large fluctuations in demand and at the same time reduce the dangers inherent in having to buy great amounts at short notice. Chamberlain had included the paragraph to provoke discussion: 'I suggest that you move its deletion and see what our colleagues think about it', he replied to Keynes's criticism which appears below. The paragraph was removed—whether through Keynes's efforts does not appear—but Keynes's expectation that the demand for silver would level off was to be upset by India's extraordinary absorption of the metal during World War I.

NOTE ON PURCHASE OF SILVER

As at present advised, I am opposed to the proposal contained in the last paragraph of this section. I believe that the circumstances of recent years have been much too exceptional for it to be prudent to build on them any prophecy as to the kind of scale on which it may prove necessary to purchase silver in the future. During these years there has been a combination of rapidly rising prices in India (prices rising, for reasons which need not be discussed here, faster than the world's level of prices) with the steady spread of a money economy into districts where barter formerly prevailed to a greater or less extent. At the same time the use of gold or notes, though showing a respectable increase in quite recent times, is still in its infancy. If either the advocates of gold or the advocates of notes have any considerable measure of success, if in the future prices do not rise so fast, or if the substitution of money for barter and for payment in kind proceeds, as it approaches completion, at a slower rate, the demand for new rupees will be on a very moderate scale indeed, and the coinages of the next ten years will bear but little relation to those of the last ten. For example, the use of gold or notes in moving the jute and rice crops, even to no greater an extent than is now the case in the Punjab, would cause an enormous falling off in the demand for rupees; and I do not think it would be safe to say that such a change may not occur within the next five or ten years. An enormous recurrent demand for additional coins of low denomination is an exceedingly abnormal condition for a country to be in, and one the long continuance of which is neither to be expected nor desired.

If the Government were to buy, by rule, £1,500,000 worth of silver every year, they would run a considerable risk of finding themselves loaded up with large quantities of silver, useless in itself and a cause of greater weakness in their general reserves than would otherwise exist.

I would ask also whether it is intended that they should buy this silver quite regardless of the likelihood of their having any immediate use for it. Suppose, for example, the rule had been laid down in 1907; ought it to have been followed in 1908? The money to be spent on these advance purchases of silver might be wanted far more urgently for other purposes.

On the other hand I do not think the saving in cost through steady purchases would, after allowances for loss of interest, be worth much (if the silver were held on the average for 3 years the loss of interest at 4 per cent would be $3\frac{1}{2}d$ per oz.); and I do not see why the Government of India is likely to [be] more successful than anyone else in speculating on the future value of silver.

But my objection to the proposal mainly is, that it must be based on the assumption that on the average of the next five or ten years the additions to the rupee currency will be very considerable—an assumption, to my mind, in the highest degree doubtful.

J.M.K.

The Report of the Royal Commission on Indian Finance and Currency was signed 24 February 1914 and published 2 March. Marshall wrote to Keynes 9 March, the day that he received his copy. The reference to his own experience in 1898 is to when he gave evidence before the Fowler Committee on Indian Currency.

Dear Keynes,

The I.C. Report came in at lunch time. I am behind hand with copy for the Press; so I thought I would not do more than get to know its general drift just at present.

But I dipped in here and there, and then read the conclusions: and finally turned negligently to the Annexe. But that held me. I had had no idea you had written it. Much of it, as of the Report itself, deals with matters beyond my knowledge and judgment. But there is quite enough of it within my understanding for me to have been entranced by it as a prodigy of constructive work. Verily we old men will have to hang ourselves, if young people can cut their way so straight and with such apparent ease through such great difficulties.

I thought of several objections as I read: but on going further, I found all of them met except one. Probably there is an answer to that also: but I did not see it. The objection is that in being generous to the shareholders in the Presidency Banks, you may possibly have been a little less than just to other credit institutions (I purposely use a broad vague term), English and Native; and also perhaps to the Indian States. I have always felt a little jealous of those Presidency Banks: they seem to me to have none of the obligations of a State Bank, and yet some of its sources of profit: and the new Bank would be able to override competitors who might have held their own against the Presidency Banks.

Again I have always thought the Bank of E[ng]land Parlour as it was described by Bagehot contained elements, which a State Bank should consider; and try to get something of them if possible. I admit that the fortunate accidents, which made it so strong say 40 years ago, are not as prominent now as then: and that state banks are for many reasons in a stronger position than then. But yet, I think, I should like to inquire—if I ever went into the matter, which of course I shall not do—whether some assessors might not be nominated (subject perhaps to conditions, including a veto in exceptional cases) by other financial authorities. Also *some* of them might perhaps have the right to subscribe for a few shares of the bank at par.

I found in talking to the Indian experts in 1898 that the work of the native financiers (Banyans I fancy they were called) was not fully understood: and I doubted even whether E[ng]lishmen in India understand it. Several natives of India have talked to me confidentially about the relations of Indians and English: and they were unanimous in the opinion that Anglo-Indians, even the best-informed, have no conception how much there is to be known about India which is beyond the knowledge of Englishmen. The extent of native hoarding was one of the subjects to which these conversations referred.

But I have made a sufficient display of matters on which I certainly know much less than you: so I will end

Yours enthusiastically

ALFRED MARSHALL

The Report was a vindication of the gold-exchange standard system; it left no doubt that in the minds of the commissioners the much-urged adoption of a gold currency would not serve the best interests of India. Its reception was generally favourable, outside of the columns of the *Times of India*; leader writers found it reassuring that no revolutionary changes were advocated.

Keynes's State Bank memorandum gave less pleasure. The chairmen of the exchange banks considered the scheme to be theory flouting the hard facts of experience. Sir Shapurji Broacha, considerably less charmed than Marshall, returned to India to campaign strenuously against it, even though he had signed the Report. The Calcutta financial journal *Capital*, which printed a copy of his reservation, described the memorandum editorially as 'the dogmatism of a professor of political economy, who knows nothing about local conditions in a continent like India' (26 March 1914).

However, one of *Capital*'s contributors, Reginald Murray, who wrote under the name of 'Rex', sent Keynes a complimentary letter (14 March 1914), asking some questions. Will it pay? he wanted to know, and suggested that it would be both fair and expedient for the Government to guarantee interest to the shareholders during the early years of the Bank. He also asked whether the Bank would be allowed to buy bills from the exchange banks other than those endorsed and rediscounted by them.

To REGINALD MURRAY, *18 March 1914*

Dear Sir,

I have been a subscriber to *Capital* and have often read with interest and profit your contributions to it. I have also read articles in the *Bankers' Magazine* on Indian subjects, which I fancy have been from your pen.

The question you ask as to whether a State Bank such as I have outlined will pay in the first instance is, I admit, a question of opinion. My own view is that in the event of a reasonable reform of a paper currency system, the use of the funds so made available, together with the use of the Government balances, ought to more than reimburse the Bank for the new expenses in which the new organisations would involve them. Provided the new Bank is not required to open new branches in a great hurry, I do not see that their expenses beyond what they incur at present need be high in relation to their total resources. If others however feel that this conclusion is highly doubtful, I personally should not feel specially averse to something of the nature of a guarantee to the shareholders in the early years; indeed I have provided for something not far short of this on page 67 of the Report, 3 a [p. 170 above]. It is there suggested that shareholders should receive ten per cent, even though the profits fall short of this, the balance being made up from the reserve. My own belief is that the shareholders have much to gain from the scheme, not only in an eventual increase in their dividends, but in the greater security and diminished risk which will in future attach to their position. In fact I have heard the scheme criticised by some competent authorities on the ground that it treats the shareholders, if anything, too generously. However, in my own opinion, a generous treatment is both just and politic, and an attempt ought to be made to meet any of their reasonable demands.

With regard to your second point, I did not mean to suggest in saying that the State Bank should take only rediscounted bills that this should exclude bills drawn by the exchange banks themselves, provided that they are drawn on some independent party, such as a London joint stock bank. I do not know, however, whether it would be wise to accept exchange bank drafts at three months' sight, drawn on their own London offices. This would practically amount to lending the exchange banks money on their own note of hand alone, without security. I do not see that three independent names need necessarily be required, but

I doubt whether less than two ought to be accepted. This, however, is entirely a matter for the banker, and I do not feel that my opinion on it is of any particular value. That the exchange banks would *like* to put themselves in funds in the way you suggest I do not doubt. But the security does not strike me as quite adequate for a State Bank to be satisfied with.

I am very much gratified to gather that to the main outlines of the scheme as a whole you are not unfavourably disposed.

Yours truly,

[Carbon copy unsigned]

Chapter 5

INDIAN EPILOGUE 1919

The outbreak of war prevented the Government from implementing the Chamberlain Commission's recommendations and the currency situation in India soon became very different. British war expenditure and a boom in exports created a tremendous demand for rupees; in one year the country was able to absorb twice the world's annual output of silver. The high world price for silver boosted the cost of the rupee until the value of the silver in the token coin outstripped its face value. After twenty years of stability at 1s 4d, it rose to 1s 8d. The shortage of silver threatened the convertibility of the expanded note issue but it also became a question of what it was to be convertible into—for the pound sterling had been turned into the Bradbury note and divorced from the gold sovereign in the ultimate departure from the time-honoured ordering of things.

The Indian Exchange and Currency Committee, under the chairmanship of Sir Henry Babington Smith, was appointed in May 1919 to examine the working of the monetary system under the new conditions and make policy recommendations to obtain stability and safeguard the exchange. The rupee ignored the Committee's deliberations and rose to 1s 10d, then 2s, reaching 2s 4d in December 1919. However, when Keynes appeared before them as a witness on 25 July, it was still at 1s 8d.

Keynes's evidence reflects the experience of the four and a half years that he had just spent in the Treasury. His duties there had largely consisted in supplying the needs of the Allies, or more specifically, the currency to finance them. During the last six months at the Paris Peace Conference he had become acquainted with the relief problems of the devastated countries and the desperation of deprived and hungry people. In this testimony he seems less interested in the technical functioning of the currency system than in the practical good that it could be made to achieve. It is taken from *Minutes of Evidence taken before the (Babington Smith) Committee on Indian Exchange and Currency*, Vol. II (Cmd. 528, 1920), pp. 166–75.

TWELFTH DAY

Friday, July 25th, 1919

Present:

Sir Henry Babington Smith, C.H., K.C.B., C.S.I. (*Chairman*)

The Right Honourable Lord
    Chalmers, G.C.B.
Sir Marshall F. Reid, C.I.E.
Sir James Brunyate, K.C.S.I., C.I.E.
Mr. F. C. Goodenough
Sir Charles Addis
Sir Christopher Needham

Mr M. M. S. Gubbay, C.S.I., C.I.E.
Sir Bernard Hunter
Mr D. M. Dalal
    Secretaries:
    Mr C. H. Kisch, C.B.
    Mr H. Denning, I.C.S.

Mr J. M. Keynes, C.B., called and examined.

(CHAIRMAN) *You have given considerable attention to questions of Indian exchange and currency, have you not?* I was in the India Office for two years; I wrote a book on the subject, and I was a member of the Royal Commission under the chairmanship of Mr Chamberlain.

Have you followed the development of the question since the date of the Chamberlain Commission? Not so closely as before, but I have followed it in a general way.

I propose not to ask you questions of an historical character on what happened during the war, but rather to ask you to give the Committee the benefit of your opinions on questions of policy and of future development. The first point with which I will ask you to deal is the general question of the economic effects on India of different levels of value for the rupee—whether a high rupee or a low rupee is advantageous in the general interest of India? In the present condition of world prices, whether measured in sterling or measured in gold, I attach more importance to fixing the rate at a high level than to the particular means of ensuring the stability of the level, whatever it is; that is to say, I should think it better to fix the rupee at 2*s* than at 1*s* 8*d* or 1*s* 10*d* and even higher, if it is practicable—which I doubt.

Will you explain your reasons for that view? My main reason for that is that, as far as I can judge, prices in India have not yet risen in proportion either to world prices or to sterling prices. They have been prevented from rising by various administrative measures which are possible in times of war but which cannot be continued permanently without very detrimental effects on the general course of industry and production. I also believe that world prices outside India are not going to fall, and may very rapidly rise to a substantially higher level than that to which they have risen already.

If the existing rise outside India was to be realised in India, and if an even greater rise was to take place, I think there would be social and political consequences of a very dangerous tendency. From the Indian point of view, the prevention of too high a level of prices in India seems to me quite to transcend any of the other issues—which, however, are also important and must be considered by this Committee.

On the question of fact, have you any figures or any definite information to give us as to the comparative rise of prices in India and of world prices? I do not carry them in my head, and I have not seen the Indian index numbers up to date, but I have followed them up to the end of last year, and I think I am right in saying that the rise in prices in India up to that date is nothing like so great as in this country or in the United States.

On what do you base your opinion that there is likely to be a further rise in world prices? It seems to me that, at present, prices in the world are kept down by two influences—one, a great variety of administrative measures in almost all countries, by means of which people are not permitted to pay for various commodities as much as they would be prepared to pay in a free market, and, secondly, because there is a good deal of unrealised potential inflation which has not yet affected prices. In almost all countries traders, companies, and others hold great quantities of funds, either in bank balances or in bank notes or in Treasury bills, which are not, from their point of view, permanent investments, and they are waiting until the time when the movement of capital and the movement of goods makes it possible for them to invest those funds. Gradually, I think, they will have those opportunities, and, as they exercise them, prices will rise still further.

Do not some of the administrative restrictions that you mention tend to keep prices up rather than to keep them down? It is often held that the guaranteed price for wheat in the United States has had that effect, but personally I doubt it. I think that the additional harvest which was called forth in the United States by that high guaranteed price is required to feed the world, certainly as long as Russia and Roumania are out of action, and I am inclined to think that if the United States Government had not guaranteed wheat last year, and if the harvest this year had been very much smaller than it actually is for that reason, and if, in addition to that, the rest of the world had competed freely for what wheat there was, the price might very well have been driven higher than the actual price guaranteed by the United States Government. I may illustrate that by saying that, as far as I know, the whole of the wheat, or very nearly the whole of the wheat, in the British Empire and in the Argentine is required by this country.

Is that assuming that there is no import from America? Apart from the

274

United States. If we got all our wheat from elsewhere, we should require nearly all the wheat there is from elsewhere.

When you speak of America do you include Canada? No, I was excluding Canada. I was assuming that we had the Canadian, so that the United States wheat is required to feed the rest of the world in present conditions. I think there would have been a tremendous scramble for wheat if this bumper harvest had not been secured by Mr Hoover.

There were large accumulations of wheat in Australia? Yes, fairly large; but not really large in relation to the entire consumption of the world; and that cannot be brought into use instantaneously.

On the other hand, as facilities for transport return to a more normal condition, will not that tend to check any rise in prices? Yes, it will tend in that direction, but I think it will be counterbalanced by the other influences.

As cultivation is restored in the other countries where the war has diminished the production of the soil, will not that tend to be a regulating factor? I do not believe that will operate fast enough. There is a third influence I have not mentioned, namely, that most of the Governments of the world are still inflating. I do not think there is any European government, including the neutrals, certainly no government of importance, whose budget balances for the present year.

Your general inference, then, is that prices are more likely to rise than to fall? Yes, in my opinion there is a serious risk of a rise of prices, the possibility of which you must consider.

You view with great apprehension a rise in internal prices in India which would correspond to the rise in world prices? Yes.

And therefore you would welcome a high rupee as acting as a corrective to that rise and tending to maintain Indian prices on a more even level? I should not only welcome it, but I consider that the establishment of a high-value rupee is the primary consideration of the problem.

The export interest in India is a very large and important one, is it not? Yes.

That interest would benefit by high prices? Yes, by high prices; that is to say, by a low value of the rupee.

You do not regard that interest as so important as the non-exporting portion of the population of India? It is a very temporary benefit in any case. If prices were to rise seriously in India wages could not lag very much behind them, and the process of adjusting them would very likely cause disturbance. It would injure the propertied interests and the export interests more than the excess profits that they would have got by the high prices that would have benefited them.

A high rupee would also be a benefit as regards the charges that the Government has to meet outside India, would it not? Certainly.

And might possibly mean some reduction of the level of taxation? Yes; it would certainly avoid any increase of it. On the other hand, looking at it from that point of view, one has to remember that the value of the very large reserve which the Government of India have accumulated in sterling would represent a smaller number of rupees.

What would be the effect on the import trade? The power of the Indian consumer to purchase cotton goods would be aided, and the upset in the trade due to the very high price of cotton would be ameliorated. It would mean that the ryot could clothe himself more cheaply, in spite of the very high price which Manchester has to give for American cotton, whether because of the high dollar price of cotton or because of the depreciation of the exchange. If you are going to weigh particular interests, I think that interest would certainly benefit more than the export interest would suffer.

Is it not possible that certain of the export commodities which compete with similar commodities from other parts of the world might suffer from a very high exchange, so that they would be unable to continue to compete? India is in a very peculiar position in respect of some of her most important exports, which are almost monopolies. In respect of certain of her exports of raw materials there is such an eager market at the moment that I should not expect any substantial fall of prices; in fact, the injury to the export interest that I should anticipate would not be that they would positively suffer, but that they might be prevented from getting the excess profits, due to a rise of prices, which they would otherwise secure. My aim would not be to reduce prices so much as to prevent them from soaring.

Are there not very important staples exported from India which are in direct competition with similar staples from elsewhere? There are some. In a sense, wheat is exported in competition because there is a great deal of wheat elsewhere. Taking the world as a whole, the export of wheat from India is not a very important factor, but there is such an eager demand for wheat that competition between sources of supply is not very effective. In the case of Indian cotton, I should not anticipate any difficulty in marketing it. In the case of linseed and oil seeds generally, India has not got as high a price as she could in a perfectly free market. In the case of jute she has a virtual monopoly, and in the case of rice a high degree of monopoly.

In the case of tea? In the case of tea she has a monopoly together with Ceylon, which I believe would follow India in anything of this kind; a monopoly of a certain kind of tea.

What about the competition of Java and Sumatra? That may be a factor to be reckoned with. I do not know the relative figures of the output in those countries.

We were told recently that the Sumatra and Java production is 120,000,000 lb., as compared with 220,000,000 lb. in Ceylon, if I remember rightly? I should not be surprised if the Government of the Dutch East Indies were not very soon faced with much the same sort of problem. They may choose so to arrange their currency as to benefit their exports; if they do, our corresponding exports may suffer a little.

(LORD CHALMERS) *For the time being?* For the time being. When I say that our corresponding exports may suffer I mean rather that they would not secure certain excess profits that they might otherwise obtain.

(CHAIRMAN) *You do not consider that any of these interests will suffer to the extent of the extinction of their trade?* No, because I am going on the hypothesis that a collapse of world prices to anything like what existed before the war is not seriously to be reckoned with in the period I had in mind.

Then your conclusion is that, looking at the interests of contentment and good government in India, for the prosperity of the country and, in fact, the interests of India as a whole, you prefer as high a rupee as possible? Yes, and I would suggest a figure such as 2s.

Have you any particular reason for selecting that figure? There are historical reasons that make that figure agreeable to sentiment. It is a round figure and it is about as high as you can go without provoking protests from various people who might feel that you were rather overdoing it if you go beyond that. If I had an absolutely free hand I think I would go a bit higher; 2s seems to me a level which could be justified on a great many grounds, and not only on the particular ground that I am putting forward at the moment.

Would you move the rupee up to 2s irrespective of any movement in the price of silver? Yes.

If silver rose above the parity of a 1s 8d rupee, do you consider that it would be necessary in any case to move the rupee up to correspond? Yes.

It is quite impossible to contemplate a rupee the bullion value of which would be higher than its exchange value? It is not impossible to contemplate it, but I think it would be very inconvenient and anomalous.

When I said 'impossible to contemplate' I meant that it would very soon cease to exist—that it would soon be melted down? I am not sure of that because there is such a tremendous volume of rupees in India. I doubt whether I should go as far as that, but you would have a great many objectionable practices going on, no doubt.

You think that, even though there was a very good profit to be made by the melting of rupees into silver, that some rupees would remain? I think so, certainly. What the Government of India might be faced with would be a

277

process by which rupees were being melted and exported contrary to regulations, and by which they were having to buy the silver back again and put it into circulation in order to maintain convertibility. If there was a large profit to be obtained it is very hard to prevent something of that sort going on. You would have to put on vexatious regulations and have all sorts of dishonest practices in relation to currency in vogue; but it could not be expected that the world would be able to absorb anything approaching the entire volume of Indian silver rupees.

If large volumes of rupees were melted and silver put on the market, probably the price would not remain for long above the level? No; you would be faced, not with the melting of great volumes, but with a constant dribble of an irregular and illegal character.

You said, I think, that you would move the rupee up to 2s irrespective of any movement in silver? Yes, in order to keep the standard of value in India more stable in relation to commodities.

If it were fixed at 2s do you consider that that would do away with any risk of the bullion value exceeding the exchange value? I do not think there would be any substantial risk. It rather raises the question of whether by 2s you mean 2s Bradbury or 2s gold.

We will come to that presently? If you mean 2s gold, so that any question of American exchange is eliminated, it seems to me to provide a pretty safe margin.

The rupee at 2s gold corresponds to a silver price of how many pence? I am not sure—I think it is about a dollar and a quarter for fine silver.

(SIR CHARLES ADDIS) *I think it is about 63d?* I was trying to do it in gold without the interposition of sterling. What one really requires to know is what dollar price for fine silver a 2s gold rupee represents.

(CHAIRMAN) *It is 64d—140 cents?* That is an even safer margin than I had thought.

What is the parity corresponding to the silver of the Latin Union? I cannot say off-hand.

I am told it is 60¾d? Then it is well beyond the parity. That is an additional safeguard.

If silver rises above the parity of the Latin Union silver a new factor would come into play in checking the rise? That is not a factor that would count as strongly as it would have at earlier dates, because the greater part of the 5-francs silver is held in the bank reserves, and whether those banks would dispose of it or not I do not know, it is very doubtful.

The amount of silver actually in circulation is not so very large? Not so large as it was, because France now has 5-franc notes. Spain has a great deal of silver in her bank which she might be willing to sell. At any rate, that strengthens my argument, because the margin is safe enough to allow for such relief as could be obtained by the Latin Union melting.

Is it not likely that considerable objections would be raised to a sudden move in the value of the rupee to 2s, if such move were not rendered necessary by circumstances over which the Government has no control? I should have thought that the main line of defence was from the popular point of view impregnable—the main line of defence being that this move was required in order to prevent India suffering from the notorious disadvantages and evils of high prices which European countries were suffering from to their great disadvantage. It is very seldom an unpopular move on the part of governments to do something which will keep prices at a reasonable level.

But it is unpopular with those who have produce to sell or export? Particular interests are, of course, affected by any action of that kind.

Are not those interests extremely widespread in India? That brings us back to the question of the exporting interests. As I have said, I think they would be losing only excess profits, but the profits they would be losing would be temporary, and they have themselves a great deal to gain from the stability of prices in India and from satisfactory conditions of labour. I should doubt whether the tea companies, to take a particular instance, would not stand to lose as much as anybody by a state of affairs under which coolie labour was constantly dissatisfied with its standard of life and its level of remuneration.

I do not know what the practice is in India, but we have been told that in Ceylon the food for the coolie labour is generally supplied by the employer, and that therefore any rise in food prices is felt by the employer and not by the labourer? In that case the exporters have all the less to gain by high prices, because there is not even the temporary lag of the remuneration of their labour.

On the other hand, as the food for the labourers is only a part of the cost of production, they get the benefit of the high prices on the whole and the detriment of high prices only on a part? Yes. It would not entirely abolish the advantage they would get from high prices for the time being.

And so far as the labourer is concerned he would not have the same cause for dissatisfaction? No. It must be admitted that a depreciating currency is a temporary advantage to certain particular interests, but that has not generally been held a sufficient argument in favour of depreciating the currency.

Turning now to the question of the practical course to be pursued, the Committee have before them proposals of various kinds. I do not know whether you are familiar with the proposal that has been made by the Government of India? Yes, I know in general terms what it is.

As you are aware that contemplates fixing now or in the near future a value for the rupee which would be intended to be a permanent value and adhering to that even though the parity of silver should rise above it? Of course a great deal would depend upon the figure chosen. If the figure were to be 1s 8d, I think it would be a mistaken policy on every ground. It would tend to cause a rise of prices in India in the trades released from control and it would run a very substantial risk both of partial inconvertibility and of the melting of Indian coin. I can see no substantial advantage which it would attain. If, on the other hand, the figure was 2s, as we have already seen, the risk of silver rising to that price may be neglected, and there only remains the question whether it is wise at this moment to fix the rupee in terms of sterling or whether it would not be better to fix it in terms of something else. When we come to the question of what else it could be fixed in, one proposal which I think has been put forward has been that, while not fixing it in relation to silver or opening the mints to silver, it should nevertheless be fixed in relation to silver to this extent, that it should provide from time to time only a small margin beyond the actual cost of silver and should move upwards or downwards with the value of silver. That is one proposal I have seen put forward, which, while not purporting to make India again a silver country, seems to me to be very near it.

The proposal to which you are referring is the proposal which has been developed before us in evidence by Sir Lionel Abrahams. His proposal, how-ever, did not assume that the course of silver would be followed downwards? I did not know that.

His view was that the course of silver must be followed upwards, and that it was inadvisable to fix any point at present at which that process should stop, but I do not think he was prepared to say that it should be followed downwards; that I think he would leave open for future consideration? That plan seems to assume that, left to yourself, you would not move the rupee up; you would only move it up to the extent you were compelled by the movement of the price of silver. I differ from that opinion, because I think there are positive advantages in moving the rupee up apart from movements in the value of silver. Therefore I should be against such movements by slow degrees. If you go to 2s immediately, there is no difference between the Government of India's plan and Sir Lionel Abrahams's plan.

Except that the Government of India, if 2s were fixed, would contemplate stopping there indefinitely and never rising any higher? That comes in practice to the same thing as Sir Lionel Abrahams's, if we are right in thinking that we may neglect the risk of silver rising beyond that level.

From the views you have expressed, I take it that you would not follow silver downwards if silver fell in future? Not merely if silver fell in future, but I should follow it downwards if world prices had very much changed in the meantime. I should aim always, subject to the limitations of the necessity of having gold coin or silver coin in India, at keeping Indian prices stable in relation to commodities rather than in relation to any particular metallic or particular foreign currency. That seems to be of far greater importance to India. Therefore, in considering at some remote date the possibility of putting down the rupee I should be influenced by the effect it had on prices rather than by its relation to a particular metal.

Putting that consideration on one side for the moment, would you have any apprehension about the possibility of maintaining a 2s rupee if silver fell to its old price, to a parity of 9d or 10d? I do not think that the movement of the price of silver would much affect the matter. If world prices were such that, at a 2s rupee, the balance of trade was against India for a long period, it might be difficult to maintain the 2s rupee simply by the exhaustion of the Government of India's reserves.

You were speaking just now of the possibility of fixing the rupee not in relation to sterling but in relation to something else. What had you in mind then? I had in mind gold, for the reason that in the near future, whatever may be the ultimate result, sterling is likely to be a very fluctuating currency. It may fluctuate downwards or upwards. It is very unlikely to remain stable.

When you speak of fluctuation, do you mean fluctuation in relation to gold or in relation to commodities? I meant at that moment in relation to other currencies, some of which would be based on gold, and to that extent it would be the same thing as saying fluctuation in relation to gold. I was not thinking of commodities at that moment.

Will you develop your idea about the possibility of fixing the rupee in relation to gold? I do not see any advantage in the rupee moving about with the daily, weekly and monthly fluctuations of sterling in the near future. If sterling settles down, as we hope it will, to a stable gold basis again, then I should like to see the rupee at as steady a rate in relation to sterling as has existed hitherto, but I should aim at doing that by fixing the rupee in relation to the gold sovereign and letting it fluctuate in terms of sterling so long as sterling fluctuates in terms of the gold sovereign, hoping that a day would come when they would come together again.

How would you do that? I would do it by the Government of India accepting gold at Bombay in return for rupees at the rate of 10 rupees to the sovereign. I would not do it by selling Councils against a deposit of gold in the Federal Reserve Bank of New York, or any scheme of that kind. I have seen a memorandum by Mr Lucas on this subject, which I think the Committee have had before them, in which he made the proposal that the rupee should be fixed in relation to gold, and in which he suggested it was necessary for that to pivot the arrangement on New York rather than on London. That seems to me a great weakness in his scheme and not a necessary feature of it. At the time he wrote it New York was the only important gold market in the world. I see in today's papers that the Treasury have now come to an arrangement with the South African mines which has long been under discussion, by which the owners of the mines will be entitled to sell their gold in London for what it will fetch and to export it. The consequence is that there will be now in London week by week a gold market fluctuating in terms of sterling more or less on the lines of pre-war conditions; and, as the supply from South Africa will be quite £30,000,000 sterling, if not more, India will be in a position to obtain her gold from the London market. I would therefore suggest an arrangement by which the shipment of gold to India was left in the hands of the exchange banks. It will always be open to the exchange banks to purchase Council drafts or to export gold to India, according to which was most profitable at the moment. When their demand for currency in India is in excess of what they could obtain by Council drafts, they would purchase gold in the London market and export it to Bombay for exchange into rupees at the rate of 10.

Is it certain that the South African gold will come to London? The newspapers do not give a full account of the arrangement. No doubt the Committee could learn from the Treasury exactly what it is, but the announcement suggested that an arrangement had been made with the mine owners by which they did undertake to bring the gold to London. That, however, was not quite clear and requires further investigation. I may add that, even if the mine owners refined their gold in South Africa and exported it direct from South Africa, there could be no doubt whatever that the business of dealing in the gold would take place in London even if the physical gold did not come here. It may be that the exchange banks would buy their gold in London, but the gold itself would be exported direct from South Africa to India. That really is not very vital to the question.

At present the Government of India does accept sovereigns in return for 12 rupees 4 annas 6 pies? Yes; but I think I am right in saying that, with the present rate for Councils, there is no substantial advantage in shipping gold to India as compared with buying Councils.

What is your view as to the relation between the price given for sovereigns and the price at which Councils should be sold? I agree with the proposal in Mr Lucas's memorandum that the Government of India should sell Councils of a total value up to their requirements, and that there should be open tender for them.

And that there should be the alternative of shipping gold in unlimited quantities at a fixed price? If the result of the open tender was so to raise the price of Councils as to make it more profitable to export the gold from London to India than to export it to some other destination, as, for example, the United States, you would have as near as is possible in the present system the old system by which the South African gold was distributed to that part of the world which was willing to bid the highest price for it.

The result would be that the sterling exchange would depend upon the price of Councils, and would vary according to the relation between sterling and gold? Yes, so long as sterling was fluctuating in relation to gold that would be the case. If a point was reached at which the Treasury and the Bank of England were able to stabilise sterling in terms of gold, whether at the old rate or at another rate, substantial fluctuation would cease, because there would only be the fluctuation round the gold point.

What would the Government of India do with the gold when they got it? I would suggest that they make it available for circulation in the ordinary way.

Do you mean by coining it? By coining it or by selling it—but probably the exchange banks would sell it best. There ought to be no regulation against that. If there was a bazaar demand for it, the exchange banks would obtain their funds just as readily by selling gold in the bazaars as by turning it over to the mint.

You are aware that there is at present a considerable premium on gold? Yes.

Would you allow importers to sell gold freely so long as that premium exists? I should deal with the premium before introducing the new system.

How would you deal with the premium? If I was not altering the relation of the sovereign to rupees I should deal with it by selling gold to the bazaars out of the Government reserves, and I should endeavour to make as large a profit for the Government as I could consistently with steadily bringing down the bazaar price to parity. If, however, I was changing the relation of rupees to the sovereign—from 15 to 12, 10, or some other figure—there might be advantages in postponing the sale in the bazaars until after the change had been made and due notice had been given. If under ordinary conditions you were to announce that for a certain period of time the Government of India would give 15 rupees for a sovereign and that thereafter they would give 10 or 12, you could make that announcement without much risk of being swamped by gold if the bazaar price for gold was above 15; but once I came down to my definite level as between rupees and sovereigns I should then free the gold market so as to bring the bazaar price for gold down to parity.

Do you think there is an advantage in the gold that goes into India being as far as possible centralised in Government reserves rather than distributed in the country? I think there are great advantages in as small a part of the currency of India as possible being metallic. I have always maintained that everything ought to be done to centralise the gold reserves with a view to utilising them when the drain was in the opposite direction. The only way of doing that is by inducing the people of India to employ notes or other means of effecting payments, not rupees or gold. As between gold and silver, the only advantage in silver would be that the Government would still be making a profit on it. I should not take artificial means of preventing gold from going into circulation, but I should continue to stimulate in every way possible other means of effecting payments. The more the gold that I was concentrating in my reserves the better pleased I should be; in fact, when the reserves had reached a satisfactory level I should increase my sales of Councils and follow the pre-war practice of accumulating reserves in foreign centres as against an increased fiduciary issue.

Am I right in saying that your view is this—that you should as far as practicable limit the putting out of gold to the actual demands for social purposes? Yes.

And that you should not encourage a gold currency? Yes. To go back to the point from which we set out, I do not see much object in having an artificial price for such gold as is required in the arts as distinct from the circulation. In so far as you do do it, you can justify it on the same lines as you may justify a tax on diamonds or pearls, on the ground that a luxury article is properly the subject of taxation; but if I was to adopt that policy I should do it as such rather than by allowing a fluctuating premium in the bazaars as a result of artificial restrictions.

If you sold enough gold to prevent there being a premium on gold, would that be a measure of the real demand for social purposes? I think so.

Do you think it would be necessary to give some notice of any change in the legal value of the sovereign? I think so. I have not a very definite view on the matter. So long as the value of the gold in the bazaar is substantially above 15 it is rather in the nature of a formality. It seems to me that on general principles it is desirable not to change the relation of legal tender units without giving the holders sufficient opportunity of saving themselves from any loss.

Would you also make the import of silver free? Certainly.

Would you remove the duty on silver? No, not necessarily. I should justify the duty on silver on the grounds I was just mentioning—as a tax on a luxury—and also on the same grounds as duties on alcoholic liquors, as tending to cause economy in a wasteful habit.

You are aware that the note issue has been very largely increased during the war? Yes.

Have you any definite view as to the proportion that the gold reserve should bear to the note issue? It is very difficult to speak of that without Indian experience. I have noticed that the present figure is round about one-third, I think, and the Indian authorities have expressed alarm at it. I am rather surprised at their expressing alarm. I should have thought that one-third was a good reserve provided the other parts of your reserve were in a form available to meet a foreign drain. For purely internal purposes one-third ought to have been adequate. I remember, however, that in the evidence given before the Commission, of which I was a member, many Indian witnesses gave strong evidence as to the very large amount of currency required by reason of the great number of currency centres in India and so forth. I was never quite convinced that further economies could not be effected in that respect. For any other country than India I should regard one-third as very much on the safe side.

Are there any other points that you would like to put before the Committee? No, I think the ground has been covered.

(SIR JAMES BRUNYATE) *Exactly how would you use the gold which was received in India by Government?* I had contemplated that the India Office in selling Councils would adjust such sales to its needs, and in its needs I included remittances due either to its bringing some of its currency reserve home to India or increasing its currency reserve abroad. If the view of the Government was that they wanted more gold in India, that would mean that they desire to turn part of their currency reserve now held abroad into coin. That would have the effect of diminishing their need to sell Councils, their requirements being met by liquidating part of their foreign reserves and they would be leaving it to trade to bring the gold which they wanted in India. If, on the other hand, they had decided that the gold they had in India was ample and that it was not a case for increasing their foreign reserve, again that would correspondingly increase their demand for Councils and so diminish the amount of gold which the exchange banks would find it worth their while to import into India. So that the question really comes back to a question of the policy of the Government of India as to the level of the gold reserves.

Do you contemplate the free use of gold as coin in India whenever the Government are relatively short of silver coin? Yes, I contemplate that, but I do not contemplate any substantial suspension by the Government of

India of the present deterrents to the use of coin generally. I should be indisposed to go back upon the policy that the Government of India has pursued in recent years of definitely encouraging notes and discouraging coin, but where for any reason coin had to be put into circulation I should see no special reason for not putting sovereigns into circulation.

Are you aware how severe those deterrents have been in the past few months? They have extended to the absolute prohibition of the movement of coin by rail and boat; and in regard to certain crops, such as jute, which it was formerly considered it would be absolutely impossible to purchase except by the remittance of actual rupees into the producing districts, in the last twelve months the Government of India have, broadly speaking, refused to send coin to those districts at all and have sent only notes? Do I understand from that that they have not only suspended the Government facilities but have prohibited private persons from sending coin by rail?

Yes? I was not aware of that. I should not be in favour of any deterrent which had the effect of bringing about a substantial premium on coin in a given district. I should do anything short of establishing a really substantial premium on coin.

You would rather see gold freely used as coin than bring about such a state of things? Yes. It seems to me very undesirable to have a difference of value that would matter to the ordinary person between two forms of currency which were equally legal tender in law.

There has been another great change in the Government of India's policy in regard to the free encashment of notes. Up to about 1913 the legal right—(and it is still the position as regards the legal right)—of securing metallic coin for notes existed only in the case of notes presented for encashment at the six or seven offices of note issue in India. Then a certain amount of encashment was done by grace at the Treasuries in India, which, as you know, are very numerous. From 1913 onwards, until the difficulties created by the war began to be so serious, the Government of India established a practice of almost unrestricted encashment of notes at all Treasuries in India. That is the second stage. In the third stage, when difficulties were experienced, they practically entirely suspended that practice. Would you advise them to stand to their present practice in that respect or would you expect that in the long run metallic currency would be less used on the whole if more facilities were given for the encashment of notes? That is very much a question of psychology and local experience. The ordinary doctrine is that by having facilities for the encashment of notes you increase the popularity of your notes. If experience shows that the increase of facilities for convertibility had that effect, I should increase the facilities; if, however, experience shows that the Indian mind does not work that way, I should continue the existing practice. I should, however, be disposed to give convertibility a good chance.

What particular kind of deterrent had you in mind when you advised that the Government of India should maintain the existing deterrents on the use of coin? I had in mind the number of centres you can encash at, and also the fact that sovereigns were not put into circulation at all, or at any rate only exceptionally.

Just a final question about bills. You do contemplate that, whether by the sale of bills or by facilities for importing gold, trade should have the means of remittance up to its entire requirements? Certainly I think that is essential.

(SIR CHARLES ADDIS) *In your opinion the chief difficulty that we have to face at present is really the want of silver in order to maintain the convertibility of the notes?* That is the principal technical difficulty, but, as I said at the beginning, the thing I personally attach most importance to is the danger of the high level of world prices extending itself to India.

But from the point of view of urgency is not that rather secondary to the immediate and urgent demand for silver? They are two rather different questions, both of them important, but I regard both of them as urgent. What has actually been the moving factor in Indian currency policy has been the shortage of silver, but I am not sure that the other question is not really the more important.

So much so that you would propose to deal with them concurrently? Yes, especially because the solution which helps what I consider the major problem incidentally solves the minor problem.

Does it solve it in time; that is to say, if, for example, you were to raise the exchange value of the rupee to 2s would you expect that to give you immediately an increased supply of silver? No, I think that the supply of silver would be largely independent of that, but the Government of India would be given the opportunity of paying up to a very high price. It would be given full facilities for getting all the silver there was and for supplementing it by gold. I cannot imagine a plan which would leave the Government of India freer to get silver.

Would you contemplate, for example, as a temporary measure, the opening of the mints to free coinage? I should not anticipate that that would obtain any more silver.

Would it not? That would create entire freedom to anyone to purchase silver at any price in order to supply his market needs, would it not? I should have supposed that the Government of India by paying if necessary a price up in the direction of the equivalent of 2s would get all the silver which could be drawn out merely by the offer of a high price.

There is another remedy which has been suggested, still bearing in mind this question of what I think is the special urgency created by the shortage of silver. Would you consider the question of reducing the silver content of the rupee? It is a token coin at present. Apart from political reasons, would there be any objections to doing that, as has been done in the Straits Settlements? I do not think there is any really decisive theoretical objection to it, but the political and practical difficulties in the case of a country like India, in which there is such an immense volume of silver already in circulation, would, I should have thought, be so great that it would not be wise to attempt to meet a temporary emergency in that way. It would not be a thing that you could carry through with any speed.

If, for example, to take an extreme case, you were to halve the silver content in your rupee while retaining its appearance, the effect would be to double the amount of silver under your control? If one were simply looking at it from the point of view of the shortage of silver, that is a solution one ought not to dismiss, but if you look at it from the point of view of Indian prices I think anything that increased the rupee circulation in India would be disastrous. If you separate the two, if you only look at the immediate silver problem, that is a solution which ought not to be dismissed, but I should have thought the practical difficulties were too great.

What are the practical difficulties as apart from the political difficulties? I was assuming that you would not merely mint new rupees of a smaller content but would try to call in old rupees and remint them. For the mints to recoin an amount anything approaching the total circulation of India would take years.

It would not operate in time? That is so.

(MR GUBBAY) *Can you give us your opinion on the effect of a high rupee on the industrial development of India; I do not think you dealt with that point in your* exposé *of the advantages or disadvantages of a high rupee?* I do not believe that in the long run the establishment of any one level has any different effect from that point of view to that of any other level. What is disadvantageous is a great change of price, and I advocate this because it means a less change of price than the alternative proposal. If you take a view of the next twenty-five years, I do not think it matters to Indian industrial development whether the rupee is 2s or 1s.

Would not a high rupee tend to stimulate imports? Yes. It comes back to the question we were discussing before. A depreciating currency is bound during the period of its depreciation to put additional profits into the hands of the employer, because some of his expenses will probably lag behind the prices he can get for his product. If, therefore, the rupee were to depreciate, the Indian employer would be able to get his labour and possibly certain of his other products, for a time, below what he really ought to pay, and that would encourage him. But personally I believe that is a very unsound way of giving a temporary stimulus to industry. It is a method by which the employer cheats his employees for a space of time. If he does it on any substantial scale he causes political and social difficulties in the long run which will far outweigh the temporary advantages which he has secured.

To the Indian cultivator a high rupee would necessarily mean that he would have to be content to accept a smaller rupee price for his exports? In present circumstances I think it would rather be that he would fail to get a higher price.

You instanced the case of the tea industry. The tea industry is almost on a footing of its own; the capital and the management are largely European; labour is imported from other parts of India and therefore it is simply a question of the payment of wages. But in regard to the staple products which India exports, like jute, wheat and seeds, the producer is the ryot, for whom you claim that a high rupee should be advantageous in regard to the articles which he consumes. Do you not think that he would resent a reduction in the price of his produce much in the same way that he resented the artificial reduction of prices of wheat under the wheat scheme of 1915? If the scheme brought his prices down a great deal I think he might, but, passing from particular commodities to commodities as a whole, I should not advocate a 2s rupee if I thought it would cause a reduction of an established price level. I advocate it because I think it would tend to keep the price level more stable than the alternative. On the other point it is quite true that particular persons would lose. In the alternative other people would lose. The Indian export trade is a very small part of the total production of the country, and you have to offset against it the imports. With a high rupee the ryot would be able to clothe himself more cheaply, and the great mass of foodstuffs that are sold in India itself would be prevented from soaring upwards in sympathy with the comparatively small margin which is exported.

I am not quite sure that I follow your answer. Would not you say that the export price in the case of foodstuffs does determine largely, if not wholly, the level of internal prices? Precisely. That is what I was arguing. It would prevent the rupee price of foodstuffs for export from rising as much as it otherwise would.

Jute stands separately. That is a monopoly. Probably you would agree that jute prices would not be affected, whatever exchange value was attached to the rupee. Would you say the same as regards cotton? I am not certain now how far for the grade of cotton which India supplies. India, now that

Germany is for the time being out of the market, commands the market. My impression is that so far as the Japanese are concerned, India does to so great an extent command the market that it might be in the same position, or very nearly in the same position, as jute, but you have so much more knowledge on that subject that I hesitate to say.

At any rate it is not part of your proposals to put up the value of the rupee to such a point as to strangle the export trade? No; it might cause a fall in the case of particular exports which have been taking full advantage of war conditions. I know that in the case of many Indian exports that has not been the case, by reason of administrative arrangements. How far it has been the case in regard to jute since the cessation of hostilities I do not know.

You would invert the order in which the Government of India places the two principal factors in the question, namely, you would attach greater value to the keeping of Indian prices low or stable than you would to the other aspect of the case, the maintenance of the convertibility of the note issue? Yes, but I cannot but believe that the difference of opinion is due to a difference of view or a difference of vividness of apprehension as to the future course of world prices. I may be right or wrong about world prices, but if the Government of India agree with me I am sure they would view with the utmost apprehension any rise in Indian local prices in sympathy with those world prices, and they would attach tremendous importance to anything which would obviate that.

The Government of India as a matter of fact have left it to the Committee to determine what particular rate should be adopted for the exchange value of the rupee, having regard, among other considerations, to the effect of a high rupee on prices and on the supplies of silver? There is a very prevalent popular belief that high prices were due to the war, and that they would fall when the war was over, and it may be that the Government of India, who would not have access to the latest information about European conditions, would share that view.

Would you agree to this—that if a fluctuating rupee is necessary, either now, in what might be called the intermediate period, or subsequently when more normal conditions are restored, the fluctuations should not take into account the fluctuations between sterling and dollar? If the rupee was fixed in terms of sterling, automatically it would take account of it. If it was fixed in terms of gold it would not, and on the whole I prefer that.

There is another way of dealing with it, is there not? Could not the Government of India bear the loss of the difference between the present sterling–dollar rate and the normal sterling–dollar rate? They could do that, but I do not see why they should. It would be very expensive.

That would enable them to buy at a 1s 8d rupee larger quantities of silver, or putting it in another way, they could pay for their silver purchases 10 per cent more on 54d? It would mean that they lost 10 per cent also on the whole of the turnover of the remittance.

In other words, they would be selling their rupees at a loss? They would not only be selling rupees at a loss, but they would be foregoing a profit on exchange which they could otherwise obtain on a very large scale.

I did not quite follow you in regard to the action which you advised that the Government of India should take on the gold question. Perhaps I may explain the present position. The Government of India are prepared to accept gold at any port of import at the rate of 12 rupees, 4 annas, 6 pies, the 4 annas, 6 pies being supposed to cover the cost of insurance and transport. Is it part of your proposal that this acquisition rate should be so improved, in other words, that more rupees should be given for the £ gold or the number of gold grains represented by a £ gold than is represented by the equivalent of the 1s 8d exchange rate? As I understand the present practice of the Government of India, my proposal would differ, in two respects, first of all in the respect that they would give only 10 rupees instead of 12 rupees, 4 annas, for a sovereign, and secondly that they would no longer continue the practice of trying to keep a parity between their rate for sovereigns and their rate for Councils. As I understand the present practice, the rate of 12 rupees, 4 annas, 6 pies, is fixed because it is approximately equivalent to the price at which they are selling Councils. They deliberately fixed it so that there is no great advantage to anybody in sending gold to India. Under my plan that would cease to be the case, and it might very well happen that a demand for Councils would so force up the price as to make it very profitable to import gold. I should not alter the sovereign rate merely because the Councils' rate had been altered.

Under your scheme, what would you do with the statutory rate for gold? I should make the statutory rate 10 instead of 15.

For the gold? Yes.

Coming to the replies which you gave to Sir James Brunyate with reference to economy in the use of rupees, you rather deprecated the continuance of the present restrictions on the movement of rupees which are sent up to the producing districts for the purchase of produce? I deprecated them in so far as they have the effect of causing a premium on currency locally.

It has been found by experience that to some extent that premium can be broken by the provision of small coin, but I wanted to bring you to another point. The use of silver rupees for the purpose of buying produce militates against a real banking development in India, does it not, inasmuch as the way to educate the people of India to the use of cheques must be through the currency note? Yes. I think that the use of actual coin for the purchase of produce ought to be discouraged so far as possible, but I think it is a very great disadvantage in a currency system if different units exchange at fluctuating rates, and I am not sure that I would discourage the use of coin to the extent of causing a fluctuating premium as between coin and notes. It is an old-fashioned view, which I share, that it is a great merit in any currency system to have an absolutely stable relation between its different units.

The currency note in India practically functions as a cheque for a large portion of the country; it is a Government cheque which passes from hand to hand among people who have no banking account. The restriction on the movement of rupees to the producing districts was not dictated by any such consideration, but in effect it has, in certain parts of the country, brought traders and others to recognise that there are advantages in the use of the note as a cheque? If there was no discount on such instruments would not their popularity be even greater than it is now?

Undoubtedly, but so far as this discount is concerned, have you any evidence on the subject? I have no evidence as to what the discount is.

Have you any evidence of the character of the discount? None. I only say that it seems to me that the existence of any discount which is at all substantial is an unsatisfactory feature of any currency system.

But you have no evidence that a discount actually has occurred? No. I say that if this system of discouraging coin only has the effect of encouraging people to use paper instruments and not of establishing any substantial premium on coin, then I think it is all to the good.

When you say 'substantial premium' do you distinguish between a discount which represents the remuneration to a money-changer for providing coin and a discount which is due to lack of confidence in the note? I am not sure that I should divide it quite in that way. I should call it a discount that did not matter if on a thousand rupee note you were charged a few annas for the convenience of changing it. I should not call that a substantial discount any more than the fact that you have to pay poundage on cheques or postal orders is an undesirable feature of our system. On any large paper instrument you naturally have to pay a little for the trouble of cashing it, but if money-changers charged anything which was caused by scarcity rather than by any trouble they were put to, then I should call it the kind of discount I am opposed to.

What other economy in the use of rupees can you suggest? I do not quite follow your question.

You suggested that it was desirable to develop every method of economising the use of metallic currency? That is part of the general question of the development of cheque banking in India.

Is that what you had in mind? I had in mind also the general convenience of obtaining and cashing notes.

I think you have given great consideration, have you not, to the study of the development of banking in India? I have not given it any study since the war.

In your study of pre-war conditions, was it not brought out that the facilities for obtaining silver and of moving silver from one part of the country to another was a means whereby the existing banking system made a large proportion of its profits? No, I do not remember being aware of that. It may be the case, but I do not remember being aware of it.

(SIR CHRISTOPHER NEEDHAM) *You have referred in the course of your evidence to the high rate of world prices. Have you any opinion upon the length of time during which those high world prices will exist?* There is no subject on which it is more dangerous to prophesy than prices, but I see no likelihood of a sensible amelioration within five years.

I am not sure that I quite understood what you would do with regard to the rupee when high prices had fallen and the price of silver had probably fallen also at the same time. What would you do with the rupee then? If there was another substantial movement in world prices, doubtless another Committee would be appointed, and the question would again be considered.

You have not formed any definite opinion as to the course of events? No. I should always be influenced in a period of any rapid changes in world prices by the importance of maintaining prices in India as stable as possible, and I should try to adapt my currency arrangements to achieve that end from time to time.

(SIR BERNARD HUNTER) *I understand that your proposal contemplates that the balance of trade in favour of India would be largely paid by the import of gold. Will you tell us what effect that might have upon the present direction of India's export trade?* I should have thought it would not have affected trade at all. It is a question as to whether the Secretary of State makes Councils available in large quantities, and piles up sterling and dollar balances, or whether he allows gold to flow to India. The mere question of allowing gold to flow into India instead of piling up foreign balances does not seem to me to affect trade at all.

Would not a country which has at present very large stocks of gold be in a position to do more trade with India than the British Empire, for instance? I do not see how it would. As I have been pointing out, there will be a very considerable supply of gold in London, and in my opinion it is just as easy for an Englishman to buy gold in New York as for anybody else to buy it here.

(MR DALAL) *Are there any debtor or creditor countries in the world which put an import duty on gold or silver?* There are a great many countries now in which there is no effective freedom of trade in the precious metals. I do not recall any country except India which puts an actual duty on silver. Whether the countries which only accept gold at their state banks or at their mints on payment of a rather heavy discount could be said to have an import duty on gold is not quite clear—it is rather a question of language; but there are several countries now in which gold is not necessarily accepted by the central bank at its full mint parity.

(MR GOODENOUGH) *If the debasement of the rupee took place, would that of itself affect prices in India?* By the 'debasement of the rupee' you mean Sir Charles Addis's suggestion of reducing its silver content?

Yes? If that was part of a policy of having a relatively low sterling value of the rupee, as I imagine it would be, it would have the effect of raising prices in India in the long run.

If it had the effect of raising prices, would that of itself create a greater demand for currency? Yes, I think it would.

If there was a greater demand for currency and it was desired to maintain convertibility, that would of itself create a greater demand for silver? It would.

So that the effect would be that although on the one hand you would reduce the silver content and therefore economise in silver, on the other hand you would have to provide a larger amount of silver to supply the currency? Yes. If you let down the sterling price of the rupee as much as you were reducing the silver content of the rupee you would gain nothing whatever, but I do not think that was what Sir Charles Addis was proposing. He would couple it, perhaps, with having the rupee at 1s 6d, instead of 2s. But that is only a reduction of a quarter, whereas he is reducing the rupee content one-half, so that you would be increasing the demand by one-sixth and reducing the content by one-half. If you were to couple the reducing of the content of silver by one-half with having a 1s rupee instead of a 2s rupee, you would gain in the long run nothing whatever.

(SIR CHARLES ADDIS) *I put it to you that the effect of reducing the silver content of the rupee in itself will have no effect on prices whatever, one way or the other?* No, as long as it was not coupled with having the sterling value lower than otherwise.

I made no suggestion of that kind. Per se it would have no effect on prices at all? But if you approach the subject from the point of view of only putting up your rupee because the silver content of the rupee forced you to, I inferred that reducing the silver content of the rupee was part of the policy of keeping the sterling value low.

(LORD CHALMERS) *It would not matter if the rupee was a real token, representative of gold, would it?* No. If the policy of reducing the silver content had no relation whatever to its sterling value, this point falls to the ground entirely.

(SIR MARSHALL REID) *The scheme you have sketched is a permanent scheme, is it not?* As permanent as any of these schemes are.

It is essential, is it not, that gold should be available to the Government if this scheme is to work? It is essential that the Government should either be able to get so much silver as to be in a position in effect to furnish Councils to an unlimited extent, or that there should be gold to take their place—that is right.

Are you of opinion that India should be allowed to import her favourable trade balance in the form of gold to any such extent as she desired? Do you mean for currency purposes or for trade purposes?

I am speaking of both really, both for commodities and for currency? It raises the difficult question of how far a Government is justified in going on discouraging what it regards as an extravagant and wasteful habit on the part of its nationals. It would be much better if you cured the inhabitants of India of the desire for so much metal, but I think there is a definite limitation to the extent to which it is wise for the Government to do so by administrative action.

Although you think India should be allowed to import as much as is necessary for currency purposes, you think that serious consideration should be given to the question whether any control should be established on the use of gold for other purposes? Yes. If you can contrive wise measures to persuade Indians not to have this preference for the precious metals, much would have been accomplished. From the point of view of the world I welcome the absorption of gold by India, but it is very wasteful for India. I would not approve measures which would have the result of making the bazaar price of gold much more than its commercial value. As long as you have gold and silver as part of your circulation you must have them circulating at a definite parity and not at a fluctuating value, but consistently with that my sympathies are entirely with those who would seek to wean the Indians from their preference for the precious metals.

Under present conditions the sterling exchange is based on 12 rupees to the £, a 1s 8d rupee? Yes.

As a matter of fact, an American who is sending gold to India and receives for it only 12 rupees 4½ annas, is buying his rupees at something like 1s 9½d? I take that from you.

India, as a matter of fact, is not offering the world's price for gold, but it is offering 12 rupees as against 1s 8d sterling exchange? On those figures that is so.

Do you think it would be desirable for the Government of India to raise their rupee price for gold? You know that it is absolutely controlled now, that there is a fixed price for it? That is so much bound up with the question of what their sterling rate is. As I have explained, I am in favour of their lowering their rupee price, but that is part and parcel of a substantial increase in the sterling value of the rupee. The present position is so transitory that it is very hard to offer an opinion as to what the Government of India ought to do at this moment. I should have thought that, pending a decision on the main issues, there was a great deal to be said for discouraging the import of gold until the matter had been settled one way or the other.

If your policy were adopted, how would you suggest that the Government should make the alteration from 1s 8d to 2s, which would of course cause a great upheaval in many directions? I have not any very decided opinion as to whether it should be done at one blow or gradually by steps. If it was done by steps I think they should be announced beforehand, and I think the Government of India should even be prepared to sell forward drafts at the new rate. It would put on offer drafts at different rates for a certain period of time, and ration them out. It is easier for practical bankers to say whether that would be more disturbing to trade than a sudden change.

You would not contemplate, perhaps, a change from 1s 8d to 2s all at once— a 20 per cent rise? I think there has been a 2d rise in the last few months, and that took place without any very great disturbance.

It happened as a matter of fact, did it not, that the movements of trade were exceedingly small at that time? It is a point on which I should accept the advice of the exchange bankers, as to whether to do it by one or two or more stages.

It is rather a difficult point, is it not? It will cause a considerable upheaval and possibly a very long upheaval? I do not know; I think it is the kind of point that looms bigger the moment before it is done than it does the moment after it is done. These sort of changes are apt to go through very easily, more easily than people expect.

(LORD CHALMERS) *The pivot of your proposal is to adjust the rupee to world prices, is it not?* Yes.

You think that Indian prices are not in their proper relation to world prices? Quite so.

And you think that by taking 2s perhaps somewhat empirically, you would accomplish that adjustment? I think it is rather too moderate a proposal to accomplish it completely, but I think it will need less disturbance of Indian prices to adjust with world prices than if you were to have a 1s 8d rupee.

If you go from 1s 8d to 2s—a 20 per cent increase—it is a very substantial amount, is it not? It used to be thought so.

And perhaps is still; it is a very substantial thing. If you were taking that step with reference not to the sterling price of silver, but on a basis of world prices, you would, to begin with, need to have very accurate statistics and a very definite basis of comparative prices, would you not? That point would have to be gone into more closely than it has been so far, but my opinion on present information is that I am sufficiently understating it at 2s for there to be no difficulty whatever on the basis of index numbers of prices in making out a justification for 2s. It is not as though I was running it fine in relation to the statistics. I have not seen the Indian index numbers for this year, so that I am not in a position to speak confidently.

Do you think that if you were the Government of India and the Secretary of State you would take the step, on a comparative scheme of prices, of altering the rupee from 1s 8d to 2s today? Yes. I should look into the actual statistics of Indian numbers more closely than I have at present, and if they were more or less as I take them to be I should have sufficient confidence in my judgment as to the course of world prices to take the step.

Do you think that traders would accept that reasoning as a basis for an increase from 1s 8d to 2s? I do not know. It is an argument which would appeal to persons who have the task of administering India more perhaps than to traders.

If traders considered it as a theoretical rather than as a practical step, that would militate against their immediate acceptance of it, would it not? Yes.

What do you think of the future price of silver in terms of sterling? In terms of sterling one has to make a prophecy about the sterling exchange; I would rather speak of it in relation to dollars. The Pittman Act makes it very unlikely that it will fall below one dollar per fine ounce in the near future.

So that there will be an upward movement? Yes, but the upward movement will depend, in my opinion, partly upon the course of affairs in Mexico—the greater tranquillity of political conditions there probably stimulating production—but more than anything else upon the policy of the Government of India itself. I should not have thought that, apart from strong buying by the Government of India, you would be likely to have the price going above a dollar and a quarter. Sir Charles Addis can speak with so much more knowledge than I can that I can hardly venture to talk about China in his presence, but I should have thought that there was no prospect of a continuous heavy demand from China.

As regards the rate of 2s which you have put forward in general terms without committing yourself to it, you feel that that is a figure which is perfectly safe from your point of view in order to harmonise prices inside India and outside India? My only reservation is that I should like to examine the Indian index number of a more recent date than I have examined it at present.

(CHAIRMAN) *When Lord Chalmers speaks of harmonising prices, does that correctly represent your proposal? Is not the object of your proposal rather to counteract the rise in world prices?* In so far as a high price level has established itself in India without trouble, I would not wish to upset it. What I am afraid of is a future rise of prices, and I think Lord Chalmers accurately expressed my mind when he said that my object is to harmonise Indian prices and world prices by so fixing the rupee that world prices can be what they are now and increase still further without too great a movement on the part of Indian prices.

(LORD CHALMERS) *With regard to the rupee people speak of a high rupee and a low rupee. What you want is a fair rupee, is it not?* I want a rupee which keeps prices in India as stable as possible.

(CHAIRMAN) *You said in reply to a question by Sir Marshall Reid that from the point of view of the world you would welcome the absorption of gold by India. Will you explain that?* One of the contributory causes—perhaps not the greatest cause—of the rise of prices in the world has been the release of the war hoards of Europe, and I should welcome any means of absorbing that redundant coin.

You agree with a view that the absorption of a certain portion of the gold supplies of the world would tend to cause a fall of prices? Yes. At the present time the United States are obliging in the capacity of a sink and many of their people talk as though they did not like the position. Many authorities in the United States feel they have too much gold and their policy, at any rate within certain limits, is likely to be to get rid of gold rather than to increase their holdings of it. I think that is rather a menace, because the state of exchange is such that gold will always be tending to flow to the United States and they will be seeking an outlet for it, and if there is no ready outlet all that will tend to force up prices. If the state banks of Europe were in the position, which they are not likely to be in, to return to their practice of hoarding reserves, it would be a different matter. India is one of the few countries which will be in a position to afford gold and also willing to take it.

You are not afraid of an undue diminution of the world's liquid stock of gold by absorption in India? No. The currency difficulties of the world are not due to any shortage of gold but to the fact that the currents of trade and indebtedness take the whole of it to the United States.

(CHAIRMAN) *We are very much obliged to you for your evidence.*

The witness withdrew.

The Babington Smith Committee, which reported in February 1920, established the rupee at 2s and fixed its ratio to the gold sovereign at ten to one, recommending the support of the exchange if necessary by the sale of Reverse Council bills. Keynes apparently saw an advance version of the Report and in the following letter to F. H. Lucas, Financial Secretary to the India Office, discusses two of its proposals. *The Economic Consequences of the Peace* had just been published—'I hear your book is sold out. Hurrah!' Lucas wrote in his reply. It is as if, having blown off the steam of his indignation with the world, Keynes had regained his feeling for the significant minutiae of a working financial system.

The two proposals, as they appear in the letter, were modified in the final Report in the direction Keynes desired, the second even more strongly in the Act giving it effect. Lucas asked for 'a quarter of an hour ghostly counsel when you are passing' and such consultations may have had some influence.

The letter first considers the possible results of repealing the wartime restriction which gave the Government first claim on all imported gold. Keynes was concerned about its effect on the demand and Lucas had given much thought to the related problem of the changeover from the old 15-rupee sovereign to the new 10-rupee one. In the final version the Report recommended the repeal of the Gold Import Act *after* the changed ratio had been accomplished, as both Keynes and Lucas favoured.

Keynes's second criticism has to do with the new regulations proposed for the paper currency reserve. The increase of the note circulation, during the war and after, together with the scarcity of gold and silver, had brought about emergency legislation increasing the invested part of the reserve. With the enlarged circulation, according to the Chamberlain Commission's requirements, it would have been necessary to have 119 crores of rupees in the cash reserve. The Committee did not think so much was needed—the actual amount then held was 80 crores—and proposed 40 per cent of the gross circulation as a statutory minimum for the metallic part of the reserve. Striving for elasticity, they settled on a fiduciary maximum of 60 per cent of the total note issue. But with a statutory cash minimum, Keynes pointed out as he had six years before, they stumbled into the very pit they wished to avoid.

The published Report held to the 40 per cent, but added that it would be desirable to keep a substantial margin of cash above the minimum, especially at the start of the busy season. The Indian Paper Currency Amendment Act of 1 October 1920 went further; after the cash reserve had become established at an amount not less than 50 per cent of the circulation, the issue of any new notes raising the total circulation to more than twice the amount of the cash in the reserve was prohibited.

My dear Lucas,

I have read the *Times* review of Shirras's book with great pleasure. It read as though it had given you a good deal of satisfaction to write it.

Blackett was in Cambridge last week-end and discussed with me some of the aspects of the forthcoming Indian Currency Report. I agreed with him in being rather nervous about the immediate repeal of the Gold Import Restriction Act. Apparently the bazaar price of gold is still very high—that is to say, above 15 rupees to the £, and much above the new ratio to be established. It might be the case therefore that the withdrawal of the Act would lead to an immediate import of gold on rather a formidable scale. It all depends on the elasticity of the demand for gold. But so large a sudden drop in the price might be expected to lead to very heavy purchases. This would be unsatisfactory and even dangerous in more ways than one. In the first place, it might lead to a total suspension of your sale of Councils for the time being. But apart from this, a drain of gold in excess of what can be met out of the weekly shipments from South Africa would have to come from the United States and be a severe burden on the sterling exchange. Moreover, you would lose the substantial profits which you would otherwise secure by selling gold gradually at a price above that finally aimed at. In short, I believe it would be wiser to go rather slower and to keep on the Gold Import Restriction Act for a bit longer. In the meantime you could issue your proclamation offering to accept sovereigns at 15 rupees and increase your weekly sales of gold with a view to bringing down the price at a reasonably rapid rate. As soon as the bazaar price approximated to the parity recommended by the Currency Committee the Act could be safely repealed and the recommendations of the Committee put in force in their entirety.

One other point of doubt struck me in the Report, with the

greater part of which I entirely agreed, namely, the recommendation that the cash reserves against the paper currency should be given a fixed minimum percentage. This is an arrangement which all experience proves to be vicious in that not a single further note can be cashed without a change in the law when once the cash has reached the minimum percentage. If the minimum is 40 per cent and the reserve falls to this figure, the whole of the reserve though still large and satisfactory is immobilised and useless until an emergency regulation has been passed amending the law. A possible variant is to prescribe that no more notes shall be issued when the cash reserve has fallen below a certain percentage. This would not interfere with the encashment of notes already in circulation.

Yours ever,

J.M.K.

[Copy initialled]

Contrary to Keynes's expectations, world prices dropped sharply in 1920. Even before the Babington Smith Report was published, the flow of gold into India had begun to turn in the opposite direction. To support the exchange the Secretary of State sold Reverse Council bills, making use of the sterling securities in the paper currency reserve. Temporary legislation permitted the disposal of investments in the reserve without a corresponding reduction of the currency, as such a sudden contraction would have caused a crisis. For a time, Indian prices stayed high in relation to world prices; the reduction of the note issue that was needed for their adjustment could not have been achieved if the originally proposed minimum cash reserve had been retained. The Government was unable to maintain the exchange at the rupee's new 2s rate. It dropped to 1s in 1921, only climbing back to 1s 4d in 1924, and in 1925 to 1s 6d.

This was not Keynes's last experience with Indian financial inquiries. In 1921 he was appointed vice-chairman of the Indian Fiscal Commission on tariff policy, but because of other work he resigned before serving (*JMK*, vol. XVII). In 1926 he gave evidence to the second Royal Commission on Indian Currency (*JMK*, vol. XVIII).

DOCUMENTS
REPRODUCED IN THIS VOLUME

DOCUMENTS REPRODUCED IN THIS VOLUME

DOCUMENTS REPRODUCED IN THIS VOLUME

UNPUBLISHED LETTERS

INDEX

Gold mint, proposed, 66, 88, 128, 231
announcement in 1900–1, 68
circumstances in which gold would be
brought to mint, 87
Keynes's opposition, 86
relation to proposed State Bank, 134, 191
Gold reserves, British
Keynes's study of, 60
view of Sir Edward Holden, 88–90
Gold reserves, Indian
centralisation of, 77–9, 82–4, 91–2
magnitude, 89, 101, 107
proportion to note issue, 285
Gold standard reserve, 90, 111–12, 128, 130,
144, 170, 183, 222, 257
accumulation of needlessly high sterling
reserves, 234–7, 255
amalgamation with paper currency reserve, 262, 264
centralisation, necessity for, 91–2
constitution of, 73–6, 88, 215, 252, 254,
262, 264–5
emergency guarantee for note issue, an,
177, 181
gold in paper currency reserve trans-
ferable to, 89, 105–6, 248
growth through profits on coinage, 75,
104–5, 227–8
proper size for, 74, 89, 101–3, 234–7
responsibility of Government through
agency of State Bank, 129, 133–4,
191–2
sacrifice of forgone investments, 236
weakened by gold currency, 84–5
Goodenough, F. C., 273, 294
Goschen, Lord, 78–9, 91
Government balances, 144
abnormally high, 237
as loan or reserve fund, 95
removal from money market by 'Independent Treasury System', 192
State Bank as custodian of, 129, 131, 148,
151, 171, 193, 199, 212
See also Cash balances, Lending from the
balances, Secretary of State's balances
Government of India, 88, 106, 114, 116,
123, 131, 223, 271
absorption of gold, recommended by
Keynes (1919), 281–6, 295–8
aloofness from banking, 196–8
attitude towards exchange banks, 201
bank rate, 194–6
circulation of gold, 79, 81–3, 85, 224,
227–8, 232, 283–4

coinage, 75, 235–6
evolution of currency system, 67–9
exchange rate for rupee, 281, 290–1, 301
gold mint, 86–7
home charges, 275
jute trade, 5–6
lending from balances and paper currency, 148, 196–7, 238–50, 257, 259–63
losses to bullion-dealers, 83–4
management of balances, 128–9, 147,
148–9, 196, 221
management of currency, 177, 179, 181–
3, 196, 231, 233–4, 277–8, 286–7, 290
management of reserves, 74, 92, 236, 283–4
paper currency, popularisation of, 74–5,
141, 193
policy of giving public form of currency
wanted, 224, 232–3
price policy, 289–90
printed Keynes's paper, 66, 86
purchase of silver, 267–8, 287
relation to proposed State Bank, 120–1,
126–7, 129–34, 136, 138–40, 151–4,
156–9, 159–63, 166–72, 174, 189–93,
197, 199–200, 216, 218–19, 269–70
relation to Presidency Banks, 124, 126,
128, 132, 141–2, 146–7, 152 (in 1900–2),
166, 195, 199
remittance, 128, 143, 148–9, 282–3
role in currency system, 71, 77, 103, 125,
129, 133, 149
silence of, 91
statistics, 11, 36
Government's Broker, the, 95–6
Government treasuries, reserve treasuries
number, 139
replacement by proposed State Bank, 139
source of loans, 237
sovereigns obtainable at, 80
State Bank to hold balances from, 131,
176, 190
Grant, Duncan, 16
Gubbay, M. M. S., 273, 288–93
Guinness & Co., Messrs, 54

Hammond, Basil Edward, 39–42
Hoarding
in India, 67, 80, 82, 87, 197, 269
in the United States, 198
Holden, Sir Edward, 88–90
Holderness, Sir Thomas, 4–5, 11–12, 15–16,
28–30, 33, 65, 97–8
Home rule for Ireland, 39, 42, 221
Hoover, Herbert, 275

Sterling reserves
  danger of needlessly high accumulation, 215, 234, 236–7
  held as sterling bills, 135
  more economical in London, 84
  proper size to support exchange, 103, 234–6
Strachey, James, 2
Strachey, Lytton, 2–3, 4

Thackersey, Sir Vithaldas (Sir V. D.), 69, 84
Times of India, the 90–1, 269
Times, The, 65, 88, 90–1, 94–5, 300
Toomey, J. A., 120–7, 219

Trade, Indian
  export, 275–7, 279, 289–90, 293
  import, 276, 288

Wakely, 28
Waldstein, Professor Charles, 43
Webb, M. de P. (the Honourable Montagu de P. Webb), 65, 90, 110–19
Wilson, Sir James, 66
Wilson, Sir Guy Fleetwood, 66, 69, 84, 256
Withers, Hartley, 95
Wyndham, George, 18

Yamamoto, Mr (Japanese Minister of Finance), 93
Young, Edward Hilton, 43